THE ARMS RACE

THE ARMS RACE

Michael Sheehan

St. Martin's Press   New York

ISBN 0-312-04947-1

Library of Congress Cataloging in Publication Data

Sheehan, Michael.
The arms race.

Bibliography: p.
Includes index.
1. Munitions. 2. Arms race – History – 20th century.
UF530.S47   1983   355.8′2   83-40068
ISBN 0-312-04947-1

Contents

List of abbreviations

ABM   Anti-Ballistic Missile
Weapon system for intercepting and destroying ballistic missiles. Also referred to as BMD (ballistic missile defence).

ALCM   Air-Launched Cruise Missile
Jet-powered (non-ballistic) missiles. Modern version of the Second World War 'Doodlebugs', capable of following the contours of the terrain to their target.

ASAT   Anti-Satellite
Weapon system for destroying or disturbing the normal function of artificial Earth satellites.

CBM   Confidence Building Measure

CEP   Circular Error Probable
A measure of missile accuracy. The radius of a circle centred on the target, within which 50 per cent of the warheads aimed at the target are expected to fall.

CW   Chemical Warfare
The chemical substances suitable for use as weapons, and the means of their delivery.

DEW   Directed Energy Weapons
Weapons such as lasers and particle beams which destroy by striking the target with intense energy beams.

GLCM   Ground-Launched Cruise Missile

GSFG   Group of Soviet Forces in Germany

IAEA   International Atomic Energy Authority

ICBM   Intercontinental Ballistic Missile
A missile with a range in excess of 5,500 kilo-

metres, which follows a ballistic trajectory when thrust is terminated.

INF   Intermediate Range Nuclear Forces
Nuclear weapons with ranges between 200 kilo-metres and 5,500 kilometres, for example, Pershing II and SS-20. Weapons with ranges of less than 200 km are known as 'battlefield' or 'tactical' nuclear weapons.

Kt   Kiloton
A nuclear explosion equivalent in yield to 1,000 tons of TNT.

MAD   Mutual Assured Destruction
(See second strike capability)

MARV   Manoeuvrable Re-entry Vehicle

Mt   Megaton
A nuclear explosion equivalent in yield to one million tons of TNT.

M(B)FR Mutual (and balanced) Force Reduction Talks
Often referred to simply as MFR.

MIRV   Multiple Independently Targetable Re-entry Vehicle
Re-entry vehicles carried aloft on a single missile, which can be directed against several different targets.

NASA   National Aeronautics and Space Administration

NBC   Nuclear Biological and Chemical

NNWS   Non-Nuclear Weapon State

NPT   Non-Proliferation Treaty

RV   Re-entry Vehicle
Portion of ballistic missile designed to re-enter the Earth's atmosphere carrying a nuclear warhead.

SALT   Strategic Arms Limitation Talks

SLBM   Submarine-Launched Ballistic Missile

SSBN   A nuclear-powered ballistic missile submarine

SSC   Second Strike Capability
The ability to survive a nuclear attack and launch a retaliatory blow sufficient to inflict intolerable damage on the attacker.

START Strategic Arms Reduction Talks

Preface

This book attempts to present a complex problem in a straightforward manner. A great deal has been written about the arms race in the past few years, but most of that writing has been either too specialized, analysing specific areas of defence planning without attempting to make the arguments accessible to the non-specialist reader, or too polemical, sacrificing objectivity to the dictates of political campaigning. The subject of the arms race is too important for either of these approaches to be satisfactory.

Karl Deutsch, writing in 1968, stated that the study of international relations had become the science of survival. 'If civilisation is killed within the next thirty years, it will not be by famine or plague, but by foreign policy and international relations. We can cope with hunger and pestilence, but we cannot yet deal with the power of our own weapons and with our behaviour as nation-states.'

The arms race therefore represents the central danger currently facing mankind. But the forces which produce arms competition, and the means by which such forces might be controlled, are complex and numerous. The aim of this book therefore is to describe and explain the nature of the contemporary arms race so that the reader can comprehend the issues clearly, but without becoming lost in detail. It is alarming without being alarmist. Though the author's own values are clearly reflected, the reader is left to draw his or her own conclusions about the questions raised.

Each chapter analyses an important aspect of the contemporary arms race, examining in turn the history of the international competition in that field, the current levels of weapons possessed, the likely trends in weapon development, and finally the prospects for arms control and disarmament.

1

Arms races and military power

The term 'arms race' suggests a certain mindlessness, as if the exercise were pure folly or mutual hysteria. Yet a closer look at the mechanics of arms interactions among two or more powers will show that there is indeed a certain unhappy logic to it all.[1]

Before looking in detail at certain aspects of the contemporary arms race it is necessary to have an understanding of why states acquire weapons, for, as George Quester notes in the passage cited above, there are compelling reasons for many states to acquire military power and these have to be taken into consideration when looking at the nature of the arms race. Military units may be purely for show, as with the Potsdam Grenadiers of Prussia's Frederick William I, or the Pope's Vatican Guard, but these are very much the exceptions.

WHY DO STATES ACQUIRE MILITARY POWER?

The foreign policies of states are the efforts of governments to achieve national objectives in the international environment. All states have a wide range of objectives of varying importance which they will be pursuing simultaneously. These are the 'ends' of foreign policy and most objectives are not ends in themselves, but rather the means to further ends.[2] Thus, for example, Britain's entry into the EEC in 1973 was not an end in itself, but was the means to another 'end', greater economic well-being, which in turn would allow other social and political objectives to be achieved.

1

The actual objectives pursued by states will vary widely, depending upon their size, population, location, climate, history, ideology, economic resources and so on. How much effort a state expends in trying to achieve an objective will depend upon how important the objective is and what sort of time-scale is envisaged for achieving it. However, having decided upon an objective a state will have to commit resources to its attainment and employ various policy instruments. These instruments include diplomacy, economic pressure, propaganda, the support of allies and so on, and one of the most important is the military instrument. The military instrument will not always be appropriate; it is of little use, for example, in settling trade disputes between the EEC nations and the USA, but there are many problems in international relations for which states will judge the application of military power to be an appropriate solution.

Note that the emphasis is on military *power* rather than military *force*. The two concepts are related, but there is an important difference between them. It is, in Thomas Schelling's words, the 'difference between taking what you want and making someone give it to you'.[3] Although in the final analysis military power is based upon military force, they are not the same thing. Military force is the actual use of instruments of violence to gain one's objective, the use of ships, tanks, aircraft and so on. It achieves the objective by hurting the opponent. Military power on the other hand is rooted in psychology — it is the attainment of objectives by the exploitation of the opponent's fear of being hurt. The possession of weaponry makes the threat credible, but achieves the state's objective without necessarily having to be used on a large scale. Thus, for example, when Britain despatched her task force to recapture the Falkland Islands in 1982, she demonstrated the efficacy of her military *force*. However, if in March 1982, Argentina had decided that Britain's strength made an invasion of the Falklands by Argentina impractical, that would have been a demonstration of Britain's military *power*.

To a large extent, therefore, the use of military force represents the breakdown of military power. A truly powerful state should not have to constantly demonstrate its power;

the threat, either implicit, or explicit, to do so should be enough to attain objectives. However, because a state's military power may be difficult to assess, it may undergo periodic challenges.

Another important point about military power is that it is relative. As a Huguenot statesman wrote in 1584: 'All states are considered strong and feeble only in comparison with the strength or weakness of their neighbours.'[4] Thus, Britain could successfully use military force against Argentina and thereby reassert her military power against comparable challengers such as Guatemala. However, the Falklands campaign could give no grounds for a reassessment of her military inferiority *vis-à-vis* the Soviet Union, any more than the British victory over the Italian army in North Africa in 1940 altered the balance of power between the land forces of Britain and the Third Reich. A state's military power is relative to the situation in which it tries to employ it.

Even the strongest military powers find that there are limitations to what they can do. In Vietnam in the 1970s and now in Afghanistan the two superpowers have found it difficult to translate their immense military superiority into political victory. Against a weak but elusive and resourceful enemy it is, in one American's words, 'like shooting a cloud of midges with a shotgun'. Ironically, having politically defeated the mighty USA, the Vietnamese found themselves likewise incapable of achieving a definitive victory over the Khmer Rouge in Cambodia.

To acquire military power is costly. It is best assessed in terms of 'opportunity cost', that is, the cost of what you were not able to buy because you spent the money on weapons. Thus, as President Eisenhower said in the late 1950s, 'the cost of one modern bomber is this: a modern brick school in more than thirty cities . . . it is two fine, fully equipped hospitals'.[5] Not all states are prepared to tolerate the high opportunity costs of defence spending. Liberal democracies, for example, have electorates who are always sceptical of the value of bombers compared with the value of hospitals. One such state, Costa Rica, actually disbanded its entire army on 1 December 1948,[6] and has managed without one ever since. The money thus saved helped Costa Rica to become the only welfare state in central America. However, there was no rush by other states to follow Costa Rica's example. So what are states gaining in return for the opportunity costs of the armed forces they maintain?

USES OF MILITARY POWER

One thing which states are trying to acquire is *security*; a scarce commodity, much sought after, but notoriously difficult to achieve. A major reason for this is that one state's security is another state's insecurity. Thus, the huge armies stationed in Eastern Europe by the Soviet Union are designed to give her security. Yet their presence makes the NATO states feel insecure. Attempts by NATO to improve the situation from their point of view make the USSR feel insecure, and so on. This condition of related insecurity is one way of explaining arms races. However, even given the virtual impossibility of achieving total security, there are a number of ways in which military power can contribute to a state's security, and more generally, to the attainment of its foreign policy goals. Among the uses of military power are the following.

1. *Deterrence.* This is essentially the prevention of the use by another state of its military power and perhaps, of other foreign policy instruments as well. Dr Henry Kissinger has defined deterrent power as being 'the ability to prevent certain threats or actions from being carried out by posing an equivalent or greater threat'. The clearest example of this is the contemporary strategic nuclear balance between the USA and USSR (discussed in chapter 2), where neither side dare attack the other for fear of the devastating retaliation this would provoke.

2. Should deterrence fail, a state is obliged to defend itself. *National defence* remains the premise upon which all foreign and domestic policy is based. As Michael Howard has pointed out, the international system is based upon the assumption that states will defend themselves against attack, and if in fact there were no extremes beyond which a state could not be

pushed the maintenance of international order would be made far more difficult. Thus all the states which have acquired independence since 1945 have felt it necessary to possess armed forces:

> . . . even when the strategic need has been as negligible as the financial capacity to support it. Such a force is not purely symbolic. The ultimate test of national independence remains in the nuclear what it was in the pre-nuclear age: whether people are prepared to risk their lives in order to secure and preserve it.[7]

An extension of this question is the defence of allies. A state may feel that it must possess forces capable not only of protecting itself, but also of rendering aid to important allies whose downfall would be detrimental to its own security.

The requirements of defence in the modern world are an important explanation of why armed forces are so large. Daniel Defoe, writing in the first half of the eighteenth century, declared that to raise a new army in Britain took three years and cost 30,000 lives before the army attained any prowess.[8] But given the slowness of eighteenth-century campaigns, Britain knew that she had considerable time to mobilize. By 1871, however, the lightning victories of Prussia over Denmark in 1862, Austria in 1866, and France in 1870, had shown that time to mobilize at leisure was a luxury no longer available. This is infinitely more true in the 1980s. To a very great extent armies must now fight with what they have at the outbreak of war, and this puts a premium upon the possession of large, well-equipped and well-supplied peacetime establishments.

3. *Coercion.* In times of peace, military power may still have many important functions. It can, for example, be used as an instrument of coercion, as when China attacked Vietnam in an attempt to pressurize her into withdrawing from Cambodia, or when Israel invaded Lebanon in 1982 in order to force back the Palestine Liberation Organization.

4. *As a backdrop to negotiations.* Even when it is not being used, military power is important. When Britain and Germany

negotiated at Munich in 1938, the military power of Germany induced Chamberlain to give in to Hitler's demands. Since 1945, the word 'Finlandization' has been coined to describe a situation in which a sovereign state demonstrates a peculiar deference towards the wishes of another. Finland, though independent, refrains from actions which would particularly antagonize the USSR, such as joining the EEC, or NATO, though she is not prevented from opposing the USSR on lesser issues.

States frequently use military power to 'signal' to each other. The USSR mobilized an airborne division in 1973 as a signal to the USA that the Soviet Union would not tolerate an Israeli attack on Cairo. During sensitive negotiations, states may stage large-scale military manoeuvres in order to remind their opponent of how strong they are. A similar tactic was practised by Britain at the end of the nineteenth century, when Queen Victoria invited her nephew Kaiser Wilhelm II to attend the Spithead naval review. The purpose of the invitation was to make the Kaiser aware of the power of the Royal Navy. Britain was subscribing to the belief of Frederick the Great of Prussia, that 'diplomacy without armaments is like music without instruments'.

5. *A shield.* More generally, military power is the shield behind which all the other foreign policy instruments are ranged. Economic pressures, diplomacy, propaganda, and so on, operate effectively as foreign policy instruments only so long as the state is independent, and in the final analysis, as noted earlier, it is her military power which guarantees that independence.

6. *Prestige.* Military power also contributes to a state's prestige; indeed, it is often difficult to determine whether a state is acquiring military hardware because of genuine military reasons or because it is felt to enhance her prestige. As far as this aspect of the arms race is concerned, like the Olympics, what matters is not so much winning as taking part. The pursuit of prestige has undoubtedly been a major factor behind the British and French independent deterrent programmes.

7. *Territorial expansion.* States still use military power directly in attempts to acquire territory, though this is now politically unfashionable in the post-colonial era. In the past twenty years, for example, India has seized Goa, Israel the Golan Heights and West Bank, while Somalia unsuccessfully attempted to annex the Ogaden region of Ethiopia, Iraq was forced back out of Iran and Argentina was repulsed in the Falklands. The appetite of states for wars of territorial conquest has declined because the military, moral, economic and political costs of aggression have risen since 1945, but such aggression still occurs and states are obliged to insure against it, either by their own efforts or in alliance with like-minded states. In either case, states attempt to maintain their independence by paying close attention to fluctuations in the balance of power.

THE BALANCE OF POWER

The idea of the balance of power is based, in David Hume's words, 'on common sense and obvious reasoning'.[9] The British statesman, Palmerston, expressed this succinctly in 1854, declaring:

> 'Balance of power' means only this — that a number of weaker states may unite to prevent a stronger one from acquiring a power which should be dangerous to them, and which should overthrow their independence, their liberty and their freedom of action. It is the doctrine of self-preservation.[10]

States go to war because they believe they will win.[11] There is no such thing as an 'accidental' war which no country wanted. Since 1700, for example, the outbreak of every European war has been characterized by a firm belief in victory by virtually all the states involved. In this century all the states in 1914, the Soviet Union in 1939, Germany and Poland in 1939, believed they would win — though most lost or at best achieved an expensive draw. If a state is convinced it will lose a war it does not fight, to do so simply extends the agony. However, a state may go to war believing that, while its own efforts would not suffice, help from allies or third parties will enable victory to be achieved.

The purpose of the balance of power system is to remove the confidence in victory of the aggressor. Power balanced is power neutralized. To deter a state from attacking, therefore, it is necessary to confront it with countervailing power approximately equal to its own. The balance need not be exact; it is sufficient 'that the deviation be not too great'.[12] It is important to note that the balance of power is not designed to prevent *war*. It is designed to prevent one state from dominating the system, and if the equilibrium it seeks produces peace, this is a valuable, but incidental, side effect.[13]

One result of the concern with maintaining equilibrium is that states develop paranoia as an occupational disease. It is necessary for their statesmen to pay careful attention to the international scene in order to ensure that no state or alliance is amassing an unbalanced, preponderant power. If evidence appears that this is in fact occurring, the other states must take counter-measures. This is one clear recipe for an arms race. In the eighteenth century, Montesquieu commented upon the results of this cycle:

> A new disease has spread across Europe; it has smitten our rulers, and makes them keep up an exorbitant number of troops. The disease has its paroxysms and necessarily becomes contagious; for as soon as one power increases its forces, the others immediately increase theirs, so that nobody gains anything by it except common ruin. Every sovereign keeps in readiness all the armies he would need if his people were in danger of extermination; and peace is the name given to this general effort of all against all.[14]

In this, as in other things, little has changed. As noted earlier, in a real sense, one state's security is another state's insecurity. It might be thought that the balance of power system would get round this problem, for if two states have approximately equal forces, neither is a real threat to the other. Unfortunately, this is not necessarily the case. For one thing, in a condition of near equilibrium, minor differences may assume a major profile. Thus, as Chancellor Schmidt noted in 1976, it was the very attainment of strategic nuclear parity between the superpowers that made the disparity in theatre nuclear weapons newly significant.

Moreover, there remains the question of balance. Statesmen frequently declare that they are in favour of a balance of power, but what exactly do they mean by this? There is more than one meaning of balance, and in particular there is a clear and important difference between balance meaning equilibrium, and balance meaning surplus, as with a bank balance. As A. F. Pollard noted in 1923: 'one has a shrewd suspicion that those who believe in a balance of power do so because they think it is like a balance at the bank, something better than mere equality, an advantage which they possess'.[15]

However much they may give verbal support to the idea of a balance of power, statesmen prefer an imbalance, one that is in their favour. A state *might* not attack you if it is in a position of equality. It *certainly* won't attack you if it is hopelessly outnumbered. Unfortunately, of course, this approach typifies *all* states. Thus, in Pollard's words, 'each aims at the balance with the idea of improving it, and the balance of power is otherwise known as the race for armaments'.[16]

ARMS RACES

Although the acquisition of arms by states is often referred to as 'the arms race', a more precise definition would be preferable. For the process of arms acquisition is the normal state of international relations, yet when people speak of an 'arms race' having begun, they generally mean to indicate a departure from the normal, and more often than not they wish to communicate a sense of alarm about this development. Martin Wight defined an arms race as:

> The competitive amassing of troops or armaments, whereby each side tries to gain an advantage over its neighbour or at least not to remain at a disadvantage. The race can be pursued by two rival powers or many; it can be local or general.[17]

An alternative definition is that offered by Colin Gray, who lists the basic conditions for an arms race:

(1) There must be two or more parties, conscious of their antagonism.
(2) They must structure their armed forces with attention to the probable effectiveness of the forces in combat with, or as a deterrent to, the other arms race participants.
(3) They must compete in terms of quantity (men, weapons) and/or quality (men, weapons, organization, doctrine, deployment).
(4) There must be rapid increases in quantity and/or improvements in quality.[18]

It is the last attribute which distinguishes a true arms race from the normal weapon procurement processes associated with international politics. A race implies the use of maximum effort in order to achieve a clear victory. A true arms race should therefore be characterized by 'abnormal' rates of growth in the military outlays of two or more states.[19]

Looked at in these terms, it is difficult to discern a true arms race in the past twenty years. The picture is not one of both sides adding to their weapons stocks at a phenomenal rate. Rather, there has been a fairly slow, but nevertheless sustained pattern of growth, so that over decades, the sum total of armaments built up is awesome. Even so, in Europe, for example, totals of manpower and weaponry have remained fairly stable. For the populations living in their shadow this is scant consolation. What impresses those calling for major disarmament is not the fact that the ground forces have not altered much in size for ten years, but rather the truism that 'no European can or should contemplate with complacency the concentration of military power which continues to occupy the centre of his continent so long after the formal closure of the events which called it there'.[20] Even so, it was not the sheer weight of armaments which produced the upsurge in popular concern in the late 1970s, but rather the perception that an arms race was indeed under way.

The explanation for this lies in the qualitative aspect of weapons acquisition. Definitions of arms races involve more than a concern with quantity. Thus, for example, Gray's definition, cited earlier, or that of Hedley Bull: 'arms races are intense competitions between opposed powers or groups of powers, each trying to achieve an advantage in military power by increasing the quantity or improving the quality of its armaments or armed forces'.[21] It is concern about qualitative improvement, and particularly the introduction and proposed introduction of certain new weapon systems such as the SS-20 and cruise missiles, Trident submarines, neutron bombs and binary chemical warheads, which have produced such alarm among Europe's citizens.

Again, from the military perspective, much of this activity is routine. Both the SS-20 and the binary chemical weapons are designed, among other things, to replace older, obsolescent and unsafe systems. Improvement in the quality of weaponry is something which takes place all the time. What distinguishes the late twentieth century from earlier periods in this respect is the diversity of weaponry and the sheer pace of technological change. Between the end of the seventeenth century and the middle of the nineteenth, military technology changed little. A soldier in the army of the Duke of Marlborough at Blenheim in 1704 would have found little or nothing to surprise him in the weapons and tactics employed at Waterloo in 1815. In stark contrast, a soldier who had fought at the battle of Sedan in 1870 would be lost in the technology of intercontinental ballistic missiles (ICBMs), tactical nuclear weapons, nerve gases, jet fighters, helicopters and tanks, which have come to dominate European defence planning in the 1980s.

Although weapon development is 'normal' to military planners, the developments in the technology of destruction seem to be occurring faster than the capacity of many people to comprehend and accept them. Because of the nature of the societies involved, attention tends to be focused more on the USA than the USSR. Weapons programmes in the USSR remain cloaked in secrecy both before and after deployment begins. To Western citizens, these weapons therefore emerge as a *fait accompli* and have to be accepted. In states like Britain or the USA, however, years of controversy surround the development of new weapons or attempts are made to block their deployment and this can give the rather lopsided picture that it is only NATO which is developing new weapons. In practice, however, there are no angels in this process, both NATO and the Warsaw Pact improve their weaponry at a fairly steady and predictable pace. This raises the question of how susceptible this process is to restraint, and particularly to arms control and disarmament.

THE ACTION–REACTION DEBATE

One of the enduring images of the arms race is the phenomenon known as 'action–reaction'. Thus, for example, Robert McNamara who was Secretary of Defence under Presidents Kennedy and Johnson in the 1960s, declared that:

> It is essential to understand that the Soviet Union and the United States mutually influence one another's intentions. Actions — or even realistically potential actions — on either side relating to the build-up of forces necessarily trigger reactions on the other side.[22]

There is obviously a great deal of truth in this statement. States to a large extent assess their military needs with the power of the most likely opponent clearly in mind. Therefore, developments in the military power of one state are likely to affect those in the other. Thus, if the USSR were to develop a powerful new intercontinental bomber and deploy it in large numbers, one would expect the USA to react by improving its continental anti-aircraft defences. The important questions are, however, how automatic is the action-reaction sequence, and what *other* explanations of weapon developments are important?

These questions are important because if the action-reaction phenomenon was as rigid as some have suggested, then arms control and disarmament would be fairly simple to achieve. If it were simply the case that state A reacts to increases by state B and vice versa, then one could break out of the spiral simply by reversing the process. Why then is the pattern of reciprocal reduction so infrequently witnessed in international affairs? It is not that it never happens — states tend to disarm after great wars. Moreover, some states have managed to remove the question of military power completely from their relations with certain states. Thus, Norway and Sweden, Canada and the USA are 'security communities' between whom the idea of war is no longer considered possible. The latter case is particularly interesting, for such amity was not always the case. The populations of America and Canada were on opposing sides in the American War of Independence and the War of 1812. The USA invaded Canada and was only driven back with difficulty. It was this legacy, and the emerging naval arms race on the Great Lakes, after 1815, that led in 1817 to the Rush–Bagot treaty[23] which effectively demilitarized the border. Despite a major war scare in the 1840s, the border has since remained the longest undefended frontier in the world.

The essential reason why such security communities have not become more common is that security is so broadly defined. States, as we have seen, accumulate military power for many reasons and some of these reasons are not affected by what the potential enemy may or may not be doing. Thus, for example, when the USSR increased the size of its armed forces in the late 1960s, it was because of the deterioration in its relations with China and the need to strongly garrison Czechoslovakia. The fact that the USA also increased its forces at this time was because it was heavily engaged in the Vietnam War. The superficial picture of a superpower arms race *against each other* was deceptive.

There are other factors than action–reaction which drive arms races. In the complex technological world of modern defence it is difficult for politicians to control weapon developments. In order not to 'fall behind' in quality, research must go on continuously, even in an era of detente, and once a new weapon has been produced or refined the scientists who worked on it must immediately be given another project so that they do not lose their military expertise. Former Prime Minister Harold Macmillan has said of politicians involved in defence matters: 'There is today a far greater gap between their own knowledge and the expert advice which they receive than there has ever been in the history of war.'[24]

Once the scientists have produced a new weapon, the armed forces can generally find a reason for having it. If the reason becomes invalidated they substitute another rather than give up the weapon. The placing of several warheads on one intercontinental missile (multiple independently targeted re-entry vehicle), 'MIRV'ing them, in the jargon, went ahead for the United States Air Force from the late 1960s onwards. The rationale for doing it changed frequently as each earlier excuse proved inadequate. Even when SALT I banned large scale Soviet anti-ballistic missile (ABM) deployments, MIRVing went ahead although the multiple warheads were finally supposed to be the counter to Soviet ABMs. Action–reaction does not operate in reverse.

Similarly, military establishments will invent new names to save their weapons. In the late 1960s, Denis Healey, then British Defence Minister, told the Royal Navy that no new British aircraft carriers would be built. During the 1970s, however, the Royal Navy designed, and had built, the through-deck, 'anti-submarine cruiser' which could also carry some V/STOL (vertical or short take-off and landing) aircraft. These ships, the 'Invincible' class, were in fact aircraft carriers renamed to allow them to sneak undetected past cost-cutting defence ministers. The Falklands War showed not only that the Royal Navy had sneakily hung on to their aircraft carriers, but also how right they were to have done so, since without them the recapture operation could not have succeeded.

Bureaucracy is in fact a major explanation of arms race dynamics. To an extent, states produce weapons almost out of habit. Thus, for example, according to Henry Kissinger, the Soviet Union goes on accumulating power 'because it is not overly imaginative about what else to do in the field of international relations'. If the Soviet Union massively reduced the size of its armed forces, it would have very little left with which to influence international relations, since economically and ideologically it has little to offer.

Bureaucracy is important in other ways. The competition for defence funds between the different branches of the armed services may encourage the development of multiple weapons systems, irrespective of what the rival states are producing. Similarly, the activities of companies involved in defence, the ubiquitous 'military-industrial complex' can pressurize governments into purchasing weapons for which there is no clear strategic rationale. In recent years, for example, the 'bail-out imperative' has been operative. Aerospace companies in Britain and particularly the USA have been awarded expensive military contracts simply to keep them in being because the economic, technological and unemployment consequences of their failure are seen as being politically unacceptable. In fact, once millions have been spent on any weapons system, governments are loath to abandon it and see the money 'wasted'. Cancellations like that of the TSR-2 bomber under Prime Minister Harold Wilson, or the B-1 bomber under President Carter, take political courage, which is always in short supply.

Domestic politics in fact plays an important role. It is electorally popular to be seen to favour a 'strong defence' and this can be presented by opportunistic politicians as being simply a question of spending more money on defence. As with that promoted by the arms companies and military scientists, spending of this kind has more to do with job security than national security. Because of the secrecy surrounding defence matters, it is easier to promote defence spending than spending in other sectors of the national budget. The rationale is more difficult to challenge because not all the available evidence is unambiguously on view. The defence establishment can therefore create its own political realities. As Lord Zuckerman has said of the technicians who promote the arms race in this way, 'they have become the alchemists of our times, working in secret ways which cannot be divulged, casting spells which embrace us all'.[25]

Geography also affects defence spending. Even if the USA massively reduced its army, the USSR might decline to do so, since unlike its adversary it has huge land borders to defend against hostile neighbours. Even its allies need policing — it has been said of the USSR that it is the only country in the world that is completely surrounded by hostile communist states! Similarly if the USSR scrapped its surface fleet, the USA, a major trading nation with huge coastlines and overseas territories, would not necessarily follow suit. Geography helps determine *which* weapons a country buys, which is one reason why arms control negotiations are marked by efforts by each state to focus attention on the kinds of weapons which it can forswear more easily than its rivals.

Most importantly of all, arms spending is the product of foreign policy objectives. Military power is an extremely important foreign policy instrument and states will wish to possess armed forces to attain certain political ends even if they do not anticipate a major war. Not all states are in this category, Sweden, Switzerland and Costa Rica being honourable exceptions, but generally all states maintain armed forces as foreign policy instruments. Thus, for example, one way in which France maintains its influence in the former French African colonies is through its ability to project French military power in support of threatened friendly regimes. Similarly, the 'Socialist commonwealth' has as its adhesive the power of the Soviet armed forces.

ARMS RACES AND WAR

The fear generated by arms races is rooted in the belief that arms races lead to war. Lord Grey of Falloden, the British Foreign Secretary in 1914, was firmly convinced that the First World War was caused by the arms race which preceded it. There is a certain logic in the argument that if states are straining their resources to amass weaponry then they must be intending to use it. To some extent the states are deliberately fostering this idea. Vegetius advised Emperor Theodosius 'if you want peace, prepare for war', and statesmen have been following this line of reasoning for centuries. Yet the opposite result may occur. Philip Noel-Baker argued that the Second World War, like the First, was to a large extent the result of an arms race. 'The arms race was not the *sole* cause of war; but it was a powerful and constant contributory cause.'[26] In particular, the arms race kept alive the idea that wars were inevitable.[27] But how strong is the link between arms races and war?

The evidence is not as strong as is often supposed. Certainly some wars have been preceded by arms races, but many have not, and there have been many examples in history of an arms race which did not end in war.

The argument that arms races lead to war is supported by the fact that most wars are preceded by accelerated arms build-ups. The real question, however, is, at what point did this acceleration take place? If it occurred only in the last year or months before war broke out, it does not follow that it contributed to the outbreak of war, for as Colin Gray has noted, 'one can argue that the existence of an arms competition shows that the states involved anticipate conflict and therefore, sensibly, are preparing to wage it as effectively as they possibly can. It is the perceived possibility of war that generates an arms race, rather than an arms race increasing significantly the possibility of war.'[28] Thus, for example, although the Second World War was preceded by an arms race, it was a brief one, and was produced by the feeling that a war was inevitable because of Hitler's foreign policy. Before 1936, there was no real arms race going on in Europe, and in fact it was the military unpreparedness of Britain and France in the late 1930s that obliged them to consistently back down in the face of Hitler's demands. Not until 1939 did Britain feel strong enough to stand up to Hitler. Since 1939, much political decision-making has been based upon the premise that one can only deter if one is strong and that 'it is not unreasonable to prefer some arms racing to a Munich'.[29]

The evidence of the pre-1914 'arms race' is equally inconclusive. In the decades before 1914, the major powers were indeed steadily increasing the amounts spent on armaments. For example, in 1860 Britain spent around £25 million on defence, whereas by 1913 she was spending £75 million.[30] However, these statistics conceal more than they reveal. Weaponry had become vastly more powerful and far more expensive in these decades. Wooden, wind-powered ships had given way to metal, steam-driven battleships. Moreover, Britain, an industrialized and increasingly socially-conscious nation, was spending more on *everything* after 1860, and, as a proportion of total government expenditure, the amount spent on defence was actually declining.[31] Nor is the belief that Britain went to war in 1914 as a result of her naval arms race with Germany correct. The Anglo-German naval competition had ended in 1912 when the two sides had reached an agreement on respective naval power. And of the warring powers of 1914, Austria which had rearmed at the most leisurely pace before 1914 was the first to go to war, while Britain, which had rearmed most energetically, was the last.[32]

Some wars, such as the Korean War, have not been preceded by an arms race at all. The Korean War in fact was preceded by a period in which the major powers had substantially *dis*armed. Nor does history 'prove' that all arms races end in war. During the second half of the nineteenth century, Britain and France twice engaged in a major arms race without going to war. The hostility and mutual tension seen by many as the key element in arms race pathology was certainly present, but war did not occur.[33]

A major fact, usually overlooked in arguments about the pre-1914 arms race, is that while war did break out in 1914, the 43 years between the wars of 1870-71 and 1914-18 constitute the longest period of peace between the major powers that Europe has known since the nation-state system came into being. Only two other periods rival this long peace: the 38 years between Waterloo and the Crimean War, and the 38 years between 1945 and 1983. For all the tension and arms build-up, since 1945 Europeans have enjoyed virtually the longest period of peace their continent has known.

War has been defined as:

> a collective form of struggle between tribes, nations or organized political groups, involving the use of all military, psychological and economic weapons. It is fought by the young adults of the opposing forces, who are trained in the use of arms (or weapons systems) and organized into military groups. Conflict is engaged until the will of one antagonist has been imposed upon the other.[34]

War as a foreign policy activity, a continuation of politics, or 'tough diplomacy' is still very much in evidence, as conflict in the Middle East and Asia demonstrates. Is Europe, or the superpower relationship, immune to this tendency? The experience since 1945 seems to indicate that it is, and that it is the deterrent power of the nuclear arsenals which has made this so.

Nuclear weapons in this context are only useful if they are *not* being used. So why are the superpowers racing in an unusable technology? A number of reasons can be put forward to explain the superpower nuclear weapons race, and many of these are examined in chapter 2. One of the most original explanations, however, has been put forward by Kosta Tsipis. He has suggested that just as animals settle disputes without fighting to the death by posturing, screaming, dancing and making complex signals, so the nuclear arms race is the superpowers 'posturing' to each other to avoid mutual destruction. The arms race enables them to display their military, economic and technological prowess without actually going to war.[35]

However comforting such a thought may be, it cannot make up for the fact that states are not monkeys. Over thousands of years, the cultural signals that sufficed to settle human struggles without war were lost until even genocide has become thinkable. Technological developments in this century have finally made the *Kriegsbild*, the war that destroys humankind, possible. Arms races may not necessarily produce wars, but they ensure that wars, when they occur, are far more destructive than they would otherwise have been, and they make the consequences of political miscalculation infinitely more dangerous. This alone makes the current level of sophisticated weaponry possessed by the major powers unacceptable, as does the diversion of resources away from unmet human needs which they represent.

There are many forces driving the arms race, but there are also forces which can restrain it, and to appreciate the nature of the contemporary arms race it is necessary both to examine the areas in which military competition is taking place and to estimate the potential for arms control and disarmament to affect those areas. Subsequent chapters will examine several such areas in turn, beginning with the weapons which can be said to have dominated international relations since 1945, the strategic nuclear weapons of the two superpowers.

2

The superpower strategic balance

In 1960 it was widely believed that the superpowers were engaged in a dramatic nuclear arms race posing unparalleled dangers to mankind. American presidential candidate John F. Kennedy alleged that the USA had allowed a 'missile gap' to develop in the Soviet Union's favour. Nobel prize-winner Philip Noel-Baker argued that 'the arms race has become . . . the most important fact in man's affairs'.[1] The Campaign for Nuclear Disarmament (CND) in Britain had dramatically alerted public opinion to the dangers posed by a strategic nuclear exchange.

Yet in retrospect the 1950s seem almost utopian. In comparison with the dangers facing mankind at present the strategic nuclear threat of 1960 seems almost insignificant. In 1960 the USA, though it possessed a variety of long-range nuclear weapons was making little effort to maintain its vast superiority over the USSR in this field. Soviet land-based and sea-based missile deployments were proceeding at a leisurely pace. Only about 50 Soviet ICBMs were in place by 1961.[2]

The real acceleration in the strategic nuclear arms build-up has occurred since 1960. The 1960s were characterized by rapid increases in the numbers of launchers deployed by the superpowers. By 1970 the pace of launcher deployments had stabilized and the effort was redirected into dramatically increasing the number of warheads carried by each launcher, a process which continued throughout the 1970s. The early 1980s have seen both superpowers, but particularly the USA, preparing to embark in another massive acceleration of effort in this field.[3] The question which arises therefore is, Why did this build-up take place in the 1960s, and what factors are combining to maintain the armament momentum?

THE REQUIREMENTS OF NUCLEAR DETERRENCE

The first nuclear weapons were *war-fighting* instruments. The bombs dropped on Hiroshima and Nagasaki in 1945 were used to force Japan to surrender. Since 1949 however, when the Soviet Union demonstrated its own nuclear capabilities, nuclear weapons have served primarily as instruments of *deterrence*. Their function is not so much to *win* wars as to prevent war between the nuclear superpowers from breaking out in the first place. This situation is achieved by threatening any attacker with reprisals so devastating that the original attack could not be justified on any rational estimation of costs weighed against gains.

Such a strategy has been made possible by the dramatic improvement in offensive capabilities since 1945. Whereas during the First World War it was the defence which dominated the battlefield, no effective defence is currently available against ballistic nuclear missiles. Thus the threat to retaliate with them carries immense credibility.

The essence of deterrence however is fundamentally psychological. What matters is that the other side *thinks* that the costs of a nuclear attack would outweigh any conceivable benefits. Deterrence therefore is about the threat of punishment, rather than the application of force, and the threat is contingent upon the actions of the state being threatened. As long as they do not attack, they in turn will not be attacked.

Stated in this way the deterrent relationship seems entirely straightforward and the stability of the strategic nuclear balance a matter of limited concern. Both sides possess and have possessed for several years, awesome retaliatory capabilities, so why is there currently so much speculation about the fragility of the strategic balance? There are in fact a number of explanations for this, the most obvious being the difference between the American and Soviet strategies of 'deterrence'.

AMERICAN DETERRENT STRATEGY

American strategic doctrine has for four years been based upon two concepts, MAD and the triad. MAD is an acronym for mutual, assured destruction. This doctrine asserted that if both sides possessed large stockpiles of nuclear weapons, neither side would attack because in a nuclear war, the holocaust would be inevitable and would consume both societies. This idea remains widely held in the public mind at present, the belief that the sheer quantity of destructive capabilities available to each side would suffice to deter.

During the 1950s, however, a number of academic strategic specialists began to challenge this assumption. They argued that it was not the total megatonnage available which counted. What mattered was the percentage of this force which could actually be delivered in wartime. It was no use the USA having vast numbers of nuclear weapons if in the event of war none of them could actually get through to their targets. In such circumstances the American deterrent would not be *credible* and therefore the USSR might not in practice be deterred from attacking.

What exercised the minds of US strategists was the possibility of the 'disarming first-strike'. American defence analysts have been obsessed with fears of surprise attack since the disaster of Pearl Harbour in 1941, when a surprise Japanese air attack devastated the American Pacific fleet. In the 1950s specialists like Albert Wohlstetter of the RAND Corporation argued that a surprise nuclear attack was equally conceivable. If the USSR suddenly attacked America, it might destroy the American nuclear weapons before they could fire back. Thus, Wohlstetter argued, what mattered was not the *absolute* size of America's nuclear forces, but rather the residual capability of those forces, that is the proportion which would still exist even after a surprise Soviet attack had destroyed the rest.[4] The USSR would only be effectively deterred if the USA had forces which could absorb a surprise Soviet attack and *still* have the capacity to retaliate and inflict unacceptable levels of destruction on the USSR.

By the late 1950s the US administration had accepted the validity of these arguments. One part of the solution was the triad concept. It was possible in nuclear war that a sudden Soviet attack might wipe out all America's land-based missiles. However if some of America's retaliatory ability was in aircraft constantly on patrol, or in missile-submarines prowling the ocean depths, then a surprise attack on America's ICBMs would not disarm the USA. Similarly it was just possible that all America's bombers might be shot down as they entered Soviet airspace, but nothing could stop incoming ballistic missiles. America therefore decided that rather than put all its strategic eggs in one basket, it would rely on the triad. Land-based missiles, submarine-launched missiles and bombers would all carry the deterrent burden. No surprise attack could possibly hope to eliminate all three legs of the triad at one go, America's ability to retaliate would thus be unquestioned, and the USSR would be deterred from launching an attack.

For the purpose of deterrence, the USA had also to define some level of destruction which the Soviet Union would find 'unacceptable'. In the early 1960s, US Secretary of Defense, Robert McNamara, defined an 'assured destruction capability' as America's ability to destroy 20 to 30 per cent of the Soviet population and 50 per cent of Soviet industry — and to be able to do this even after a surprise Soviet nuclear attack on the United States.[5]

An immediate effect of these decisions was a dramatic increase in the size of the American nuclear arsenal during the 1960s. Each leg of the triad was designed to be able to deliver a devastating retaliatory blow on the USSR *after* absorbing a Soviet first-strike. Thus each leg had to be large enough to destroy all the targets called for in McNamara's 'assured destruction' doctrine, even after many American weapons had been knocked out. Thus a huge margin of 'over-kill' was built into the system. And each leg of the triad had to have the power to destroy the USSR *on its own*, in case of a dramatic failure of the other two. Secretary McNamara announced that America would require 1,054 ICBMs, 41 ballistic missile submarines, and some 500 bombers, in order to carry out the strategic mission.

In the early 1960s the vast majority of American nuclear weapons were targeted on Soviet cities. This was known as 'counter-value targeting', that is threatening the things people value, most obviously their lives and the productive capacities that support life. As missile accuracies have improved, the emphasis has gradually shifted towards targeting the Soviet Union's ability to wage nuclear war, but since most Soviet industry and ICBM sites (the targets for US 'counterforce' attacks) are adjacent to Soviet cities the difference would have little practical effect. In any case, attacks on Soviet cities remain the central element of the American deterrent strategy. As recently as 1978, Harold Brown, President Carter's Secretary of Defense, declared that it was essential that the USA 'retain the capability at all times to inflict an unacceptable level of damage on the Soviet Union, including destruction of a minimum of 200 major Soviet cities'.[6]

Thus in order to fulfil her self-defined strategic requirements, the USA deployed forces well in excess of the minimum needed to destroy the Soviet Union as a functioning society. A recent study of the Kennedy administration's strategic programme has suggested that the reason for the American arms build-up had more to do with domestic politics than with strategic doctrine — that having demanded such a build-up as a candidate in 1960, President Kennedy could not back away from the commitment even when he found that the alleged 'missile gap' was nothing more than a myth.[7] Cynics have even suggested that the reason for the build-up was so that even if all the nuclear warheads failed to explode, the sheer weight of falling metal would be enough to kill everyone in the USSR!

The pursuit of mutual assured destruction also led the USA to look again at the state of their strategic forces. In order to reduce America's vulnerability to a surprise attack, a larger proportion of her missile forces were based in submarines rather than being in land-based silos. Those that remained on land received protection, the silos being reinforced to withstand greatly increased blast pressures so that they could survive anything short of a near miss or a direct hit. The older, vulnerable and slow-to-fire missiles were replaced by modern Minuteman ICBMs, solid-fuelled, rapid-reaction missiles. The vulnerability of the bomber force was reduced by dispersing the aircraft to more diverse locations and by keeping part of the force constantly on alert.

These changes made the American forces rapid reaction instruments. Efforts were therefore made to reduce the danger of 'accidental' nuclear war by increasing the 'fail-safe' precautions. Kennedy was encouraged in this both by the dangers highlighted during the 1962 Cuban missile crisis, and by his own reading of Barbara Tuchman's *The Guns of August*,[8] in which she described the outbreak of the First World War almost as an unintended consequence of the rigid alliance systems and mobilization plans of the period. Kennedy feared that the Third World War might similarly be triggered by mechanical failures or inflexible defence contingency plans. The efforts to avert this were symbolized by the 1963 Hot-Line agreement between the USA and Soviet Union.

By 1967 the USA had reached the force-levels laid down by McNamara's strategic plan. The American force stabilized at this level at which point it comprised 1,000 Minuteman ICBMs, 54 older Titan II ICBMs, 41 submarines carrying 656 SLBMs and a reduced bomber force of around 465 B-52s and 60 FB-111s. With this force, the USA was deemed perfectly secure since no attack could threaten its assured capability to retaliate. Nuclear war was thus by 1968 seen as virtually unthinkable by US strategists. US Strategic Air Command felt confident in the validity of their motto, 'Peace is Our Profession'.

SOVIET DETERRENT STRATEGY

One of the advantages of the superpower dialogue, established by the arms control negotiations of the 1960s and 1970s, was the growing realization in the USA that the Soviet approach to deterrence was fundamentally different from the American one. Because deterrence is primarily a psychological phenomenon, concepts are all-important. What matters in deterrence is what the *other* side thinks. It is extremely dangerous to assume that the other side will respond to strategic cues in the same way that one's own side would.

The difference between the Soviet approach to deterrence and the American was prompted both by Russia's historical experiences and by Soviet Marxist-Leninist ideology. Historically the USA had little to fear after 1815. Its wars were fought against enemies unable to compete on equal terms. In the World Wars, although the dangers were greater, the continental USA was never seriously threatened. America's armies fought as expeditionary forces. The idea of passive deterrence therefore seemed eminently logical to Americans. No one would attack the USA if such an attack would serve no political purpose.

For the Soviet Union, the historical experience demonstrated different lessons. Russia has always been militarily powerful. Her huge expanse and large population allowed her to amass huge military forces. These forces saved her in 1812 and 1941, being largely responsible for the defeat of Napoleon and Hitler. But they did not deter the original attack, nor could they prevent Russia from being brought to the very brink of defeat. In 1917 Russia actually had been defeated and suffered a punitive peace as a result. For the Soviet military therefore the lesson of history was that deterrence was not enough. Deterrence might break down and in that case if Soviet forces were not superior to those of the enemy, defeat would follow. For Russia therefore deterrence was to be maintained by having forces so large that in the event of war the USSR would *win*. No state would attack the Soviet Union if it knew in advance that it would lose. And if deterrence failed the USSR would be secure in the knowledge that it would win the war anyway.

This approach is buttressed by the dictates of Soviet ideology. The USSR sees itself as the vanguard of the socialist states and the leader of the working classes around the world. Because they see international relations as an extension of the class-struggle characteristic of national societies, they have little faith in the idea of an enduring detente. In Soviet eyes the years since 1917 have seen steady advances in the socialist cause. The 'correlation of forces' between East and West — a compendium of military power, economic resources, domestic political forces and ideological security, is seen as steadily shifting in the socialist camp's favour.[9]

According to Marxist doctrine, the capitalist class can be expected to fight rather than peacefully release their wealth. If the correlation of forces continues to move in Moscow's favour, therefore, the Soviet leaders anticipate that the West will at some stage be inclined to resort to war, even nuclear war, to destroy the USSR and its allies and prevent the victory of socialism. Such an attack would be a last mad paroxysm brought about by the 'death throes' of capitalism.[10]

Again this belief encourages the idea that passive deterrence is not enough. If such capitalist aggression is inevitable then at some point deterrence *will* break down and the Soviet Union must therefore possess forces sufficient to fight and win the resulting war. Soviet strategic nuclear forces are therefore structured with a war-fighting strategy clearly in mind.[11]

It is important to understand what the Soviet leaders mean by 'winning' a war. They do not mean achieving a political superiority through military means in the classic Clausewitzian manner. Rather, Soviet leaders such as Brezhnev, Grechko and Ustinov, during the 1970s defined a Soviet victory in terms of minimizing damage to the USSR while maximizing the damage done to any attacker. The Soviet forces would deliver a 'crushing rebuff' to any such attack. Thus, for the USSR 'war survival' is the operational key.

A further important point is that although the Soviets' force posture is geared to cope with a possible capitalist war of aggression, such a war is no longer seen as being inevitable; Krushchev announced that war was no longer 'fatalistically inevitable' and his successors have echoed this belief.

During Leonid Brezhnev's period in office, the Soviet Union's conception of deterrence moved closer to the American view in emphasizing the *preventative* aspect of deterrence.[12] However, the Soviets refrained from adopting the word 'deterrence' itself because, they argued, it was too closely linked with a status quo concept of international politics based on an arms-race fuelled balance of terror, a concept which the USSR has officially condemned. To accept such ideas would be to undercut Soviet socialist self-belief. It would be to admit that technological change might have undercut the inevitability of socialist triumph, something Moscow could never accept.

Soviet strategic thinking has, in turn, helped determine the make-up of Soviet strategic forces. Thus, for example, because it is assumed that the capitalists will be taking the offensive, a prime requirement of Soviet strategic planning is to minimize the number of weapons that can attack the

USSR by destroying as many as possible in their silos and bases. Soviet targeting therefore stressed 'counterforce' strikes, long before America came to support such a policy. Soviet missiles are aimed at American missile-sites, military bases and centres of heavy industry. Targeting of cities was less heavily stressed, partly because it did not directly contribute to a reduction in the threat to the USSR and partly because it went against the tenets of dialectical materialism. If the working classes in the West are truly struggling for liberation and socialism it is hardly justifiable to incinerate them with Soviet weapons for the crimes of their leaders. Indeed, since 1970, several Soviet writers have stressed that not even the goal of furthering the classless society could justify Soviet countervalue strikes. In October 1973 Colonel Ye Rybkin wrote that 'a total nuclear war is not acceptable as a means of achieving a political goal'.[13]

If nuclear war is not acceptable, the second-strike concept is unpalatable. Unlike the USA, the USSR does not subscribe to the notion of 'riding-out' a first-strike before retaliating. This would allow too much destruction to befall the USSR. The suffering experienced in the Second World War makes this policy unacceptable to Soviet leaders. Thus pre-emptive Soviet strikes are not clearly ruled out in Soviet doctrine, nor can they be. Because they are not committed to enduring a first-strike, the USSR has not gone as far as the USA in dispersing its nuclear forces. The USSR has 75 per cent of its warheads deployed in vulnerable fixed-site land-based ICBMs, whereas the USA has only 24 per cent of its warheads deployed in this most vulnerable situation.[14] The USSR is therefore highly vulnerable to an American first-strike, which would eliminate 92 per cent of the USSR's total deliverable megatonnage.[15] This is almost certainly one reason why the USSR has reacted so fiercely to the NATO decision to deploy cruise and Pershing missiles in Europe. They *might* be used to attack Soviet ICBM strength. The technical characteristics of the NATO missiles make them extremely ill-suited to such a task, but the Soviet fear of being strategically outflanked is probably genuine.

US STRATEGIC WEAPON TRENDS

Since the late 1960s the USA has held the *size* of its strategic forces fairly constant. The *quality* of those forces has been steadily improved however. The USA has retained 54 older Titan II missiles in service. This is the largest missile yet deployed by the West and the first which could be launched directly from the bottom of its reinforced silo. It has a launch-reaction time of only one minute and the final version can carry a GE Mk 6 warhead of nine or 18 megatons, vastly more powerful than any other American missile. A new guidance system, the USGS was installed as recently as 1978–79. The Mk 6 has also been fitted with sophisticated new penetration aids to enable it to get through any ABM defences it might encounter. Though liquid-fuelled and relatively inaccurate compared with later American missiles, the Titan II is a powerful weapon and is likely to remain in service for many more years.

During the 1960s the main American ICBM became the 'Minuteman' missile. Minuteman I entered service in 1963. About 350 had been deployed by late 1965. However these have been superseded and replaced by Minuteman II and III. Minuteman II entered service in 1966 and there are currently 450 in the American inventory. This was the first US missile to carry penetration aids, with the Tracor Mk Ia warhead. The missile carries a single warhead in the two-megaton range.

Minuteman III marked the major qualitative breakthrough of American ICBM technology between 1965 and 1980. It was the first 'MIRVed' missile. The MIRV (Multiple Independently Targeted Re-entry Vehicle) enables a single missile to deliver more than one warhead. These can either attack several targets, or attack a single target from different angles.[16] Thus without changing the number of missiles deployed, the USA was able to dramatically increase the number of warheads targeted on the Soviet Union. Each Minuteman III carries three warheads. The Mk 12 warhead was extremely accurate and has now been superseded by the even more accurate Mk 12A with three 350 Kt MIRVs. It is estimated that the Mk 12A is so accurate that each warhead has a 50 per cent chance of destroying any Soviet missile silo it is aimed at. If two warheads are targeted on one Soviet silo, the estimated 'kill-probability' increases to 40 per cent.[17] Some 300 Minuteman IIIs have been fitted with the Mk 12A warhead. The Minuteman III also carries penetration aids, chaff and decoys, to confuse Soviet radar.

The MIRVing of the ICBM forces was the most significant and disastrous twist in the arms race which has occurred since 1960. When both sides relied on single-warhead missiles, the missile balance was stable. As the two sides approached numerical parity there was no incentive for either side to attack. If both sides had the same number of missiles even a totally successful strike against the other side's silos would use up all the aggressor's missiles, leaving him no better off. Since a proportion of the attacking missiles would undoubtedly fail to destroy their targets, the aggressor having used all his missiles would find himself facing empty-handed the other side's remaining missiles. In such circumstances an initial attack would be insane.

With MIRVing, however, there were now more warheads than silo-targets. An attacker could use one missile to attack several targets. Thus he would not need to use all his missiles to attack all the enemy silos, even allowing for double targeting to insure against 'operational degradation' — warheads missing the target, failing to explode and so on. Having destroyed the enemy ICBMs, the attacker would still have ICBMs left with which to blackmail the victim-state by threatening his cities.

TABLE 2.1
US ICBM deployment 1981[18]

Missile	Number deployed	Range (km)	Throw-weight (lb)	Warheads	CEP (km)
Titan II	54	12,921	7,500	1 × 8 mt	1.28
Minuteman II	450	8,633	1,500	1 × 1 mt	0.48
Minuteman III Mk 12	250	11,224	1,500	3 × 170 kt	0.32
Minuteman III Mk 12A	300	11,224	1,500	3 × 350 kt	0.16

The failure to prevent the MIRV revolution was the gravest failure of the arms control process since 1960. The Minuteman IIIs, equipped with the Mark 12A RV, were a formidable counter-silo weapon, and the introduction of the NS 20 guidance system at the end of the 1970s made the basic American ICBM a weapon with formidable counterforce first-strike potential. The Minuteman silos have also been upgraded to increase their capacity to survive Soviet attacks, and their command and control elements have been improved.

THE MX AND THE PROBLEM OF SILO-VULNERABILITY

During the 1970s the USA began to lose faith in itself. A number of factors contributed to this phenomenon: the loss of her leaders to assassins' bullets, the Vietnam experience, Watergate, economic difficulties and the growth of Soviet capabilities, being the most obvious, though there were many others. One of the results of the growing American self-doubt however, was a retreat from the certainties of Robert McNamara's 'mutual assured destruction' theory. The essence of McNamara's thesis was that deterrence was finite, that what mattered was not how many of any particular weapon each side had, but rather whether America had the weapons it needed to carry out their preordained tasks. 'Once we are sure that, in retaliation, we can destroy the Soviet Union and other potential attackers as modern societies, we cannot increase our security or power against them by threatening to destroy more.'[19]

The key words were 'retaliation' and 'sure'. In the 1970s Americans began to express doubts about whether their forces were sufficient to provide for certain retaliation. These doubts focused on the ICBM leg of the strategic triad. The essence of the sceptics' arguments was based on the assumption that American ICBMs had become vulnerable to a Soviet first-strike. As a result of the Soviet Union MIRVing its missiles and increasing the accuracy of its warheads, while maintaining the high average nuclear yield of those warheads, the American silo-based ICBMs could be destroyed by a Soviet missile attack.

This development it was argued, had produced a 'window of vulnerability' for the USA, a period when it could be black-mailed by the USSR. Thus, if a Soviet first-strike eliminated 90 per cent of US ICBMs, America would have only enough missiles left to retaliate against Soviet cities. But if she did so, the USSR could use its massive remaining missile stocks to exterminate the American population. Therefore America would *not* retaliate to the initial Soviet strike, instead it would simply surrender.

Such a scenario was deeply alarming and prompted the USA to increase massively strategic defence expenditure in an attempt to close the 'window'. However, before looking at the question of the MX response, the validity of the initial threat to Minuteman has to be examined.

HOW VULNERABLE ARE ICBMs?

The calculations of silo-based missile vulnerability are in practice based upon a number of dubious assumptions. Esti-mation of warhead accuracy is calculated as CEP — circular error probable, that is the radius of a circle within which a warhead can be expected to land 50 per cent of the time. That is already a fairly dubious proposition. Who would buy a telephone that only worked every other time they rang someone up? The more the assumptions about warhead accuracy are examined, the more dubious they become.

The American fear of Minuteman vulnerability is largely a result of the fact that the USSR has MIRVed its missiles, so that more than one warhead can be aimed at each silo. Logically, if one gets two shots at a target then the chances of hitting it are much better than if only one shot is possible. But is this necessarily true? A MIRVed missile is not as accurate as a single-warhead missile. A single-warhead ballistic missile is launched at its target by a rocket that burns for only the first few minutes of the missile's flight. It is during this part of the flight that the missile is 'lined-up' with its target, using an inertial guidance system that compensates for all minor deviations except those produced by gravita-tional variation. By the time the rocket's fuel is exhausted and the engine shuts off, the missiles trajectory and speed is such that it will terminate on the target.[20]

However, with a MIRVed missile the process is more complicated than this. As well as the rocket booster, the MIRVed missile has a 'post-boost control system' or 'bus'. Once the main rocket engine has shut off, the bus, carrying the warheads, separates from it. After coasting for some distance the first warhead is gently ejected. The recoil from this action tends to deflect the missile slightly and the bus therefore briefly fires its engine to compensate and to increase speed. Further warheads are released in the same way.[21] Because it is impossible to compensate with total accuracy for the effects of warhead release, the second warhead fired will tend to be less accurate than the first, the third less accurate than the second, and so on. The CEP for a MIRVed missile is therefore an average of the CEPs of the separate warheads, an aggregate of estimated inaccuracies. Targeting the same object from different angles, with warheads from the same 'bus', thus does not *automatically* confer certain success, since CEP suffers through MIRVing.

Aiming at the same target-silo with warheads from different missiles is not an automatic guarantee of success either, because of the phenomenon known as 'fratricide'. The explosion of a warhead above or near a target-silo will produce a number of effects, blast, heat, radiation, electro-magnetic pulse, and so on, which would have a major effect on any second warhead arriving to strike at the same target.[22] No one knows how great an effect fratricide could have, and this must reduce the confidence of any first-strike planner, particularly since some of the fratricide effects would still be active an hour after the first warhead detonated.

MIRVing of missiles has therefore not proved an unmixed blessing for first-strike planners. In the same way, the widely-held assumptions about dramatically improved warhead accuracies are open to question on grounds other than MIRVing effects.

Both American and Soviet missiles are test-fired on an East-West trajectory. If ever used in war however, they would be fired northwards over the pole, the shortest route between the USA and USSR. The gravitational effects over the north polar region are, however, quite different to those over the Pacific, and would have considerable influence on inertially-guided ICBMs. The American and Soviet planners use computers to try to allow for the differences, but since test flights are impossible, these remain guesses. Secretary of Defense Schlesinger told Congress on 4 March 1974:

> As you know, we have acquired from the western test range (Vandenberg Air Force Base to Kwajelein atoll) a fairly precise accuracy, but in the real world we would have to fly from operational bases to targets in the Soviet Union. The parameters of the flight from the western test range are not really very helpful in determining those accuracies to the Soviet Union.[24]

Even if the polar gravitational variation is successfully allowed for, confidence in missile accuracy must be tempered with caution. Any number of minor miscalculations could fatally undermine a missile's accuracy. If the rocket's engine shuts down a few moments early, or burns for a few moments longer than planned, the warhead(s) will not come down on their programmed target. If the weather over the target area produces unforseen effects the warheads will be diverted. If any of the initial guesses that went into the inertial guidance calculations were wrong, the missile will miss. Moreover, the missiles sit ready and waiting in their silos year after year. Over time this must degrade their reliability, when absolute perfection is essential. The NASA experience with the Space Shuttle has demonstrated clearly that on a modern missile a great many minor, but crucial, technical problems are constantly emerging. And for an ICBM salvo launch there could be no question of putting the count-down on 'hold' while last-minute checks are carried out. Everything has to work, without a flaw, first time.

The question of salvo-launching is itself crucially important. Is it reasonable to assume that if one missile test-fired comes close enough to the target to give a kill-probability of 50 per cent, as with the Mk 12A cited earlier, one can derive a 90 per cent kill-probability if two warheads are used? On the basis of the problems examined so far, even this seems contentious. But to then go on to extrapolate that 1,000 missiles carrying 2,000 warheads would also have an overall 90 per cent kill-probability against 1,000 silos — as US planners do when calculating the threat to Minuteman — is rather stretching the data to say the least.

No one has ever fired a full salvo of 1,000 missiles. To do so would panic the other side into believing that a full-scale attack had been launched. Yet for the Minuteman forces to be disarmed in a Soviet first-strike, the USSR would have to fire all its missiles within an hour or so. The missiles would *not* be launched simultaneously because the USA has missile fields in both the north and south of the country. Therefore to *hit* all the silos simultaneously, the USSR would have to fire the ICBMs aimed at the targets furthest away, some time before it fired at the nearest targets. Thus before the northern ICBM silos were immediately threatened, there would be clear evidence of a Soviet strike, in the shape of the missiles heading towards the southern targets. The USA would therefore have time to fire its northern-based ICBMs well before the Soviet ICBMs arrived, leaving the Soviet missiles to explode above empty American silos.

With all these uncertainties, with so little operational data and so much that could, and almost certainly would, go wrong, would the USSR's leaders launch their missiles in the greatest gamble in human history? The evidence of history suggests that Soviet leaders are by nature cautious rather than rash. It is unlikely that they would take the risk. Even if they did there is no reason to suppose that the USA would not launch its ICBMs before the incoming Soviet missiles arrived. America has never forsworn its option to do this *in extremis.*

The threat to Minuteman is therefore a danger produced by computer modelling. As one defence writer has pointed out: 'strategic analysis is a dream world. It is the realm of data-free analysis. There's no test data, no combat data.'[25] Another writer has compared discussions of strategic nuclear theory with the speculations about the physical characteristics of angels which used to occupy the time of medieval theologians.[26] This does not necessarily mean that ICBMs have not become more vulnerable since 1970. However it is important to maintain some sense of proportion about the extent or immediacy of the threat. Even assuming that such a threat exists one may ask, 'Does it matter?'

IS ICBM VULNERABILITY IMPORTANT?

Many critics of the MX missile plan have emphasized the argument that America does not depend solely on ICBMs to maintain deterrence, but rather on a triad of strategic forces. Former Defense Secretary Harold Brown has stated that 'survival of Minuteman against a surprise attack is not the same thing as survival of the United States'.[27] What Brown was alluding to was the retaliatory power of America's B-52 bombers and nuclear-missile-carrying submarines. The whole purpose of the triad was to avoid becoming dependent upon a single system. Only about a quarter of America's nuclear warheads are carried on ICBMs and this percentage will be further reduced as cruise and Trident II become operational.

The sea- and air-based legs of the triad are more than enough to devastate the Soviet Union. The US Congress has estimated that even after a massive Soviet first-strike, two of the three legs could destroy at least 65 per cent of Soviet industrial targets, and the military targets other than ICBM silos. Fewer than 60 B-52s would be enough to wipe out 80 per cent of the Soviet industrial base,[29] and a mere 15 submarines would suffice to do the same damage.[30] In Harold Brown's words, even after the USA had endured a debilitating first-strike, 'we would ... have surviving bomber and submarine forces still fully capable of selectively attacking military, economic and control targets, thus negating any gain the Soviets might imagine they could attain by an attack on our ICBM force'.[31]

TABLE 2.2
Soviet and American nuclear warheads by carrier

	Total	Bombers	SLBMs	ICBMs
USA	9,200	26%	50%	24%
USSR	6,000	5%	20%	75%

But if the deterrent function is maintained by the other two triad legs, why need Minuteman's alleged vulnerability cause any anxiety at all? The simple answer to this is that one of the basic functions of the triad system was to provide a hedge against the breakdown of any of its component parts. If one leg became threatened the other two would bear the burden of deterrence during the period when the weak leg was being restored to health. Since another leg of the triad might also become threatened it is important to redress the *perceived* weakness of the ICBM component. In Harold Brown's words:

> Even though we have known for some time that the survivability of the ICBM force was eroding, we have not been driven into panicky and costly crash programmes — largely because the other two legs of the Triad were (and remain) in good order. That does not mean that our only options are to abandone the ICBM force or adopt a policy of launch on warning. If we want to be able to keep equally cool and level-headed in the future, when another leg of the Triad might become vulnerable, we must restore the survivability of our ICBMs.[32]

Other reasons for restoring American ICBM potency are also put forward. Having three systems means that the USSR cannot devote all its attention to countering any of them. However, if the American ICBM threat could be ignored, then the USSR might be able to switch sufficient resources to anti-submarine and anti-aircraft technology to negate the other two legs of the triad as well.[33] ICBMs also have a certain political visibility lacking in the other two systems. When most people think of the balance of terror, it is the ICBMs poised in their land silos which spring to mind. Thus some might argue that 'a decision not to modernize the land-based missiles would be interpreted by military observers around the world as a sign of inferiority, whatever other strengths we might have'.[34] Because in deterrence *perceptions* are all-important a new missile system is seen as necessary by some simply to demonstrate resolve, irrespective of whether or not Minuteman is seriously threatened. However, if perceptions of American weakness are the real problem, it is not Soviet commentators who have created such perceptions. They have said little, if anything about ICBM vulnerability. Rather it is American 'hawks' who have trumpeted claims of Soviet superiority, and thereby created the perceptions that they now insist can only be redressed by massive new weapons programmes, and in particular the MX missile.

THE MX DEBATE

The planned replacement for Minuteman is MX — or Peace-keeper — a system designed to overcome the threat posed by the powerful and accurate new Soviet missiles such as the SS-19. The MX weighs twice as much as Minuteman III, has a throw-weight of 8,000 pounds, and with the Mk 12 warhead and Advanced Inertial Reference Sphere (AIRS) guidance system, can carry ten 350 kiloton warheads to within 400 feet (120 metres) of its target.[35] It will be the most accurate nuclear weapon ever deployed.

However, it was not the accuracy of the MX which prompted the Carter administration to invest huge sums in developing the missile. The problem which MX was designed to solve was the increasing vulnerability of American land-based missiles to accurate Soviet ICBMs. The Carter administration's solution was deceptively simple — to make the missile mobile. The favoured plan was known as the 'racetrack' basing mode. The initial scheme was truly colossal in scope. It envisaged the spending of $33 *billion* to build 200 MX missiles, mount them on huge lorry transporters and shuttle them around 10,000 miles of road. Each MX missile would move between a pattern of 23 reinforced launch silos. A total of 4,600 such silos would be needed. The missiles would be kept moving between their silos. The USSR therefore, in order to be sure of destroying a single MX missile, would have to attack all 23 silos, thus 'wasting' 22 warheads at least. In order to be sure of eliminating all the MX missiles it would have to expend at least 9,000 warheads,[36] a huge proportion of the Soviet total.

The missile would confuse Soviet efforts to pinpoint it by

being moved every few weeks. The container moving the missile was designed in such a way that the Russians could never even be certain that a missile was inside it as it moved from one silo in the network to another.[37] This transporter-erector-launcher (TEL) would visit each silo in the loop, while shielded from observation, so that the USSR could not determine into which shelter the missile had moved — if it had moved at all.

The MX therefore combined two important features. It was a potent first-strike weapon and it was mobile — and therefore far less vulnerable to a Soviet first-strike. This combination aroused alarm in some, who argued that such a weapon was inherently destabilizing — posing a far greater threat to the Soviet ICBM force than the SS-18s and SS-19s had posed to the Minuteman missiles.

Many alternatives to the 'MX racetrack' system have been proposed, such as putting the new missiles in small submarines off America's coastline, or even launching them after parachute-dropping from aircraft. One of the more interesting alternatives proposed was put forward by the Committee on the Present Danger, a group of leading American 'hawks'. They suggested adopting the racetrack 'Shell-game' approach to hide the missiles, but rather than develop MX, use existing Minuteman III missiles in the system.[38] The suggested cost for this was 'only' $12 billion, far less than the $33 billion of MX (a figure expected to reach $100 billion if the scheme were fully implemented in the time-table envisaged). The Committee's scheme had several advantages. For one thing it used mainly tried and tested technology. It could have been brought into service in four years—in time to meet the alleged Soviet danger—and while it would be less vulnerable to a Soviet first-strike, it would have posed a less potent first-strike threat to Soviet forces.

In the event this rational scheme was rejected. However, as the Reagan administration came into office, the wisdom of the MX scheme became more and more doubtful. After many months of consideration the Reagan Government decided not to proceed with the Carter administration's scheme. After a further two years reappraisal the favoured deployment which emerged was the so-called 'dense-pack' system.[39]

Dense-pack involves placing 100 MX missiles in silos less than 2,000 feet (600 metres) apart. The system relies upon the concept of 'fratricide' to provide security for the missiles. Warhead fratricide is: 'The tendency of one warhead to destroy or deflect another when it detonates, through the release of radiation, the production of intense pressures, or the elevation of dust and debris.'[40]

Dense-pack predictably ran into a storm of congressional opposition. The rationale for MX is the need for a less vulnerable ICBM force, yet dense-pack offers no secure guarantee of ICBM survival. On the contrary, it simply offers the USSR a bigger target at which to aim. The system's viability has been deduced purely through computer modelling, without any empirical data; already defence writers have pointed out a number of ways in which the USSR could overcome the dense-pack system.[41]

That the Pentagon could accede to such a dubious solution only serves to confirm the widely held belief that support for MX has little, if anything, to do with Soviet counterforce-targeting improvements. MX support derives rather from a combination of the strategist's desire for a missile large enough and accurate enough to be perceived as a war-fighting tool, and secondly from bureaucratic in-fighting within the Pentagon. In the early 1980s the American army was to receive new nuclear missiles, cruise and Pershing; the Navy was getting new Trident submarines and missiles. Quite simply, the US Air Force insisted that it too should have a new missile. Putting air-launched cruise missiles on the ancient B-52 bombers was not seen as being sufficient compensation. The Air Force wanted a new ICBM. President Carter's political vulnerability at the end of the 1970s gave them their wish. Carter wanted the SALT II Treaty confirmed by the Senate, and therefore needed supporting testimony from the Air Force chiefs. The price was the acceleration of the MX programme. As Paul Warnke, President Carter's chief SALT negotiator, put it 'Forget the other arguments. Politically, there was no choice.'[42]

The choice of a basing mode as controversial as dense-pack, appears to confirm the fact that what is important for the USAF and the administration, is possession of the *missile itself*, rather than its vulnerability to attack.

THE TRIDENT MISSILE SUBMARINE

President Reagan's MX plans fall within an overall strategic programme designed in Senator John Tower's words to 'modernize all three legs of the strategic triad, land, sea and air'.[43] The modernization of the sea-based leg has, in fact, been under way for some time.

Three of America's Poseidon submarines have already been retrofitted with the Trident I missile and another nine will be converted in this way. The USA is also producing the huge 'Ohio'-class submarines, specifically designed to carry Trident. Eight Ohio-class boats are due to come into service. Each will carry 24 missiles, the Mk 4 RV, eight warheads to each missile. The Trident I (C-4) missile is essentially an improved version of the existing Poseidon missile, having a similar accuracy (estimated CEP being half a mile). Trident C-4, unlike Poseidon, has a third-stage motor which doubles the missile's range to some 7,000 km (4,350 miles). There are plans to replace the Mk 4 RV with the General Electric Mk 500 MARV (Manoeuvrable Re-entry Vehicle) which can manoeuvre in space, should improvements in Soviet ballistic missile defences warrant it.

Already the US Navy is committed to the C-4's successor, the Trident II, D-5 missile. The D-5 will have a substantially increased range of about 6,000 miles. The great advantage of increasing the range of SLBMs is that it increases the area of ocean in which the submarine can patrol and thereby increases the submarine's chance of remaining undetected. The new missiles will not enter service until the mid-1990s, but with an accuracy equivalent to that of Minuteman ICBMs they will mark a major increase in the US Navy's counterforce capabilities. Certainly the increased range of both the C-4 and the D-5 should ensure that the submarine-based element of the triad remains secure well into the next century.

The Trident system will also equip the SSBNs of Britain's Royal Navy under present plans. The Conservative Government of Mrs Thatcher is committed to the purchase of the

D-5 missile to be placed in a new 14,680 ton SSBN, to super-sede the present Polaris force of four 'R' class submarines in the 1990s. Because Britain's strategic nuclear weapons are designed as last-gasp countervalue weapons, the D-5 missile has far greater sophistication and performance than British requirements would determine. However, since Britain is no longer in the business of producing strategic missiles, she must accept what is on offer from the USA. Initially Britain wanted the C-4 missile, but since this will be going out of service with the US Navy just as the new British submarines are entering service, Britain has opted to wait for the D-5. Had she not done so, spare parts and maintenance for the C-4 would have been increasingly hard to obtain as the American production lines closed down.

In the USA the modernization programme for the sea-based deterrent has gone ahead steadily without the military and political controversy that has accompanied the efforts to modernize the land-based ICBMs. This relative acceptance is probably due to their reduced political visibility out at sea, and to the fact that submarines do not invite retaliatory counterforce strikes in the way that land-based missiles do. According to opinion polls, 65 per cent of the inhabitants of the area designated for MX deployment are opposed to the scheme.[44] While the fact that the USSR would have to fire 9,000 warheads to destroy all the MX missiles might appeal to strategists, it can hardly be expected to appeal to those who live in the target zone. This political opposition undoubtedly influenced the Reagan administration's decision to delay finalizing MX deployment plans.

BRITAIN AND THE TRIDENT DECISION

In Britain the controversy has centred around the Trident submarine system. Arguments over Britain's decision to purchase Trident are centred around the question of what kind of deterrent does a medium power like Britain actually need? There are two different aspects to this question. The first is that since British nuclear deterrent strategy is of the crudest kind, why should Britain purchase a system as sophisticated as Trident? Britain's retaliatory strategy is simply to destroy Soviet cities. To destroy huge, undefended Soviet cities hardly requires a missile as sophisticated as the Trident II. However it has also always been part of Britain's targeting strategy that one of the Russian cities to be destroyed must be Moscow, and Moscow *does* have an ABM (anti-ballistic missile) defence. The targeting of Moscow is based on the belief that Soviet decision-makers will only be deterred by the threat of their own destruction rather than 'just' that of the rest of their compatriots. Opposition to Trident is therefore partly based on the belief that the ability to destroy Moscow is superfluous and that a less sophisticated delivery system such as cruise, or a new aircraft, would suffice.

Another aspect of opposition to Trident is the argument of those who believe that Trident *weakens* rather than strengthens deterrence. Supporters of this case argue that for a second-rank power the opportunity-costs of Trident are all-important. Thus they argue Trident will cost some £7,000–£12,000 million over the next 15 years — and this money can only come from the equipment budget of the armed forces as a whole. Thus Trident means a weaker British Army of the Rhine, a smaller Royal Navy with a depleted surface fleet, and the continuation of the present lack of credible air-defence of Britain. It can be argued that by weakening her conventional forces to pay for Trident, Britain makes nuclear war *more*, not less, likely. Weaker British forces would give way faster on the European central front, forcing decision-makers to 'go nuclear' even sooner. Against this, if Trident was cancelled and the money put towards a major conventional reinforcement programme, NATO and Britain would benefit far more than they would from the dubious marginal utility of one more nuclear missile submarine on station.

This argument would have force at any time. However one of the 'lessons' of British history is that eventually the cheese-paring attitude of treasury ministers is paid for not by them, but by the dead and mutilated British servicemen who go to war with inadequate equipment. During a long peace this argument invariably loses its force, but the fighting in the South Atlantic in 1982 served as a painful reminder that money 'saved' by conventional force cutbacks is false economy if it encourages others to pursue a military option. War is always more expensive than peace and adequate, if expensive, armed forces are a vastly better bargain than short-sighted cutbacks which leave the armed forces too weak to deter. It is here that the moral argument against British nuclear weapons becomes significant. Is the deterrent an expensive but necessary possession which prevents the greater cost of a nuclear war, or, given the inherent incredibility of all the scenarios in which Britain might use her nuclear weapons on her own, is the deterrent a useless and expensive white elephant, which weakens rather than strengthens British security? Increasingly, the latter interpretation is being seen as the more accurate. And because three of the four major British parties oppose the Trident programme, a cancellation of the project is quite possible, particularly should the decision be taken before the late 1980s when little of the expenditure will have occurred.

THE B-1 BOMBER

The third leg of the strategic triad is the manned long-range bomber force. For three decades the USAF has depended on the B-52 as its strategic bomber. It was used in large numbers for conventional bombing during the Vietnam War, but its major role was and remains as part of the strategic triad. During its long years of service the basic aircraft has undergone a number of improvements designed to maintain its ability to penetrate Soviet air-defences. Originally designed as a high-altitude bomber, the B-52 is now designed to fly in low, just above the tree-tops to defeat Soviet radar.

The airborne leg of the triad, though more vulnerable to detection and destruction than the other two legs, has a number of advantages. One is that the weapon can be recalled after launch. The flight plan can be changed *en route*, or abandoned altogether, in a way that is impossible with a ballistic missile. Bombers can also be dispersed to many airfields during periods of tension, or numbers can be kept aloft during crises. Moreover, the B-52 carries a bomb-load of 75,000 lbs and can attack more than one target.

Against this, the manned bomber is vulnerable to interception. Compared to a missile, a bomber is large and slow.

Soviet anti-aircraft defences have improved dramatically in the past 15 years, and there must now be serious doubts as to the ageing B-52's ability to penetrate these defences in any number. The first B-52 was produced in 1952 and many of the bombers are now older than the pilots who fly them. The last aircraft was produced in 1962 and spare parts are extremely difficult and expensive to supply. Even so, the active life of the B-52 has now been given yet another extension. One hundred and seventy-three B-52-Gs[45] are being converted to carry air-launched cruise missiles (ALCMs). Twenty will be carried inside the aircraft and eight fitted externally. Because of the cruise missile's accuracy and long range, the B-52s can then be used as 'stand-off' weapon platforms. That is, instead of flying directly to their target and risking destruction by Soviet air defences, the B-52s can fly the cruise missiles much of the way to the target, but then launch them while still outside the main Soviet air-defences. The use of the B-52 in this role after 1985 will extend the aircraft's life into the 1990s.

The question of a successor to the B-52 has been the subject of political controversy several times since 1954. In the late 1950s and early 1960s the B-70 was the planned follow-on aircraft, but this project was abandoned in 1966. By the 1970s a new strategic bomber, the B-1, had been designed and a small number of prototype aircraft were flown. However, in 1977 this aircraft too was cancelled, leaving the B-52 with no designated successor. The decision to scrap the B-1 was controversial since it implied a move away from the triad concept, and it was no surprise when the Reagan administration revived the project. On 4 December 1981 the Senate overwhelmingly approved a plan to build 100 B-1 bombers. Opponents described the B-1 as the most costly single weapon system ever built. The cost of the programme was estimated at $20,000 million though one congressional office put the cost at nearer $40,000 million.[46]

The B-1 generated the kind of opposition in America that in Britain fell on the Trident system. Opponents of the B-1 argued that its huge cost would be met by making cuts in conventional forces which would lower the nuclear threshold. A group of 28 Democrat Senators had in fact tried to cancel the B-1 and spend the money instead on improving the combat readiness of America's conventional forces.[47] There is no doubt that such a move would be immensely valuable. America's forces, despite the huge amounts being spent on them, suffer from many weaknesses, such as inadequate training and shortage of basic equipment. These weaknesses are not remedied because they lack political appeal. In war absence of reserve ammunition would be disastrous, but there is no glamour in voting to increase the size of ammunition stockpiles in Europe. By contrast, a shiny new jet aircraft looks impressive, and to be photographed at its commissioning can help a Congressman's re-election prospects in a way that being photographed in front of a pile of 200 spare tank treads does not.

One effect of the delay in the B-1 programme is that the new aircraft will probably now incorporate elements of the new 'stealth' technology, first revealed during the 1980 presidential election campaign. Stealth refers to a number of technologies designed to make aircraft less visible on radar. This includes such techniques as designing aircraft which have few of the flat surfaces, cavities and straight edges which produce a clear radar echo. The aircraft will also be coated with material which absorbs rather than reflects radar energy.[48] Where flat surfaces are essential, as for example in the tailplane, these will be constructed out of plastic materials which absorb radar, while still being strong enough to cope with the structural stresses associated with the strategic bomber's low-level penetration role. The B-1 is due to come into service in 1986–87, so how far it incorporates some or all of these stealth technologies will depend upon the current state of this highly secretive art.

SOVIET STRATEGIC WEAPON TRENDS

The 'mix' of Soviet strategic weapon systems is somewhat different to that favoured by the USA. Although the USSR also has ICBMs, SLBMs and long-range bombers, there is no comparable Soviet 'triad'. The submarine and bomber elements of the Soviet force are — in some indicators — small in comparison to the ICBM element, and are not designed to be able to carry the entire Soviet deterrent burden should the ICBM force be elininated.

At present the Soviet force consists of some 989 SLBMs carried on 84 submarines, 1,398 ICBMs, and 150 long-range bombers.[49] The ICBM is by far the most important element. As noted earlier, whereas the USA has only a quarter of its warhead total carried by ICBMs, the USSR deploys three-quarters of its warheads on ICBMs. For this reason the development of its ICBM force is even more important to the USSR than it is to the USA, where fears of ICBM vulnerability have produced such concern.

The Soviet Union has some 1,398 ICBMs deployed. Despite the failure of the US Senate to ratify SALT II, the USSR has abided by the terms of the agreement, as has the USA,[50] in the absence of anything better. The Soviet force consists of 580 SS-11, 60 SS-13, 150 SS-17, 308 SS-18, and 300 SS-19.[51]

The SS-11 comes in three versions (Modifications 1–3) all with a range of nearly 6,000 kilometres. Only the third version has more than one warhead, carrying three each of 350 kilotons. The others carry single one-megaton warheads. The USSR has been engaged in modifying its SS-11 force for some years. In the early 1970s, 120 were retargeted on Western Europe, while since 1978 the missile has been gradually replaced by the SS-17 and SS-19.

The SS-13 is a missile similar to the American Minuteman III, though it is far less sophisticated. Solid-fuelled, it carries a single one-megaton warhead, and has a range of 8,000 kilometres (5,000 miles). The SS-17 is a successor to the SS-11 and was the first Soviet missile to carry MIRVs. Most of the deployed SS-17s carry four warheads each of 200 kilotons.

Of the newly-deployed present generation of Soviet ICBMs, it was the SS-18 which caused most consternation. According to one writer 'this is the missile that has demolished almost all the West's bargaining power and ability to deter aggression'.[52] This is rather overstating the case, but certainly the SS-18 has been the focus for the American fears of silo-vulnerability. The SS-18 is the largest ICBM deployed by either superpower. A number of the missile's features cause concern. It has a throw-weight that is ten times greater than Minuteman III, it can carry either a single warhead with an awesome 25 megatonnage or eight MIRVs with warheads in the one–two megaton range. The SS-18 is cold-launched, that is its engines do not ignite until after the missile leaves the silo, so in theory at least, the USSR could re-use SS-18 silos to fire more stockpiled missiles. The feature which produced most alarm, however, was the missile's accuracy. The single-warhead version has an accuracy estimated at 350 metres. When combined with a 25 MT warhead, such a missile could devastate fixed-silo ICBMs, and its megatonnage would make any degree of silo-hardening a waste of effort. One author has argued that in the absence of the SALT II treaty, or a similar restraint, by 1985 the SS-18 could be expected to be totally successful if used to attack the American silos, leaving not a single US ICBM with which America could retaliate.[53] Although the USSR has traditionally opted for large missiles, the special characteristics of the SS-18 could not simply be dismissed as the end result of Soviet design inertia, and were seen as a deliberate attempt by the USSR to design a 'silo-busting' missile capable of eliminating the American ICBM force. The only comfort to the West was that Moscow,

TABLE 2.3
Currently deployed Soviet ICBMs[54]

Missile		Number deployed (1982)	Range (km)	Warheads	CEP (m)
SS-11	Model 1 & 2	492	11,000	1 × 950 kt	1,256
	Model 3	88	10,600	3 × 350 kt	975
SS-13		60	9,400	1 × 600 kt	1,355
SS-17	Model 1	125	10,000	4 × 700 kt	398
	Model 2	25	11,000	1 × 3.6 mt	380
SS-18	Model 1	20	12,000	1 × 2.4 mt	380
	Model 2	288	11,000	8 × 900 kt	380
SS-19		300	9,550	6 × 550 kt	231

abiding by the terms of the much-maligned SALT treaties, has refrained from deploying more than the 308 'heavy' SS-18s permitted by those treaties.

The last of the so-called 'fourth generation' Soviet ICBMs was the SS-19. This seems to have been produced by a rival design team of that which created the SS-17, since the missiles seem to answer the same requirement. The SS-19 is slightly larger than SS-17, is hot-launched and carries six warheads. It appears that the SS-19 is to be the basic replacement for the SS-11 and large numbers are being deployed. Like the SS-18 it is extremely accurate with a CEP of about 230 metres.

As noted earlier, the USSR has even more to fear from growing warhead accuracy than does the USA. And this imbalance of insecurity is likely to grow, since while the USSR will be continuing its MIRVing programme for ICBMs in the 1980s, the USA plans to reduce the number of its ICBMs and deploy large numbers of air-launched cruise missiles. As a proportion of total deliverable megatonnage, therefore, the Soviet ICBM delivered proportion will rise above 75 per cent while the US equivalent will fall to less than 20 per cent.

The Soviet Union is already investing heavily in its next generation of ICBMs. Four new missile types have been identified and two have already completed their pre-flight testing. These latter two are solid-fuelled and extremely accurate. One of them is a mobile missile similar in size to the American MX missile.[55] The missile's accuracy is the same as that of the more advanced versions of the SS-18.

THE SOVIET SUBMARINE FORCE

The Soviet strategic nuclear submarine (SSBN) force has traditionally been less important than its American counterpart. The Soviet leadership has shown far less confidence in a submarine-launched ballistic missile force (SLBM) than in the land-based ICBMs. Political, geographical and technological constraints held back Soviet developments in this area in a way that they did not in the USA.

Politically, the Soviet leadership seems to have exhibited a nervousness about the command and control problems related to SSBNs. A submarine can communicate on long-wave radio by means of an antenna protruding above surface, but to do this raises the risk of discovery dramatically.[56] It is possible to communicate with a submarine running submerged by using very long-wave transmitters, but this facility will not work at great depths, again forcing a submarine to risk detection. To perform its strategic deterrent function a submarine needs to patrol undetected, thus it must remain silent, out of communication with its home base. This situation, militarily necessary, is politically offensive to Soviet leaders. The Soviet system is based on rigid hierarchy and adherence to the party line which in turn is based on the tenets of Leninism. It is deeply alarming for Soviet leaders to know that deep at sea are relatively low-ranking Soviet officers who, by launching their missiles in an unauthorized manner, could plunge the Soviet Union into a fatal war. The Kremlin goes to enormous lengths to guard against such an accidental release, but concern of this kind has slowed the development of the Soviet SSBN force until very recently, and kept it clearly subservient to the ICBM force.

Geographical constraints have also been important. The USA has an immense warm-water coastline from which its SSBNs can depart on patrol. The USSR has a huge coastline as well, but most of it borders the Arctic region where, for much of the year, navigation is obstructed by ice. Murmansk is the only northern port which the USSR can use all the year round. From here Soviet SSBNs can reach the northern Atlantic, but to sail further south they must pass through comparatively narrow waters, the Greenland–Iceland–Faroes–UK gap. In these areas NATO has sophisticated listening devices to detect Soviet submarines.

To use any other Soviet port is to run an even greater risk of detection. The Baltic exits are blocked by narrow waters monitored by Denmark, a NATO state. The exit from the Black Sea is the Dardanelles, watched by Turkey, another NATO member. On the Pacific coast, the Soviet Union has three main naval bases at Petrapavlovsk, Sovetskaia Gavan and Vladivostok. Petrapavlovsk is blocked by ice in winter, while to reach the Pacific from one of the other two bases, a Soviet SSBN must pass through seas whose exits are monitored by

Japan and the USA. Again, the difficulty of avoiding detection as they head out to sea on patrol has discouraged heavy Soviet commitment to SSBNs.

Finally, technical difficulties have constrained the USSR in this area. Although the Soviet Union has always been interested in SLBM technology, carrying out their first launch in 1955, the early Soviet SSBNs were primitive. The first Soviet SLBM, codenamed SS-N-4 'SARK' by NATO, was so large that it could barely squeeze into the space between the keel of the submarine and the top of its conning-tower. Only three missiles could be carried and the submarine had to surface in order to launch them. Each missile's range was limited to 600 km (373 miles). An improved missile, the SS-N-5 'SERB' appeared in 1963 and was installed in 'Golf' and 'Hotel' class submarines. Unlike its predecessor, the SS-N-5 could be launched underwater. It carried a single-megaton warhead, but range was still less than 1,600 km (1,000 miles). Still only three were fitted per submarine.

The breakthrough in Soviet SLBM technology came with the Yankee-SS-N-6 combination deployed in the late 1960s. For the first time, the Yankee-class submarines were purpose-built to accommodate SLBMs. Although the missiles were still large in comparison with hull diameter, they could at least be stored in the body of the submarine, rather than in the conning-tower. This meant that 16 launch-tubes could be used, the same number as the comparable American and British submarines: Polaris and Poseidon. The SS-N-6 missile itself, although still limited in range, could hit any soft target on the continental USA. To do so, the submarine had to move fairly close to the coast, but this gave the advantage of allowing the Americans virtually no alert time once they were fired. Some 34 Yankee-class submarines began regular patrols off the American coasts from 1967 onwards. The Yankee-class boats are now being gradually de-activated as their more modern replacements are deployed.

Yankee-SS-N-6's successor was the SS-N-8 missile carried by Delta-class submarines. This combination marked the attainment by the USSR of parity with the USA in terms of SLBM technology. The SS-N-8 missile's appearance was deeply disturbing to Western analysts. Monitoring of Soviet tests after 1971 showed that the N-8 had a range of 4,847 miles (7,800 kilometres) comparable to ICBM range, and twice the range of the Polaris and Poseidon missiles. The N-8, in fact, was superior in quality to the Trident I (C-4) missile which the USA was planning to deploy in the early 1980s. In terms of warhead size and accuracy (CEP was estimated at 1,312 feet (3,936 metres)), the SS-N-8 was in fact on a par with the Minuteman III ICBM.

This fearsome weapon required a massive launch-platform. The Delta class is the largest submarine in full operational service with any navy. Eighteen Delta I boats were launched by 1982, with an overall length of 450 feet. Delta I carries 12 SS-N-8 missiles, while the later Delta II can carry 16 SS-N-18s. Eleven Delta IIIs are in service. The N-18 is the first Soviet SLBM to carry MIRVed warheads and penetration aids. The missile's range is 9,600 km (6,000 miles).

Already, however, the USSR is moving forward in this technology. In September 1980 she launched the first of the new 'Typhoon'-class submarines. This submarine has a displacement of between 25,000 and 30,000 tons (the British aircraft carrier *Invincible* by contrast is only 19,500 tons). The Typhoon submarines will become operational during the 1980s at about the same time as the USA is deploying its Ohio-class Trident submarines. Typhoon will probably carry 20 missiles, the SS-NX-20, an improved version of the N-18, and each missile will have up to 12 warheads.[57] Like the N-18, the NX-20 has a range sufficient to enable it to cover virtually all American targets without leaving Soviet home waters.

THE SOVIET LONG-RANGE BOMBER FORCE

Unlike the USA, the Soviet Union has never relied heavily on long-range bombers. Two bombers, the jet M-4 'Bison' and the turbo-prop Tu-95 'Bear', with ranges in excess of 7,000 miles (11,200 kilometres) entered service in the mid-1950s, but the USSR has produced no new long-range bombers since then. Only 43 Bisons and 113 Bears remain in a bomber role, the rest being used as tanker and reconnaissance aircraft. The

Soviet bombers pose virtually no threat to the USA, and so complacent has the USA become about the danger that it has now virtually abandoned anti-aircraft defence of the continental USA. Occasional rumours of a new Soviet long-range bomber have emerged and NATO has given the codename 'Blackjack-A' to one such, a design slightly larger than the American B-2, but a major Soviet effort in this area is unlikely.

TABLE 2.4
Changes in inventory since 1970[58]

		1971	1973	1975	1977	1979	1981
ICBM	USA	1054	1054	1054	1054	1054	1054
	USSR	1527	1575	1477	1398	1398	1398
SLBM	USA	656	656	656	656	656	656
	USSR	348	628	784	709	1028	989
Long-range	USA	360	397	397	373	365	316
bombers	USSR	140	140	135	135	156	150

TABLE 2.5
Total of delivery vehicles since 1973[59]

	1973	1975	1977	1979	1981	1982
USA	2140	2079	2058	2057	2000	1919
USSR	2280	2464	2460	2475	2504	2504

TABLE 2.6
Warhead totals on strategic systems since 1973[60]

	1973	1975	1977	1979	1981
USA	6784	8500	8500	9200	9000
USSR	2200	2500	4000	5300	7000

As the first two tables illustrate, in terms of launchers there has not been much of a strategic arms race since 1970. Rather the reverse, for in nearly all instances the totals have been falling rather than rising. This may be seen as a direct benefit from the SALT-type arms control process.

However this picture is misleading. While it is true that the number of delivery vehicles — aircraft and missiles — have been falling, the number of warheads have been rising dramatically. Cynics would argue that the superpowers were willing to limit launcher totals in the SALT agreements precisely because they were no longer seen as being decisive. The strategic power of the superpowers has grown since 1970, even while launcher totals have fallen. This is because of the advent of the so-called 'force-multipliers', MIRVs and cruise missiles, which enable one delivery system to carry more than one warhead. Attempts to control this 'vertical proliferation' foundered in the 1970s, but their control remains the central strategic question of the 1980s.

STRATEGIC NUCLEAR ARMS CONTROL — SALT AND START

During the 1970s the efforts to control the strategic nuclear arms race were centred upon the process known as SALT, the Strategic Arms Limitation Talks. Before describing these briefly it is important to make a fundamental point. The SALT talks were not about *disarmament*. The superpowers were not attempting dramatically to reduce the size of their nuclear arsenals. What they were trying to do was to control the speed and directions in which these arsenals were growing. SALT then, was more 'an attempt to regulate an evolving strategic balance than to create a static one'.[61] As might be expected from an approach inaugurated by President Nixon and Dr Henry Kissinger, and welcomed by Leonid Brezhnev, it was a profoundly conservative exercise.

This remained true during the administrations of Gerald Ford and Jimmy Carter. The emphasis was on *control* of weapon development rather than *reduction*, and arms control was seen as being complementary to weapons procurement and development, rather than an alternative to it. As President Carter put it in 1978: 'when necessary, we will maintain our security and protect our interests by strengthening our military capabilities. Whenever possible however we seek to enhance our security through arms control.'[62]

The fundamental advantage of the SALT process to its

proponents was that it introduced an element of certainty into medium-term strategic planning. One of the engines of any arms race is the need to plan ahead. It takes many years to conceive, design, test, modify and deploy a modern weapon system, around ten years for a strategic nuclear delivery system. The planner has to cope with the world not just as it is today, but as he expects it to be in ten or fifteen years time. The assessment will be based on intelligence reports of existing adversary capabilities and their likely development. However this estimate can never be entirely accurate. If the planner overestimates the threat, he will authorize more effort and expenditure over the next ten years than is, strictly speaking, necessary. Money will be wasted, but at least security will be assured. If, however, he underestimates the threat and his country is too poorly armed to counter the enemy's strength, a decade later the results could be disastrous. In the absence of certainty, the 'safe' thing to do, therefore, is to overestimate to cope with the possible 'greater than expected threat'.

Obviously the adversary will not stand idly by as this build-up goes on. Once the build-up is recognized he is likely to respond. If in fact his own planned build-up was less than expected, he is likely to accelerate it to redress what he perceives as his opponent's attempt to pull ahead. The 'greater than expected threat' is therefore something of a self-fulfilling prophecy.

The SALT approach offered a way out of this dilemma. By limiting each side to verifiable launcher totals and placing some constraints on the MIRVing process, SALT established the upper parameters of the possible threat. As former Defence Secretary Harold Brown declared to the Senate Foreign Relations Committee on 9 June 1979, the SALT process was preferable to an unrestrained arms race because 'First, it tends to make the future balance more predictable and stable and less likely to become one-sided. Second, it provides more certainty to each side about the current programme of the other. Third, it is obviously less costly for both sides. Overall it is less risky for both sides.'[63]

The SALT process consisted of two major treaties and a number of related agreements. SALT I, signed in Moscow on

26 May 1972, consisted of two major documents. An interim agreement to limit offensive arms was signed limiting the superpowers' ICBM and SLBM forces to those either existing or under construction in mid-1972.

This agreement was important in that for the first time it limited the two sides' arsenals, and in doing so marked a major step forward for the arms control process. However, the interim agreement was marked by important omissions. Long-range bombers were left out and, more importantly, although missiles were limited, the number of warheads they could carry was not.

The second part of the 1972 agreement was the ABM Treaty. By this treaty, the two sides limited themselves to two ABM systems each, one around an ICBM site, one around the national capital. Only 100 missiles and a set number of radars could be deployed at each site.

On a first consideration, the euphoria which greeted this treaty is puzzling. ABMs (anti-ballistic missiles) are designed to intercept incoming nuclear missiles and destroy them before they reach their target. As Soviet Prime Minister Alexei Kosygin put it in 1967, an ABM system is designed 'to save human lives, not murder people'.[64] Yet arms controllers rejoiced that the American and Russian peoples were to be left virtually naked to the threat of immolation, even more so after 1974, when a protocol to the 1972 Treaty reduced the number of ABM sites permitted, to one each.

The logic of the arms controllers was brutally simple. The second strike was what was important. As long as neither side could defend itself against nuclear attack, a nuclear attack was highly unlikely since the adversary's retaliation would wipe the attacker out. However, if a state possessed ABM defences it might calculate that if it attacked first it could destroy so many of the adversary's forces that its ABM defences could cope with the retaliatory strike. In other words, possession of an ABM system would make nuclear war *more* not less likely.

The ABM treaty was of indefinite duration. Its signing was made possible because, among other factors, neither side had confidence in its technological capacity to produce an effective ABM system, and because neither side wanted the enormous costs that the construction of an ABM system would entail. Both sides also recognized the value of avoiding entering another area of strategic competition. Marshall Kulikov, Chief of the Soviet General Staff, praised the 1972 ABM treaty for 'preventing the emergence of a chain reaction of competition between offensive and defensive arms'.[65] An ABM system would not only be destabilizing as such, it would trigger off greater investment on *offensive* weapons designed to smother the ABM defences.

Despite this, the past few years have seen a resurgence of advocacy of ABMs by leading American thinkers, including a senior adviser to President Reagan who has argued that 'the United States should pursue the development of effective ABM systems'.[66] Although one can see the moral attraction of such defensive systems, it is notable that the advocates of ABM argue that they should be used to defend missile sites rather than cities. It is also significant that ABM advocates in the USA are calling for an acceptance of nuclear weapons as 'war-fighting' tools. In technical terms, ABM systems remain unproven, and the case against them remains that against a weapons system 'that makes nuclear war just a little bit more likely'.[67]

SALT II

The 1972 Interim agreement on offensive systems was designed to last for five years, during which time a comprehensive treaty would be negotiated. In fact it was not until 1979, after seven years of arduous negotiations that SALT II was signed. The delay was partly due to the complexity of the negotiations and partly the result of American politics. A draft SALT II, ready in 1974, remained unsigned because Gerald Ford did not want to be seen as too friendly towards the USSR, at a time when Ronald Reagan was opposing him for Republican nomination. After Ford lost the subsequent general election, the Carter administration abandoned the 1974 draft, Carter because he felt the cuts did not go far enough, Brzezinski (the national security adviser) because he would have nothing to do with any plan concocted by his predecessor Dr Henry Kissinger. The resultant delays meant that nearly four years passed before a Carter SALT II Treaty (very similar to the 1974 Ford–Brezhnev treaty) was ready, and by that time another US election was imminent. The electoral considerations that plagued Ford came to affect Carter (even his eventual opponent, Reagan, was the same) and the SALT II Treaty was never presented to the Senate for ratification. However, in the absence of anything better, both sides are abiding by its provisions (despite President Reagan's description of the treaty as being 'fatally flawed'.[68] It is therefore worth noting the main features of SALT II before going on to look at the Reagan administration's own arms control effort, the 'START' talks.

SALT II limits the USA and USSR to 2,400 strategic nuclear delivery systems. Within that total a maximum of 1,320 launchers may be equipped with MIRVed missiles, or cruise missiles with a range in excess of 600 kilometres. MIRVed systems are limited to 1,200 and of these only 820 can be ICBMs. The number of warheads carried by any one missile is limited to ten on an ICBM and 14 on an SLBM. Each side may introduce one new ICBM with ten warheads. Ceilings on launch-weight and payload of ICBMs are also laid down, as are certain technical restrictions on missile modernization and conversion. With regard to cruise missiles, no existing bomber may carry more than an average of 20, no new bomber may average more than 28.

THE START TALKS

The Reagan strategic arms control initiative marked a move away from the SALT approach, or at least a major acceleration of pace compared with SALT. When the START (Strategic Arms Reduction Talks) opened at Geneva on 29 June 1982, the American proposal was for major reductions rather than mere limits to growth. The American plan called for cuts in the total number of warheads by one-third to a level of 5,000 each. No more than half of these could be carried on ICBMs. A total of 850 ICBMs and SLBMs would be allowed to each side.

These proposals are dramatic, all the more so coming from a President who has initiated a 7 per cent increase in defence spending. They are not entirely new, since in 1977 the Carter administration made a similar proposal for sweeping reductions, which the USSR rejected out of hand. Will the START proposals suffer the same fate?

There is not much ground for optimism. The American proposals, while they may not actually be *designed* to be rejected by the USSR, are clearly an effort to obtain unilateral American advantages, though in an opening round of bargaining, this is to be expected. The real question is whether the Reagan administration is prepared to modify its proposals later in the negotiations in order to reach an agreement.

The reason why the proposals are unlikely to impress the USSR is that they ask Russia to make substantial cutbacks in its forces, involving a massive restructuring of their strategic posture, yet in return the USA gives up virtually nothing. On the contrary, under the Reagan proposals, while the USSR is forced to cut back, most of the planned US build-up can go ahead unhindered. Thus, for example, no mention is made of bombers so the B-1 programme can go ahead, while the USSR has no bomber programme. Submarines are virtually unaffected also, leaving the Trident programme intact. The emphasis is upon ICBMs, and here the USA is in any case planning to reduce its launcher total by replacing the three-warhead Minuteman III with the ten-warhead MX.

As noted earlier, nearly three-quarters of the USSR's strategic power is invested in ICBMs, so major cutbacks would almost exclusively affect them. This may be desirable in many ways, and in terms of counterforce potential it clearly is, but is it *negotiable*? The USSR is left the option of turning more to SLBMs, but as noted earlier, historically and for geographical reasons, the USSR has not seen SLBMs as a satisfactory solution. Even now, while the USSR has more SSBNs than the USA, technical and geographical problems mean that the USA is always able to keep far more SSBNs at sea than the USSR.

The USSR for its part would prefer to 'freeze' the totals at their existing level, to codify the SALT II environment. Many influential Americans, including Senator Edward Kennedy, favour this solution. It would have the advantage that it could be done immediately, it would not need years of protracted negotiations. However, it would leave the balance asymmetrical, with the USSR possessing some advantages such as the 308 'heavy' ICBMs, the USA possessing other advantages such as its bomber force.

What seems most practical is a combination of the approaches. A freeze, represented by ratification of SALT II, followed by staged reductions towards, and beyond, the Reagan proposals. In a bureaucratically inert state such as the USSR it is asking too much to expect it to restructure its forces virtually overnight. However, the SALT talks in the 1970s did affect the Soviet programmes — SALT II, for example, calls for the USSR to abandon four of its five new ICBMs. Gradual redirection of Soviet effort would be compatible with their bureaucratic restraints. The USSR can probably contemplate some ICBM cuts immediately — if only because of the weakness of the Soviet economy, but these cuts, even if modest, should be seized upon by the USA and placed in a treaty. The USA should not squander a decade of precious time by insisting on its preferred option to the exclusion of rapid compromise.

3

The spread of nuclear weapons

Attempts to control the spread of nuclear weapons have been part of the diplomatic agenda since the dawn of the nuclear age. As early as 1946, the USA put forward the Baruch Plan which tried to establish international control of nuclear material in order to prevent its use in weapons. However, the USSR rejected the plan, partly because it called upon the Soviet Union to disarm before America gave up its nuclear weapons, and partly because the inspection procedures required were seen as being too intrusive. In the absence of controls, the number of nuclear weapons states (NWS) grew slowly but steadily, the USA being joined by the USSR in 1949, Britain in 1952, France in 1960, and China in 1964. In 1974 India exploded a nuclear device but insisted that it was not a weapon-test.

The increase in the number of NWS is normally referred to as 'nuclear proliferation'. However 'proliferation' implies a process far more rapid than the one which has actually occurred since 1945. There has not been the rapid increase in the number of NWS that many foresaw, and in terms of weapons *testing* only India and perhaps South Africa come into this category since 1964. Where proliferation has occurred has been in the number of nuclear weapons possessed by *existing* nuclear powers, particularly the USA and USSR. In other words, 'vertical' proliferation rather than 'horizontal' proliferation has been the dominant feature of the nuclear age.

Given that the nuclear spread has not been as rapid as some feared in the 1950s, a number of questions arise. Why has it occurred at all? Why should states wish to possess nuclear weapons, and what would be the likely consequences of a continuing, although gradual, increase in the number of NWS?

How strong is the link between the spread of nuclear energy technology and the spread of nuclear weapons capabilities, and what can be done to limit the spread of nuclear weapons?

WHY SHOULD STATES WISH TO ACQUIRE NUCLEAR WEAPONS?

In some ways the acquisition of nuclear weapons is seen as providing a solution to age-old military and diplomatic problems. All states, to a greater or lesser extent, feel insecure in a basically anarchic world. The more power they can acquire, the safer they feel because other states are less likely to attack them. Moreover, the more power they have, the more they can *do*, the more they can try to influence the course of world events, rather than being a victim of events over which they have little control. Thus, because of their awesome destructive power, a state may see nuclear weapons as immeasurably enhancing its power, its ability to influence others. These elements of 'power' as a rationale for acquiring nuclear weapons can be subdivided into military and diplomatic incentives.

MILITARY INCENTIVES

The most frequently used arguments for developing nuclear weapons are the military arguments. A state may acquire nuclear weapons because a potential enemy has already done so. Thus it is hoped that by having the ability to retaliate in kind, a state will be able to deter a nuclear attack upon itself. Thus, once the USA had demonstrated the power of its nuclear weapons against Japan in 1945, the USSR felt obliged to develop a similar capability in order to avoid being blackmailed by the USA. Even the *likelihood* that a potential enemy will produce nuclear weapons may spur a state into acquiring them first,[1] as, for example, with Argentina and Brazil.

The American nuclear attack on Japan in 1945 illustrates another use for nuclear weapons — to achieve a decisive military advantage over a state that does not possess such weapons. A variation of this is the desire of some states to acquire nuclear capabilities which can offset a potential enemy's advantages in conventional weaponry. Thus NATO in the 1950s increasingly relied upon nuclear weapons to compensate for the USSR's advantage in tanks and soldiers. Similar arguments could be advanced to justify the acquisition of nuclear weapons by Israel or Pakistan.

Finally, a state may want to acquire nuclear weapons in order to make itself more independent. A state can shelter behind the protective 'umbrella' of another state's nuclear weapons, as Japan and most of the NATO states do with regard to the USA. This, however, has two serious consequences: first, criticism of one's ally at times of divergent interest is muted for fear of alienating a state upon whom one is, in the final analysis, dependent; second, one is always haunted by the fear that *in extremis* the nuclear ally will not come to one's aid. To avoid these two consequences and restore at least the illusion of independence, a state may acquire its own nuclear weapons, as has been the case with both Britain and France within NATO.

Once a state has 'gone nuclear' its rivals may find themselves under pressure to do likewise. The USSR, Britain, France and China, in developing nuclear weapons were all to some extent reacting to the threat posed by the nuclear weapons of a potential adversary. China's 1964 weapons-test led India to begin reassessing its earlier support for non-proliferation, with the result that by 1974 India too had exploded a nuclear device. Since 1974 the same pressures have encouraged Pakistan to undertake a serious nuclear weapons development programme.

The disturbing logic of nuclear weapons is that 'the same arguments that led to the emergence of five (or six) nuclear powers can be used by the seventh, eighth and ninth nuclear powers'.[2] However, states may indicate that they will forswear nuclear weapons so long as their rivals do likewise.[3] Nor would a state necessarily have to develop large numbers of weapons carried by sophisticated delivery systems similar to those possessed by the great powers. If a state with few nuclear weapons and limited delivery system options were the only NWS in a particular area it would have an overwhelming military advantage in that particular region. And even if it lost its monopoly it would still possess a powerful *deterrent* against attack.

For these reasons a number of near-nuclear states have kept their nuclear option open by not becoming parties to the Non-Proliferation Treaty (NPT). These states include Argentina, Brazil, Chile, Cuba, India, Israel, Indonesia, Pakistan, South Africa and Spain. Even the states that did sign the NPT can, under the terms of the treaty, withdraw at three months notice, and some like Taiwan and South Korea, could produce nuclear weapons very rapidly should they decide to do so.

DIPLOMATIC INCENTIVES

As well as the purely military arguments in favour of acquiring nuclear weapons, a number of diplomatic reasons are also put forward. It is argued that by demonstrating the technological ability and military resolve required to produce nuclear weapons, a state can enhance its prestige and international status. Britain and France are cited as examples of states where international standing is artificially enhanced by their possession of nuclear weapons. States may therefore seek nuclear weapons in order to gain great power status. India, Brazil and Argentina have shown themselves to be sensitive to such thinking. Even if nuclear weapons could not confer global great power status, they may be seen as being sufficient to establish regional great power status, as with India and Brazil.

Nuclear weapons may be acquired in order to demonstrate political independence, as was clearly the case with General de Gaulle's France. There is also the rather disingenuous argument used by British statesmen that possession of nuclear weapons guarantees 'a seat at the head table', that is, it allows a state's voice to be heard among the other great powers in discussions about nuclear weapons. There is in fact little evidence to support the idea that Britain's possession of nuclear weapons has made her more influential in international forums since 1952 than she would otherwise have been.

For certain developing states, the acquisition of nuclear weapons may seem attractive as a way of improving their position in the international hierarchy. A state like India, for example, with a huge land area, massive population and many strengths may feel that she is being accorded less respect than is her due by the developed states. Joining the 'select few' of NWS might seem a solution to this problem, and certainly both the USA and the USSR have been far more careful not to offend India since she exploded a nuclear device.

The idea that possession of nuclear weapons automatically enhances prestige in a unique way can of course be challenged. Indeed some states seem to have gained increased international stature by pursuing the opposite course. Sweden, for example, which *could* have gone nuclear enhances her standing by not doing so, and thereby avoids hypocrisy in her calls for global nuclear disarmanent. Similarly Canada won a great deal of approval from the developing world when she ceased equipping her troops with nuclear weapons in the 1970s. States like Britain which call for nuclear disarmament while demonstrating that they themselves prefer to possess nuclear weapons cannot avoid hypocrisy, and the double standard which is so evident makes it extremely difficult to persuade near-nuclear states that they should refrain from crossing the nuclear weapons threshold, as a number of states may be on the verge of doing.

WHICH STATES MIGHT GO NUCLEAR?

Pakistan

At present the clearest candidate to join the nuclear club is probably Pakistan. Pakistan is a signatory to the Partial Test Ban Treaty, banning atmospheric nuclear testing, but has not yet ratified the treaty. Like India, Pakistan has not signed the Non-Proliferation Treaty. Thus there is nothing in international law to prevent Pakistan from carrying out a nuclear weapons test. Whether she does so or not will depend on two factors.

The first factor is the stability of the Pakistani regime. A weak regime might wish to explode a device in order to

reap the domestic political support which benefited Mrs
Gandhi's Government immediately after India's 1974 test.
The second, and probably more decisive factor, is the relationship with India itself. Even after the intrusion of vastly
increased Soviet influence in Afghanistan, and the upheavals
within Iran, it remains true to say that Pakistan's primary
security concern is India. India has an overwhelming advantage in the balance of conventional forces and has already
demonstrated a nuclear weapons capability. In these circumstances, and given India's failure to sign the NPT or join the
nuclear facilities safeguards regime, it is hardly surprising that
Pakistan, at the very least, wishes to keep its nuclear option
open.

The 1974 Indian test had a profound affect upon the
Pakistani leadership. It is true that as early as 1965 Zulfikar
Bhutto had declared that if India acquired the bomb, Pakistan
would 'eat grass if necessary' in order to keep up with her.
However Pakistan reacted calmly to Indian nuclear research
and it was only after the 1974 test explosion that Pakistan
began to make the tremendous effort necessary to emulate
India's nuclear achievement.

Although Mrs Gandhi assured Pakistan that India had no
intention of producing nuclear weapons, the Pakistani leadership was understandably alarmed by the 1974 explosion.
Bhutto noted that it was a question not only of intentions
but of capabilities:

> Testing of a nuclear device is not different from the
> detonation of a weapon. Given this, how is it possible
> for our fears to be assuaged by mere assurances which
> may be ignored in subsequent years? Governments
> change, as do national attitudes. But the acquisition of a
> capability becomes a permanent factor to be reckoned
> with.[4]

How far Bhutto was the driving force behind the Pakistani
bomb project is open to dispute. In 1972, two years before
the Indian test, Bhutto announced that Pakistan ought to
have the bomb.[5] The Indian test doubtless reinforced this
resolve. Bhutto at one stage even spoke of the bizarre concept

of the 'Islamic bomb', arguing that since Christian, Jewish, Hindu and Communist peoples possessed nuclear weapons it was only right that Islamic civilization should also have access to such a weapon.[6] Certainly, he seems to have believed that nuclear weapons would make Pakistan pre-eminent in the Islamic world. Some commentators, however, place the acceleration of Pakistani nuclear weapons research much later. According to Ashok Kapur, for example, it was the generals who overthrew Bhutto who gave the nuclear programme its real momentum. The Pakistani Foreign Office has generally remained unenthusiastic about nuclear weapons,[7] unlike successive heads of government in Pakistan.

The amount of uranium which Pakistan is currently producing means that few bombs could be manufactured. Indian intelligence sources believe that Pakistan could not prepare a weapon before 1984, but the Carter administration believed that by late 1981 Pakistan would have had the ability and material to explode a bomb.[8]

Producing a device is one thing; developing a credible weapon system is quite another. Pakistan would face major difficulties in producing a delivery system with assured penetration capability. India has a large advantage in numbers of conventional aircraft, so that any Pakistani bomber equipped with nuclear weapons would have little chance of getting through. It has been estimated that an airborne nuclear force would need to use two or even four bombers to attack each target if it hoped to get one aircraft through.[9] At present, although Pakistan is being re-equipped with new sophisticated nuclear-capable aircraft, she almost certainly has not produced enough weapons-grade nuclear material to arm numerous aircraft. She lacks therefore a *credible* delivery system and, in the absence of this, has limited incentives to demonstrate, as distinct from *acquire*, a nuclear weapon capability.

India, by contrast, may be overcoming such constraints. A missile programme is sometimes seen as being beyond the economic and technological capabilities of a developing country. The French missile programme for example consumed 50 per cent of the equipment portion of the French military budget in 1965, and between 1965 and 1970 accounted for

17 per cent of the French defence budget each year.[10] Expenditure demands on this scale caused the abandonment of the technically flawless British Blue Streak missile in 1960 and may well cause Britain to abandon her Trident missile programme in the 1980s. However, India seems to have overcome some of these problems. On 18 July 1980, she placed a satellite in orbit using a four-stage, 17 tonne rocket, the SLV-3. This launch vehicle could be adapted to serve as an Intermediate Range Ballistic Missile (IRBM) should India so choose.

Without a missile programme, the value of a Pakistani nuclear weapons programme is open to question. It would excite deep concern in its neighbours because it would lack any sort of second-strike capability. Relying on aircraft delivery-systems, Pakistan would be vulnerable to the effect of these aircraft being destroyed in a pre-emptive air attack by India. Even if this did not happen, the Pakistani aircraft would probably not get through in wartime. To have any chance of success therefore Pakistan would have to use its nuclear weapons *before war was declared*, and the military and diplomatic consequences of such an act would be so devastating as to seem to eliminate it from rational consideration.

If Pakistani nuclear weapons are of such doubtful utility, and are a response to Indian activities, there are clear reasons why India should want to allay Pakistan's fears of her neighbour. This seems to be well understood in New Delhi. In July 1981, Mrs Gandhi indicated that India might be turning away from the nuclear weapons path: 'I don't know how it would help if we also had nuclear weapons', she declared.[11]

Pakistan may yet be convinced by such assurances. She has herself displayed a reluctance to take the path followed by Britain, France and China. Even in the period of Pakistani nuclear development she has kept her nuclear facilities open to International Atomic Energy Association (IAEA) inspection safeguards, and has pursued diplomatic initiatives to curb nuclear arms development in the area.[12] Thus, while Pakistan is close to the brink, she is not rushing blindly towards it.

Argentina

According to Brazilian intelligence, Argentina already possesses a nuclear bomb. One senior Brazilian military official has said: '. . . either the Argentines already possess a nuclear device, or they can make it at short notice, depending only on their own political wish to do so'.

Argentina itself has been careful to keep its nuclear options open. Jorge Sabato, a former member of the Atomic Energy Commission of Argentina, has declared that while Latin American countries might not be actually producing nuclear weapons: 'we also wish to have our own capacity to judge, our own technical autonomous capability to decide what is best for our countries in that matter. For that reason we try to learn and develop as much as possible'.[13]

Like Pakistan, Argentina has not signed the Non-Proliferation Treaty or the Partial Test Ban Treaty. It has signed, though not yet ratified, the Treaty of Tlatelolco which established a Latin American nuclear-free zone. Argentina's refusal to sign the NPT or to ratify the Treaty of Tlatelolco has raised fears that it is bent upon the acquisition of nuclear weapons. This led President Carter to attempt, unsuccessfully, to prevent Switzerland from selling a heavy-water production plant to Argentina.

Argentina has five research reactors and one power reactor, all of which operate under IAEA safeguards. It has the largest known reserves of uranium ore in Latin America,[14] and Argentina's first nuclear plant 'Atucha' is a German-built natural uranium reactor. Thus, unlike other near-nuclear states, Argentina does not need to depend upon proliferation-conscious states like Canada or the USA for its supply of processed uranium. Already Argentina's nuclear expertise is felt to be well ahead of her regional rival Brazil and is buttressed by a nuclear co-operation agreement with India.

In addition to being able to pursue the uranium route to nuclear weapons, Argentina can pursue the plutonium option. It has its own plutonium reprocessing plant. 'Atucha' was switched off twice during 1978 and it is believed that this was to enable the spent fuel containing plutonium to be removed from the reactor core. Thus Argentina can produce its own plutonium and is almost certainly already in a position to explode a nuclear device should it choose to do so. However, many experts believe that at present Argentina has produced only enough plutonium for one, or at most, two weapons, and this is why it is reluctant as yet to 'waste any by conducting a test.

In terms of delivery systems, Argentina possesses French Mirage III, American A-4 Skyhawk and British Canberra bombers which could deliver a nuclear payload. Research is under way in Argentina to produce large surface-to-surface missiles.

Brazil

Argentina's great rival is Brazil. Brazil has long seen itself as an emerging great power and as the natural leader of Latin America. It is certainly not going to allow Argentina to usurp this position. Since 1978, Brazil has markedly accelerated its nuclear development programme. This is all the more significant because there are no apparent reasons why Brazil should be interested in nuclear energy for any purpose. Even Brazilian government ministers such as Delfim Netto, have criticized the nuclear programme for aiming at an alternative energy source that Brazil neither needs nor can afford. And if Brazil does not need nuclear energy, still less does it need to worry about its security. Brazil is by far the dominant military power in the region, and none of its neighbours or rivals are in a position to challenge it militarily. Only if Argentina demonstrated its possession of nuclear weapons would that position change. The transparently obvious attempts by Argentina to acquire such weapons have therefore led to a regional nuclear arms race as Brazil works energetically to close the gap with her rival. Although Brazil is still behind, the gap is narrowing rapidly.

Despite economic difficulties, Brazil has invested hugely in nuclear research in the last few years. The nuclear holding company Nuclebras was the only state enterprise granted a budget increase in 1980, and has been allocated huge amounts of capital since 1978. If present plans are adhered to, Brazil will reach Argentina's present position of having the *capability* to produce nuclear weapons sometime between 1985 and 1990.

Brazil is being helped by a nuclear co-operation agreement with West Germany. German-Brazilian collaboration is also going on in the field of missile technology;[15] since 1965 Brazil has conducted over four hundred test launches. In terms of currently available delivery systems, Brazil has Mirage III and American F-5 aircraft. It has been speculated that by the turn of the century Brazil will be in a position to produce her own IRBMs with Brazilian nuclear warheads.[16]

South Korea

Unlike the previous cases discussed, the decision of South Korea about whether or not to produce nuclear weapons is dependent primarily upon the actions of its major ally rather than those of its most likely enemy.

South Korea is a firm proponent of the advantages of nuclear energy. By the year 2000 the South Korean Government plans to increase the nuclear contribution to total electricity generating capacity to 52 per cent. In terms of technological capability and the amount of weapons-grade material already being produced as a by-product of the peaceful nuclear energy programme, South Korea already has the wherewithal to produce a small number of nuclear warheads. At present, however, it is under no great pressure to do so. The key determinant is the attitude of the USA.

Under American pressure South Korea ratified the NPT in 1975. However, two months after doing so, the South Korean President called for a research programme to develop nuclear weapons. Most significantly, he declared that South Korea could and would develop its own nuclear weapons if the American nuclear umbrella were withdrawn.

This is the key point. South Korea has no need for nuclear weapons *per se*. It is concerned with the security that they can provide. Thus, so long as South Korea remains secure behind a strong South Korean and American conventional military shield, buttressed by the implied American nuclear guarantee, there is no incentive for South Korea to develop nuclear weapons of her own. At present South Korea's conventional forces are a match for those of the North and as long as the USA maintains a strong military presence in South Korea, that country is unlikely to feel that nuclear weapons must be added to its military inventory.

However, even if the USA did withdraw its forces and South Korea produced its own nuclear weapons, this would not necessarily trigger a regional nuclear arms race. North Korea is not in a position to produce nuclear weapons un-aided, and neither China nor the Soviet Union would be keen to supply it with the necessary technology. On the contrary, they would be energetic in dissuading it from doing so.

Taiwan

Taiwan may be numbered among the 'pariah states' of the international system, a group of states with few friends and a large number of idological enemies. Israel and South Africa also fall into this group. This very isolation makes them strong candidates to join the nuclear club. Of the three Taiwan is probably the least likely to do so.

Taiwan has been an enthusiastic supporter of the NPT regime. It signed the treaty on the first day possible, 1 July 1968, and had completed its ratification process by 1970. Taiwan supported the NPT because it seemed to mirror their own attitudes to nuclear power — condemning military proli-feration while leaving the road clear for the peaceful exploita-tion of nuclear energy.

Taiwan had acquired its first nuclear reactor in the 1950s, and by 1980 had four large reactors, two research reactors and a plutonium reprocessing plant. Certainly Taiwan has the capacity to produce several small nuclear warheads each year if it chose to do so. It has the nuclear facilities and it has more than enough competent physicists and engineers.

Whether it does so depends, as with South Korea, to a large extent upon the actions of the USA. As long as the USA is committed to defending Taiwan against any Chinese attack then Taiwan need not undertake the production of nuclear weapons. However, since the American *rapprochement* with China in the early 1970s, the USA has steadily reduced its military and diplomatic support for Taiwan. Should American support ever be completely withdrawn, Taiwan might feel obliged to acquire nuclear weapons in order to offset China's overwhelming conventional military superiority. Taiwan has therefore taken steps to keep its nuclear option open, with a number of small steps being steadily taken in the direction of acquiring nuclear weapons.

One further factor *might* operate to deter Taiwan from going nuclear – and this may, without being made public, also influence South Korean nuclear decision-making. This is the question of targeting. Both Taiwan and South Korea claim to speak for all their people, Chinese and Korean respectively. They argue that the Peoples' Republic of China and North Korea are bandit regimes keeping their people imprisoned by force. In such circumstances it would be difficult for either government to use nuclear weapons against its *own people*. Premier Chiang Ching-Kuo of Taiwan said in 1975 that when he had broached the subject of Taiwanese nuclear weapons to his late father, the former Premier Chiang Kai-shek: 'he rejected it flatly on the ground that we cannot use nuclear weapons to hurt our own countrymen'.

South Africa

South Africa is strongly suspected of having tested a nuclear device in 1979. On 22 September of that year an American 'Vela' satellite detected a flash of light over the South Atlantic which, American scientists declared, bore the unmistakeable 'signature' of a low-yield nuclear explosion, one estimated to be in the 2.5 to 3.0 kiloton range. South African warships were in the area at the time.

It has been an accepted fact that for several years South Africa has been able to explode a nuclear device, but it has not been known how far, in practical terms, that ability has been exercised. A report by the United Nations[17] declared that, because overt possession of nuclear weapons would entail diplomatic risks, South Africa would prefer covertly to stockpile nuclear weapons, but without actually testing or deploying them.

Within South Africa itself even critics of the regime doubt whether a device has actually been tested. However, there has been speculation that the flash seen by the Vela satellite was the testing of an 155 mm shell fired by a howitzer from a South African warship.[18] American scientists in the US Office of Science and Technology Policy have been cited as believing that the 1979 blast may have been a 'neutron' bomb explosion.[19] The low yield — one quarter of the yield of the Hiroshima bomb — supports this contention. Because such a weapon reduces blast effects and dramatically cuts risks of fall-out, it would have some military uses for South Africa in a way that a normal nuclear weapon would not. The CIA investigation of the 1979 blast concluded that the flash *was* an explosion and that it was either South African or Israeli, or part of a co-operative research programme between those two states.

Such tests may have occurred before 1979. The Vela satellite was slightly out of position when it photographed the 1979 blast and earlier tests may have been timed to avoid satellite surveillance of this kind. In 1977 Soviet and American satellites spotted a nuclear test range being built in the Kalahari desert. This was dismantled following Western diplomatic pressure.

The South African Government's position is one of deliberate ambiguity. South Africa is not a party to the NPT, and although the 1977 and 1979 incidents produced routine denials of Western accusations, government spokesmen never give a direct 'no' when asked if the country has, or intends to have, nuclear weapons. They simply repeat the assertion that South Africa is only interested in the peaceful application of nuclear energy.

However, there are few pressures for South Africa to follow even the peaceful nuclear path. South Africa has massive coal resources and is an exporter of coal. Although South Africa is vulnerable to interference with her oil supplies, she uses much less oil as a proportion of total energy production than do other developed countries. Moreover she has two SASOL plants for converting coal into liquid fuel.[20]

Despite this existing energy wealth, South Africa has two research reactors and two light water reactors. She also possesses a fifth of the non-communist world's uranium reserves and is developing her own capacity to enrich uranium. Thus there are no technical or resource barriers standing in the way of a South African nuclear weapons programme.

As early as 1965 the then South African Prime Minister, Dr Verwoerd, referred to the Government's 'duty' to consider the military uses of nuclear material. The South African Government sees itself as being faced by major security threats. Prime Minister Botha has spoken of the 'total onslaught' facing the country. South Africa is faced by implacably hostile neighbours and near neighbours, and, unlike Israel, cannot rely on the support of a major power. Even so, it is difficult to see what military use nuclear weapons are to South Africa.

The country's conventional military forces are vastly more powerful than those of neighbouring states. The only black African state with the resources to challenge South Africa is Nigeria, and her army is under-equipped and too far away to threaten Pretoria. The real threat to South Africa's regime is that posed by guerrilla warfare and internal dissent, where nuclear weapons would offer no conceivable advantages.

South Africa could use the threat of her nuclear weapons to intimidate Angola, Zimbabwe and Mozambique into closing their frontiers to anti-South African guerrillas, but such a policy would be diplomatically reckless; the same strategy could in any case be pursued using South Africa's conventional military superiority and economic dominance for leverage. However, as South Africa becomes increasingly isolated, diplomatically such reckless behaviour may come to be seen as being less costly. And the rationality or otherwise of such action must in any case be judged in the light of the South African leadership's record, which is already lacking in rationality by many internationally accepted criteria.

In this regard the South African leadership benefits from what, in another context, has been called 'the rationality of irrationality'. Because the regime has *already* demonstrated its utter ruthlessness and indifference to international opinion, its threat to unleash a holocaust if pressed too far is not totally without credibility, in which case South Africa does not need to demonstrate its possession of nuclear weapons, its likely possession is a sufficient deterrent. A South African newspaper asked in 1979: 'Who needs a real bomb? Rumours are a cheaper deterrent.'[21] Thus, since South Africa does not *demonstrate* its possession of nuclear weapons it incurs no diplomatic costs for so demonstrating, while the generally-held belief that it does in fact possess them gives it the military and diplomatic advantages accruing to a nuclear weapon state.

In terms of international restraint upon proliferation, South Africa poses a particularly difficult problem. It has been noted that the best way to stop South Africa deploying nuclear weapons might be to give her something such as greatly increased supplies of conventional weapons for not doing so.[22] However, the international opprobrium in which South Africa is held makes the offering of anything significant essentially impossible, enabling her 'deterrence by uncertainty' to continue.

Israel

Israel has long been suspected of possessing nuclear weapons. In 1974 President Katzir said: 'it has always been our intention to develop the nuclear potential. We now have that potential.' In the same year a CIA document was accidentally released which declared:

> We believe that Israel already has produced nuclear weapons. Our judgement is based on Israeli acquisition of large quantities of uranium, partly by clandestine means, the ambiguous nature of Israel's large investment in a costly missile system designed to accommodate nuclear warheads.[23]

The CIA put the number of Israeli nuclear warheads at between ten and twenty, but concluded that it was unlikely that Israel would confirm their suspicions either by testing or by threat of use, unless the existence of Israel was gravely threatened.

There are indications that this may have occurred in 1973, when Egypt and Syria drove back Israeli forces in the first days of the Yom Kippur War. Israeli nuclear weapons are alleged to have been taken out of underground emplacements in the Negev Desert and placed on specially adapted bombers ready for use, should the need for them have arisen.[24]

Israel's governments have used ambiguous statements to deny possession of nuclear weapons. Spokesmen always declare that: 'Israel will not be the first country in the Middle East to introduce nuclear arms into the region.' Like South Africa, Israel is following a policy of 'deterrence by uncertainty'. It has not threatened anyone with its nuclear weapons, but the persistent reports are enough to caution Israeli's neighbours. There is physical evidence of the Israeli efforts in the research facilities at Dimona in the Negev desert, and at Nahal Sorek near Tel Aviv. In terms of delivery systems, the Israelis are well equipped with nuclear-capable aircraft and missiles.

Iraq

Israel's declaratory policy of not being the first state to introduce nuclear weapons into the Middle East extends beyond restraint in nuclear testing. She has worked actively to sabotage the nuclear programmes of her rivals and the most obvious victim of this policy has been Iraq.

President Saddim Hussain of Iraq said in July 1980 that Iraq had 'no programme concerning the manufacture of the atomic bomb'. However, he then went on to imply that the Arab world would develop nuclear weapons soon, and that 'whoever wants to be our enemy can expect that enemy to be totally different in the very near future'.

Iraq is the most advanced Arab country in nuclear development, and since 1968, when the USSR supplied an IRT-2000 reactor, the Iraqis have steadily developed their nuclear expertise. The USSR has been careful, however, to ensure that Soviet-supplied material can only be used for peaceful purposes. Iraq's other main supplier, France, has not been so careful. The French-supplied reactor in Iraq will use weapons-grade uranium fuel, and France is supplying 72 kilogrammes of fuel in advance. Encased in a beryllium reflector, as little as 16.5 kilogrammes would be needed to produce a crude, but effective, nuclear weapon. Since Iraq also has 12 Soviet-built 'Blinder' bombers, Israel has made every effort to obstruct the Iraqi nuclear programme.

In April 1979 the naval yards at Seyne-sur-Mer in France were attacked by commandos who destroyed metal casings about to be despatched to the Iraqi French-built reactor. In June 1980 Professor Yahia el Meshed, an Egyptian scientist working on the Franco–Iraqi nuclear programme, was found beaten to death in a Paris hotel room. His wallet was untouched. As with the Seyne-sur-Mer attack, the Israeli secret service Mossad, was suspected. In September 1980 the Franco–Iraqi Osirak reactor was attacked by Phantom F-4 fighter-bombers. Iraq was at war with Iran by then, but although the aircraft carried Iranian markings, Iraq alleged that Israeli F-4s had carried out the raid, which had entailed precision-bombing to a degree uncharacteristic of Iranian air attacks.

Finally, on 7 June 1981, Israeli aircraft attacked and destroyed the Osirak reactor. The following day an official Israeli Government statement justified the attack, declaring that: 'Under no circumstances will we allow our enemy to develop weapons of mass destruction against our people. We shall defend the citizens of Israel in good time and with all the means at our disposal.'

Whether or not Iraqi intentions justified the attack is an open question. The Israeli Prime Minister, Menachim Begin, has been accused of timing the Osirak raid to boost his chances in the Israeli election campaign then in progress. Certainly Iraq's activities in the nuclear field have been far more above-board than Israel's. Iraq, unlike Israel, has signed the NPT and is open to IAEA safeguards. Both the Congressional Research Service in Washington and the IAEA refuted the Israeli claim that Iraq was able to produce a bomb.[25] Moreover, the Iraqi plant was operating under an agreement with France by which all spent fuel was returned to France for treatment. This enabled France to take back the plutonium produced. Iraq has no uranium retreatment plant. In addition, the French engineers at Osirak were to remain in charge of the facility until 1989,[26] thus giving them a veto over military activity.

If the Israeli action was premature, it was certainly decisive and has opened up the danger of other pre-emptive attacks of this kind: India against Pakistan, or Brazil against Argentina. By Premier Begin's own logic, the Israeli nuclear facilities would themselves be legitimate targets for Arab attacks.

The dangers which such measures and counter-measures might provoke are heightened by the involvement of the superpowers in the region. Newspaper reports quoting 'well-informed sources' state that a secret clause in the Syrian-Soviet Treaty of Friendship deals with nuclear weapons. In it the USSR has promised to take all necessary steps — including military reprisals — to prevent Israel using nuclear weapons against Syria.[27]

The dangers of such involvement are clear. There are many areas of the world where the superpowers support opposing sides in international conflicts. The Middle East is simply one example. In 1956, during the Suez Crisis, the Soviet Union threatened to use nuclear weapons on behalf of Egypt. In 1973, the threat of Soviet troops being airlifted to Egypt to defend Cairo against Israeli attack, caused President Nixon to place America's strategic nuclear forces on full alert. An Israeli nuclear strike against Syria, followed by a Soviet reprisal on Syria's behalf under the terms of the Syrian-Soviet Treaty, might well trigger direct superpower conflict. The superpowers therefore have a common interest in restraining the spread of nuclear weapons.

THE CONFLICT OF SUPERPOWER INTEREST OVER PROLIFERATION

The accepted view of the leaders in Moscow and Washington has been that the more countries that acquire nuclear weapons, the greater the danger that these weapons will be used. The danger to stability, it is argued, lies in the relative lack of sophistication of the systems available to developing states compared with those in the superpower arsenals. Thus, for example, because Pakistan would rely on aircraft to deliver its nuclear weapons, she might be tempted to use her bombs before those aircraft could be destroyed, and in practice that would mean a pre-emptive, undeclared attack. The situation between hostile states with primitive or non-existent 'fail-safe' precautions would be similar to that which prevailed

between the superpowers in the early 1950s—a period characterized by high tension and a constant fear of nuclear war
occurring virtually by accident—a danger savagely satirized
in the film 'Dr Strangelove'.

The case of South-West Asia also illustrates how susceptible
non-proliferation efforts are to the currents of the prevailing
international atmosphere. Although generally opposed to
proliferation, the USA in particular is vulnerable to policy
shifts based upon diplomatic expediency. For example, since
the Soviet invasion of Afghanistan in December 1979, the
USA has allowed the delivery of uranium to India, overturn-
ing an earlier embargo caused by India's 1974 test and refusal
to sign the NPT. Similarly Pakistan's nuclear efforts no longer
attract American criticism, now that certain US policymakers
detect a Soviet drive for the Persian Gulf. A nuclear Pakistan,
the logic runs, is more likely to deter the Soviet Union from
such an effort.

Moreover, the experience of India shows that Pakistan may
have little to fear, in terms of American disapproval, if it
goes nuclear, and much to gain. US Secretary of State, Henry
Kissinger, made a rapid move to improve relations with
India following the nuclear test of 1974. In addition Pakistan
might hope to gain from the thinking which has benefited
Israel in its relations with the USA. Several Pakistani generals
have drawn attention to the fact that the equipment of the
Pakistani armed forces is of Korean War vintage, clearly
inferior to Indian equipment, let alone that of the USSR. Yet
until 1979, Pakistan's attempts to buy more sophisticated
weapons from the West fell on deaf ears. Even the US arms
offer which followed the invasion of Afghanistan was described as 'derisory' by President Zia of Pakistan. However, the
conviction that Pakistan, like Israel, either has, or soon will
have, nuclear weapons, has made Washington more inclined
to supply sophisticated conventional weaponry in the hope
that this will prevent Pakistan from reaching a military situation in which they feel obliged to resort to their nuclear
weaponry.

THE PROSPECTS FOR CONTROL OF PROLIFERATION

The main political barrier against nuclear proliferation is the Non-Proliferation Treaty (NPT) of 1968, which came into force in 1970. By 1982, 115 states had signed the treaty. The NPT is essentially an agreement between the small group of nuclear weapon states and the non-nuclear powers.

The first group, which is dominated by the two super-powers, sees the essence of the NPT as being in the first two articles. Article I states that the nuclear weapon states will not provide non-nuclear states (whether or not they have signed the treaty) with 'nuclear weapons or other nuclear explosive devices' or help in their acquisition. Article II is an agreement by the non-nuclear states not to receive nuclear explosive devices or help in their acquisition.

For a number of reasons, the parties to Article II have become extremely disillusioned with the NPT. Their discontent with the NPT has centred upon three issues, covered by Articles III–VI of the treaty. Article III of the treaty obliges the non-nuclear weapon states (NNWS) to accept international inspection. This is seen as being politically inequitable, since the same restrictions are not placed upon the NWS.

Article IV of the treaty obliges the nuclear states to contribute to the spread of civil nuclear energy. Many of the NNWS feel that this obligation has been avoided and its spirit undermined by the manner in which states with nuclear energy programmes are constantly criticized as potential NWS even when their record of adherence to the NPT is perfect. In the same context there has been criticism that the NPT acts to perpetuate the commercial advantages of the nuclear powers, especially since Article V reserves to them the right to carry out peaceful nuclear explosions.

The most significant criticisms, however, centre around the requirements of Article VI. This states that the NWS will 'pursue negotiations in good faith on effective measures relating to the cessation of the nuclear arms race at an early stage'.

These complaints, and particularly the criticism that the

superpowers have failed to live up to the requirements of Article VI, led to the total failure of the Second NPT Review Conference in September 1980. Most of the states attending attacked the patent hypocrisy of the NWS, who argued that among the developed states, nuclear weapons were a factor making for peace and stability, whereas their possession by developing states could only have the opposite effect. The racism implicit in such a belief is deeply offensive to Third World leaderships. Even so, the inequitable bargain was tolerable while some progress towards disarmament on the part of the superpowers was evident, as seemed to be the case in the early 1970s. By the late 1970s such hopes had proven illusory, and the 1970s were seen to be a decade of massive vertical proliferation, as the superpowers dramatically increased the number of warheads they could deliver against their opponents.

In particular the NNWS have been disappointed by the lack of progress towards a comprehensive test ban ending *all* nuclear weapons testing. There is a clear belief that such a measure would be the simplest and most dramatic way in which the superpowers could demonstrate the honesty of their commitment to arms control.[28] Genuine moves toward an anti-satellite weapons treaty, a chemical warfare treaty, strategic arms reductions and progress in the European arms control talks would have similar effect. But would this really act as a dam to the rising waters of proliferation?

On the one hand, it can be argued that serious efforts by the superpowers to halt and reverse the arms race would create a moral climate favouring arms restraint and weaken the pro-nuclear lobby in the threshold states, in particular by undermining the aura of prestige which at present is attached to the possession of nuclear weapons.[29]

On the other hand, there is probably more truth in the argument that the problems facing the threshold states are increasingly being seen by them as unrelated to the sterile confrontation of the Cold War. If this is true, then even major superpower disarmament would have little effect on the likelihood of further nuclear proliferation, because the decisions of the threshold states 'will be based on more local and regional kinds of concern'.[30] Given this, is the proliferation process necessarily one to be feared?

HOW DANGEROUS IS THE SPREAD OF NUCLEAR WEAPONS?

That proliferation is a thing to be feared is a rarely challenged belief. The late Senator Robert F. Kennedy argued in 1965 that proliferation was the most vital issue facing the world and that should the process of nuclear proliferation go un-checked, every passing crisis 'might well become the last crisis for all mankind'.[31]

That position has, however, recently come under challenge. A number of American specialists, notably Kenneth Waltz, have argued that proliferation is in fact to be encouraged. In his opinion, the possession of nuclear weapons concentrates people's minds wonderfully and just as it has brought peace and stability to the superpower relationship, it can do the same for other groups of states in conflict. Waltz argues that the record of the past 30 years indicates that nuclear weapons will not spread with a speed that exceeds the ability of their owners to adjust to them, and 'the measured spread of nuclear weapons is more to be welcomed than feared'.[32] Waltz accepts the argument of Winston Churchill that 'safety will be the sturdy child of terror and survival the twin brother of annihi-lation',[33] and feels that is true whichever are the states concerned.

The Waltz thesis rests on the major assumption that it is the presence of nuclear weapons *alone* which has maintained peace between the superpowers for 30 years. While the exist-ence of nuclear weapons has been vital to that effect, it has been successful because it was buttressed by a number of other factors. The USSR after 1945 was, it seems, not irreden-tist, and more concerned at seeking international guarantees for the territory and political position it had acquired as a result of the Second World War. The nuclear balance is under-pinned by the broad balance of conventional forces between the Warsaw Pact and NATO. The two superpowers have stable political systems. Their nuclear deterrents are secure in their second-strike capabilities and insured against accidental release. Not all these kinds of supportive realities exist among the threshold states. For these reasons, the assumption that a secure balance of terror can be safely extended by nuclear proliferation is an unwarranted gamble.

Moreover, the superpower balance of terror is hardly something to be esteemed. Its saving grace is that, to date, it has not failed us, but that situation may not endure for ever, and the price of failure would be inconceivable. To reduce that danger by addressing the problem of vertical proliferation should be the urgent task of diplomacy, and that task would be made more difficult by the further horizontal proliferation of nuclear weapons, however slow and measured.

NUCLEAR POWER AND NUCLEAR WEAPONS

The optimistic view on this issue is neatly expressed by Sir John Hill, Chairman of The British Atomic Energy Authority, who has argued that producing nuclear material through a peaceful energy programme does not result in automatic weapons proliferation. In the last thirty years only a handful of states have acquired nuclear weapons while over a hundred have signed the NPT.[34] Hill therefore believes that the NPT should be strengthened by massive provision of nuclear energy facilities to those states who desire it.

Most observers however would be far less sanguine about such a development. This is because of the belief that a nuclear energy programme, however peaceful, creates expertise that brings with it the temptation to produce nuclear weapons — a temptation which would otherwise not exist, or at least be unattainable.[35] Thus, in the process of operating a peaceful nuclear programme: 'The technologists of the recipient state inevitably acquire at first hand some of the skills required for the operation of an independent reactor system for manufacturing military plutonium.'[36]

There are basically two kinds of nuclear explosive, plutonium-239 and uranium-235. The first can be obtained as a by-product of the reaction in uranium-fuelled reactors, the second requires the separation of uranium isotopes. 'Would-be nuclear powers will ordinarily choose reactors that can use natural uranium as a fuel.'[37]

Where nuclear energy programmes may be important is in justifying the costs of a weapons programme.[38] Such a programme is far easier to justify if it can be presented as a low overhead spin-off from an economical domestic nuclear energy programme. Certainly it makes military research possible in a way that would otherwise not occur. As one group of authors has written: 'arguing that reactors have little to do with bombs is like arguing that fishhooks do not cause the catching of fish, since this can also involve rods, reels and anglers'.[39]

This is important because it offers a so far unexploited means of limiting the spread of nuclear weapons. One of the major criticisms made of the NPT by the non-nuclear weapon states is that the weapon states have not lived up to their promises in terms of helping to spread peaceful nuclear energy expertise. This co-operation, however, inevitably raises fears that the programme will be turned to military uses, if not immediately then perhaps by some future government.

Yet the search for nuclear energy does not derive from a love of nuclear energy *per se*. Nuclear programmes were sought by developing countries in the 1960s because they seemed to promise virtually limitless supplies of energy in a period when an energy shortage of crisis dimension loomed on the horizon. However, the assumptions of the 1960s have not been borne out. In the first place, the energy shortage has not materialized in the way that was anticipated. Changes in energy consumption patterns that would have occurred anyway have been drastically accelerated by the oil price rises of the 1970s, and the industrial recession which has accompanied them. Thus states have found that they do not need energy supply increases on the scale which prompted the crash programmes of nuclear investment characteristic of the 1960s. Secondly, nuclear energy is now no cheaper than its rivals and shows every sign of becoming more expensive than coal or oil.[40]

Nuclear energy has other drawbacks. It is not a straightforward replacement for oil. Nuclear energy is used as a source of electricity, and only 10 per cent of the world's oil is used to produce electricity. The rest is used to fuel vehicles, to heat buildings, and in petrochemical-based feedstocks.[41] Moreover, it poses long-term waste disposal problems incomparably greater than those of rival fuels.

Given the patent drawbacks of nuclear energy, an alternative route to fulfilment of Article IV of the NPT presents itself. Research into very promising renewable energy sources and other 'soft-energy' paths is being held back by the vast amounts being invested in nuclear energy research. If this priority was reversed, major advances in soft-energy technology, particularly solar and tidal energy sources would enable the developed world to address the *spirit* rather than the *letter* of Article IV. What the developing world wants is cheap energy. That energy need not be nuclear, indeed for the reasons noted above, it is far better that it should not be so. Thus the NPT bargain should be 'reformulated' in a manner which is both ecologically sound and beneficial for the prospects of halting the proliferation of nuclear weapons.

MILITARY SECURITY AND PROLIFERATION

The other major element in the proliferation equation is military security. States seek nuclear weapons if they believe that their security will be enhanced if they possess them, and damaged if they do not. To some extent, therefore, restraint breeds restraint. Thus if India forswears nuclear weapons, the pressures upon Pakistan are correspondingly reduced. That is not the whole picture however. States may seek nuclear weapons to solve the problem of diplomatic isolation or 'conventional' military inferiority. How can these questions be addressed?

It has been pointed out by Ashok Kapur that, to date, proliferation has been slow and controlled due to the caution of Third World élite: 'They are not moving madly towards economically and diplomatically expensive nuclear weaponry when other sources of power and influence (such as resource diplomacy and conventional military power) exist and, in fact, may be more usable in the foreseeable future.'[42]

Thus, Kapur believes, the NPT will be strengthened if the nuclear weapon states follow policies which increase the sense of security of Third World nations. One way in which this might be done is by giving specific security assurances similar to those given by the nuclear weapon states to the parties to the Treaty of Tlatelolco, which established a Latin American Nuclear-Free Zone.

Another way would be to give specific conventional or nuclear guarantees to non-nuclear states. Thus a number of NATO states such as Denmark and Turkey, which might have developed nuclear weapons, have not done so because they feel sufficiently secure behind the nuclear umbrella provided by the USA. Similar considerations at present restrain South Korea. However this kind of extension of superpower commitment can carry its own dangers, as was noted earlier in the context of the Syrian–Soviet Friendship Treaty. Even so, acceptance of a greater 'world policeman' role for the superpowers is probably a necessary concomitant for restraining proliferation at present.

The outlook in terms of nuclear proliferation is not as grim as is sometimes painted. Certainly the danger is real. The more countries that acquire nuclear weapons, the more complex becomes the problem of nuclear disarmament. But the acquisition of nuclear weapons by a state is not automatic. It is 'a profound and deliberate act of the will, a result of long and painstaking calculation of costs and benefits'.[43]

States will seek nuclear weapons if they believe it to be in their strategic interest to do so, if they feel that their security will be enhanced thereby. They will treat the nuclear weapons option more seriously if they already possess a degree of nuclear expertise through a peaceful nuclear energy programme than if they do not. The effort to limit proliferation should therefore take place on two fronts — providing adequate security guarantees to states who might otherwise be tempted to go nuclear, and encouraging the rapid development of non-nuclear alternative energy sources. Success in these fields would in turn limit the knock-on or 'domino' aspect of nuclear proliferation. There is no reason why proliferation should be viewed as an inevitable process, a force beyond human control. As President John F. Kennedy once said: 'No problem of human destiny is beyond human beings.'[44] To control the proliferation of nuclear weapons it is necessary to address its causes, and these are still at present amenable to influence.

4

The arms race in space

Today and henceforth the United States must be prepared to defend itself against aggression *in* space and *from* space. We cannot surrender the 'high ground' without contest. We must be in space to acquire knowledge of what others are doing there and to prepare to counter that which threatens us. . . . Americans have no choice but to move aggressively forward in this development of space power.[1]

These comments were made in 1974, at a time when, if anything, the danger of superpower confrontation in space appeared to be lessening. By the early 1970s the superpowers had abandoned some of the schemes touted in the 1960s to build weapons in space, such as the USAF's Manned Orbiting Laboratory; they had signed treaties such as the 1967 Outer Space Treaty and 1972 ABM Treaty, which appeared to limit their scope for militarizing space; they were even committed to the symbolic linking of Soviet and American spaceships in orbit, the Apollo–Soyuz Test Project, which was perhaps the most dramatic manifestation of the period of superpower detente. Even at this highpoint in US–Soviet space co-operation, however, there were warning voices, and as the atmosphere of detente soared, these voices grew louder. In the USA at least, the point at which concern began to translate itself into action, producing the beginnings of an arms race in space, may be dated to 1977. The reaction was produced by the resumption of anti-satellite (ASAT) experiments by the Soviet Union. As the US *Military Review* put it: 'the loss of our satellite network would be a crippling blow to us, especially during time of war. It is therefore with no small concern we learn of Russian experiments to destroy our space allies.'[2] Secretary of Defense Harold Brown, with characteristic understatement, said that he found the development 'somewhat troubling'.[3]

Before going on to look at the history and nature of US–Soviet military competition in space, it is important to understand why space has assumed such strategic significance. The basic reason is that the coming of the space age, and in particular, the age of the satellite, has made possible tremendous advances in communications and 'aerial' surveillance. 'Space is the high ground in today's world' as General Richard Henry, Commander of the recently established Space Division of the USAF has put it.[4] Traditionally, possession of the high ground during military conflict has offered several advantages, such as being able to see further, to see more clearly what the enemy is doing, to be able to strike at the enemy without being vulnerable to a counter-strike, and so on. The use of satellites operating in the near-Earth orbit has conferred and dramatically increased many of these advantages for the superpowers, without, so far, limiting the benefits to only one of them. So important have these considerations become that, according to the well-informed *Aviation Week and Space Technology*, 'space-based systems will constitute within 5–10 years the first line of defense against a Soviet strategic nuclear weapons attack'.[5] The first of the vital functions carried out by satellites is reconnaissance.

It has been aptly said that 'for the superpowers, space is primarily a place to carry on espionage'.[6] President Johnson, in an off-the-record comment, said in 1967 that the information gained by the USA from military reconnaissance satellites was worth ten times the $35–40 billion spent on space up until then.[7] Johnson was probably not exaggerating. Whereas the most sophisticated reconnaissance aircraft in the world, the SR–71 'Blackbird' flies at 2,000 mph, at a height of 80,000 feet, photographic reconnaissance satellites orbit at an altitude of about 150 kilometres. Satellites can therefore survey an area nearly 18 times larger than high-flying aircraft can manage.[8] At such height more than four million square kilometres are visible to the satellites' cameras.[9] Moreover, satellites, unlike aircraft, do not violate another state's

air-space as they observe, nor are they vulnerable to interception and destruction in the way that aircraft such as the U2
have been, though this invulnerability may not last much
longer.[10]

Reconnaissance satellites can be fitted with sensors to
gather information across the whole of the electromagnetic
spectrum. For example at low frequencies with radio and
radar, satellites are able to sweep across a potential enemy's
territory, listen to and record radio, telex and radar transmissions, and then as they return over friendly airspace, relay the
recorded transmissions to a ground station. Communications
monitoring of this sort is now the most widely used of the
superpowers' intelligence instruments. The USA, for example,
launches two or three 'ferret' satellites each year, in order to
gather electronic intelligence. There are also special launches
during times of crisis, such as the US 'Big Bird' satellite
1974 20A which was put into an orbit carrying it over the
Pokharan Test Site in India on 10 April 1974. On 18 May
1974 India tested its first nuclear device at Pokharan. Three
days earlier the Soviet Union had launched Cosmos 653,
which, curiously enough, also had an orbit which carried it
over the Pokharan Test Site.[11]

In addition to visible-light cameras, reconnaissance satellites can also be equipped with cameras operating in the
infra-red portion of the spectrum. Infra-red cameras detect
radiant heat energy, so they are not dependent upon the sun
for illumination.[12] Infra-red reconnaissance has a number of
uses. It can, for example, be used to detect subjects that are
underground or disguised by camouflage.[13] It can even be
used to detect the presence of something that is no longer
there, such as aircraft that have already taken off, but which
while warming their engines prior to take-off have left a
characteristic heat-signature on the concrete of the runway.[14]
Perhaps the most vital role played by infra-red surveillance at
present, however, is the provision of early warning of ballistic
missile attack. The US programme, IMEWS (integrated missile
early warning satellite) consists of satellites capable of detect-
ing the heat emissions from the exhaust trails of ballistic
missiles within seconds of their launch. During the 1980s the
USA plans to upgrade this system. Under the programme

codenamed Teal Ruby, a multispectral mosaic sensor is being designed to detect aircraft movements from space, with the aim of monitoring Soviet strategic bomber flights.[15] The Soviet Union has a similar warning network. Molniya satellites, which spend much of their orbit over North America, while remaining visible from Soviet ground stations, are almost certainly performing missile detection missions. The USSR also has satellites gathering information across the rest of the electromagnetic spectrum. Most satellites launched by the Soviet Union are designated COSMOS. They are launched either from Tyuratam (45.6°N) near the Aral Sea, or Plesetsk (62.9°N) which is about 1,100 kilometres north of Moscow. The figures in brackets are the latitudes of the launch sites. These are important because, for any satellite, the plane of the orbit must pass through the centre of the Earth. This means that a satellite can only be placed directly into an equatorial orbit from a launch site on the equator. From any launch site, the minimum inclination which can be achieved is the same as the latitude of the launch site. Thus, for example, a Soviet satellite launched from Tyuratam cannot achieve an initial orbit inclined at less than 46° to the equator.[16]

This is significant because there are distinct advantages to having an orbit which follows the equator. The higher above the Earth a satellite is, the longer it takes to circle the Earth. At a height of about 35,000 kilometres a satellite takes 24 hours to complete one orbit. If this orbit is equatorial, then the satellite will appear to hover motionless over one point on the equator. Such a satellite is said to be in geostationery orbit. An important advantage of a satellite with a synchronous (24-hour) orbit is that it can be tracked by an almost stationery aerial, rather than having to be followed across the sky.[17] In addition, it can be seen from about one-third of the Earth's surface.[18] Because a synchronous, and particularly a geostationery orbit is so useful, it is desirable to place satellites in this orbit if possible. It is here that geographical position has favoured the Americans over the Russians. The USA's launch site at Cape Canaveral, the Kennedy Space Centre, is 28°N. For the USA, moving satellites into a synchronous orbit involves a complex manoeuvre after launch in which, as the satellite crosses the equator, power is applied in order to turn the satellite into the equatorial plane. This requires an enormous amount of energy, and therefore fuel, and is a difficult operation. Nevertheless the Americans have mastered the art of the 28° plane-change. For the Soviet Union, managing a 46° or 63° plane-change is far more difficult. Not until 1975 with Cosmos 775 did the Soviet Union succeed in putting a satellite (almost certainly an early-warning satellite) into a synchronous orbit on the equatorial plane. The satellite was placed over the Atlantic Ocean where it could watch for American submarine-launched ballistic missiles. Because it is so much further from the equator, the Soviet Union prefers to place its satellites in an orbit which keeps them over the northern hemisphere for most of the orbit, thus the majority of Soviet Molniya satellites have orbital inclinations of about 63°. Soviet and American satellites therefore generally move in quite different orbital paths.

In addition to reconnaissance, satellites now perform a number of other vital military functions. Communications is the foremost of these. The USA launched its first military communications satellite, Courier 1B in 1969, and although a lack of sufficiently powerful rockets held up developments for several years, by 1966 had established its first satellite communications network, the Initial Defense Communication Satellite System (DCSS), later renamed Defense Satellite Communication System 1 (DSCS 1). This consisted of a network of 26 satellites. It was replaced by DSCS 2 in the early 1970s, a system requiring only five satellites, four operational and one back-up. The DSCS 3 system is currently replacing this. The main US military networks are the Air Force Satellite Communication Network (AFSATCOM) and the Fleet Satellite Communication system (FLTSATCOM) of the US Navy. Both are designed to provide unjammable communications systems, while in addition FLTSATCOM provides intelligence and weather data. AFSATCOM is designed to link up with DSCS, and the DSCS system will eventually provide an integrated data bank for the US military and diplomatic service, known as the World Wide Military Command and Control System (WWMCCS).[20]

The Soviet network is not quite so complicated[21] and

consists of three groups. Most Soviet communications are carried by Molniya 1 satellites[22] with high elliptical orbits. The Soviet Union also has s system of satellites of the storage/ dump type. A third group consists of those used for espionage purposes.[23] The Soviet Union has built a number of ships integrated into their communication network, such as the 'Kosmonaut Yuri Gagarin'. For communicating with Soviet forces abroad the USSR also has the Statsionar satellites which they began launching in 1975, placing them in geostationery orbit.[24]

Satellite-based communications allow unprecedented control over strategic and tactical situations, enabling secure links to be maintained between ground forces, ships, aircraft, tactical commanders and the strategic planners in the homeland. About two-thirds of all US military communications are now performed by satellite.[25] Between them therefore the surveillance and communications satellites have become the eyes, ears and voices of the superpowers' armed forces. But the value of military satellites does not stop there. Navigation satellites transmit, on very stable frequencies, signals that provide a constant reference point. Positions can be accurately obtained by calculating the satellite's known orbit and the signal's Doppler shift. The first US navigation satellite was Transit 5A, launched in 1962. The Soviet system, which uses the same procedures and frequencies as the Transit satellites, did not become operational until 1972. About five Cosmos navigation satellites are launched each year.[26] Transit, however, is being replaced by the US Navstar Global Positioning System. Navstar, a system consisting of 24 satellites grouped into three rings of eight in circular orbits, will enable a navigator to gain a position fix in three dimensions accurate to within ten metres (33 feet). It also allows velocity to be determined to within six centimetres per second. The system's advantages include high precision, global and permanent coverage, no possibility of identifying the system's user, no limit as to the number of those who can use it, a common reference system for all users, continuity of operation even when some satellites are not used, and the possibility of coupling it with other navigation systems.[27] Such accurate fixes also enable weapons to be aimed more accurately, particularly strategic weapons such as ICBMs and cruise missiles. Navstar will enable the Pentagon to synchronize the automated battlefield.[28]

Meteorological satellites also have important military functions. They can be used in conjunction with reconnaissance satellites, so that planners know whether a generally overcast area such as Moscow will be clear of cloud when the reconnaissance satellite makes its pass. In addition, any military operations dependent upon meteorological factors are planned on the basis of weather forecasts gained from satellites. As well as land, sea and air operations, this includes targeting data for ICBMs whose vector trajectories are influenced by prevailing weather conditions *en route*.[29] Until 1967 the Soviet Union did not make strenuous efforts to deploy a system of meteorological satellites, but the Meteor satellites began routine operations in 1969. The Meteor 2 system, started in 1975, is said to provide data comparable to that of the US weather satellites.[30]

Satellite-based systems have become crucial to the American and Soviet military. Not only do they perform many vital military functions far more efficiently than would be possible with other techniques, but their very success has focused attention on their vulnerability. This success has meant that earlier methods of doing the same jobs 'have been abandoned to an extent which would make it very difficult now to turn away from the convenience of satellite-based systems'.[31] It was this reliance upon satellites which caused the USA to show such alarm when the Soviet Union resumed its testing of anti-satellite (ASAT) weapons in 1976.

ANTI-SATELLITE WARFARE

The likelihood of conflict in space is now widely accepted by American defence analysts. According to one Pentagon official: 'there is general agreement within the research and development and operational communities that any nuclear weapons exchange with the USSR will start in space. That is why there is such a frantic effort to harden, shield and hide our satellites.'[32] American fears were based on the Soviet

ASAT programme which was resumed in 1976. This programme had begun in 1968, and over the next decade the Soviet Union demonstrated a clear capacity to intercept, inspect and destroy a satellite by a controlled explosion near the target.[33] The test programme began with the launchings of Cosmos 217 and 218 on 24 and 25 April 1968. The large number of fragments left in orbit after the launchings of Cosmos 249 and 252 pointed to their deliberate destruction. In 1970 a second series of launchings began. In this series, the Soviet killer-satellites flew some way *beyond* their target before exploding, leaving the target intact. This was because the target satellite contained instruments capable of monitoring the effects of the explosion and relaying the information to Soviet ground stations.[34] By the time the test series ended in December 1971, the Soviet Union had demonstrated 'an ability to place hunter-killer spacecraft in the vicinity of targets characteristic of electronic ferrets, meteorological and navigation satellites and photo-reconnaissance payloads.[35]

All these target satellites and hunter-killers were launched with orbital inclinations of around 62°. Since most American satellites orbit in quite different orbital planes, the Soviet action was alarming, but not unduly so. Between 1959 and 1976 the USA launched 223 photographic reconnaissance satellites of which only eight had an orbital inclination anywhere near 62°. Similarly, of the 97 US communications satellites launched in this period, only five had orbital inclinations of 62° or thereabouts.[36] To an extent therefore, what the Soviet Union had demonstrated was an impressive capacity to blow up its *own* satellites! It had not carried out tests placing targets in the orbital patterns in which US satellites are usually found. As US Congressman Bob Carr noted in 1977: 'they haven't demonstrated any capability against our satellites in synchronous orbit, which I believe are the most important'.[37] American defence specialists have expressed puzzlement as to why the Soviet Union has developed such weapons, seeing little use in them.[38] In addition, the Soviet ASAT experiments indicate that their hunter-killer satellites are not capable of reaching higher than about 1,250 miles, so most US communications and early-warning satellites would be out of range. In 1971 the Soviets suspended test flights because the SALT I talks were in progress. The tests were resumed between 1976 and 1978, but were halted again because on 8 June 1978, American and Soviet negotiators began on ASAT arms control measures at a conference in Helsinki. In 1980 after the Soviet invasion of Afghanistan, and the disappearance of the SALT II treaty into an unratified limbo, Soviet ASAT tests resumed once more with the launch of Cosmos 1171.

The Soviet ASAT record demonstrates a number of points. Over a period of 12 years the Soviet Union has invested large amounts of money, material and expertise in a military programme of dubious value, conducted in a way which undermined its utility as a preparation for attacks on the most likely enemy. The dominance of political over purely military considerations is shown by the ability of the Politburo to ensure testing ceased during times when good relations with the USA were at a premium. The Soviet programme in fact seems to be the result of one of the constant pressures towards arms 'racing' — the continuing desire of military establishments to assess the military utility of existing technology with a plausible strategic purpose. The reaction of the USA to this period illustrates another aspect of arms race behaviour — the tendency to emulate the opponent. As has already been noted, the USA was not particularly convinced of the usefulness of ASAT weapons before 1976, the ones being tested by the USSR did not immediately threaten US satellites, and the several Soviet pauses in testing showed that the programme was not all-important to them. Despite all this, the very fact that the USSR was 'up to something' in space prodded the USA into a military response. Any threat to American satellites, however remote, had to be countered, the USA dared not risk being 'blinded' in the event of war. Moreover, just because the USSR was testing its hunter-killers in the 62°–65° orbital planes, the USA felt it could not simply assume that the Kremlin was not intent on developing an ASAT system aimed at US satellites. Faced with the existence of a Soviet ASAT capability, the USA felt it had to develop something similar, if only to deter the USSR from ASAT warfare.[39] As one defence planner put it: 'the more you rely on space as a force multiplier, the more probability of action there is against space vehicles. When that threat becomes a real danger you have to put money into counter-measures.'[40]

In the 1960s the USA had possessed two missile bases with an anti-satellite capability, on Kwajalein Atoll and Johnston Island in the Pacific. The bases were closed down in the early 1970s because the missiles would probably have done as much damage to American satellites as to Soviet ones. In 1962 the USA had damaged one of its own satellites 22,000 kilometres (14,000 miles) away by exploding a nuclear device 248 miles above the Pacific.[41] Shutdown was completed in 1975. Yet, responding to the Soviet ASAT tests, President Gerald Ford, two days before he left office in 1977, ordered the rapid deployment of a new American satellite killer.[42] Unlike the Soviet Union, the Americans were not impressed by the satellite-to-satellite interception technique using conventional explosives. Of the various developments being pursued by the Pentagon, the one closest to development is a system which uses a rocket fired into space by a high flying F-15 aircraft using target data supplied by the NORAD tracking network. Called the Miniature Homing Vehicle the device consists of a cylinder ringed with small rockets. Once fired it would seek out its target using infra-red sensors and an on-board computer and would destroy the target by ramming it. A back-up system consists of a weapon mounted on a missile or satellite which would destroy its target by impacting fragmentation warheads.[43]

Evidence of the seriousness with which 'space war' is being contemplated is shown by the fact that the USAF is building a $100 million control centre in Colorado to co-ordinate its future ASAT operations. Although publicly described as being for satellite control and space shuttle missions, the Consolidated Space Operations Centre (CSOC) will be primarily used for ASAT operations.[44] The American ASAT system, by using the F-15 will be far more flexible than the current Soviet system. The US reaction to Soviet ASAT tests includes efforts to increase the survivability of its satellites. In 1980 the USA funded $80 million for space defence and $30 million on satellite survivability programmes.[45] Six different projects for enhancing satellite survivability are being funded, directed towards protecting US satellites from explosive or laser attack. Projects during the period 1980–81 included efforts to develop 'electrical-optical and electronic countermeasures technology for the Defence Meteorological Satellite, Defence Support Programme and Global Positioning System space-craft'.[46] The USA has already carried out studies developing on-board sensors to detect attackers, for example by sensing whether a satellite has been illuminated by laser energy. Ways of 'hardening' satellites, and particularly their vulnerable solar-panels, are being sought. Among techniques being investigated are the use of cork and other materials to coat satellites so as to diffuse laser energy long enough for the satellite to manoeuvre out of the beam, or to fire back.

Active countermeasures are also being examined. These include the use of decoys and measures to increase the ability of satellites to manoeuvre in space. Manoeuvres in space are difficult, a problem ignored in some of the excited specula-tion that followed the resumption of Soviet ASAT flights in 1976. One American newspaper immediately declared that 'the United States and Russia are moving toward satellite dogfights in space — perhaps as soon as the early 1980s'.[47] In fact, as the *RAF Quarterly* noted in 1973, 'dogfights' in space are out of the question; there are far too many constraints operating in orbit to allow the kind of manoeuvres which aircraft can carry out.[48] In space, without the possibility of using aerodynamic forces, changing direction means changing velocity, which requires a great deal of energy and scarce fuel. As well as improving satellite manoeuvrability, America is examining the use of 'dark satellites' or 'silent spares'. These back-up satellites would orbit, dormant and camouflaged to make detection as difficult as possible, until switched on by a command from Earth. Their function would be to replace sister satellites destroyed by Soviet ASAT attack. Increasing the number of satellites in orbit doing the same job is another way of achieving this purpose. In future the USA also intends to make wider use of disguising the purpose of satellites about to be launched into orbit. The developing contest in space is also producing rapid rises in terrestrial expenditure. The ground stations that control the satellites are themselves extremely 'soft' targets and destroying them would be as effective as destroying the satellites themselves. Programmes are therefore under way to duplicate ground stations and to increase the use of mobile receiving terminals.

'Active countermeasures' for defence can of course produce capabilities for offensive action. A number of American military officials believe that space is the ideal environment for *offensive* operations, and even that such space warfare could take place without endangering the population on Earth. Lieutenant General Thomas P. Stafford, USAF deputy chief-of-staff for Research, Development and Acquisition, is one such advocate. Ironically, Stafford was the astronaut who commanded the Apollo spacecraft during the 1975 Soviet–American rendezvous in space. Subsequently his interest was drawn to rather more violent Soviet–American orbital encounters. In 1980 he told a closed meeting of the Senate Armed Forces Sub-committee on Research and Development that:

> Under certain circumstances, space may be viewed as an attractive arena for a show of force. Conflict in space does not violate national boundaries, does not kill people and can provide a visible show of determination at a relatively modest cost. Because of this possibility, it is desirable to provide the national command authorities with the additional option of ordering response-in-kind to a space attack.[49]

Stafford's arguments must raise strong doubts. Given the reliance of both the USA and USSR upon satellites, in the event of war potential adversaries can be expected to deny use of these systems to their opponents. However any such attack would be a clear sign to the victim, that hostilities had been initiated.[50] And precisely because significant satellite losses could cripple a superpower's military capability, an ASAT offensive could very well prompt the other side to initiate all-out nuclear warfare while it still had the reconnaissance, meteorological, navigational, communication and command capabilities in orbit to do so. The existence of an ASAT capability in the other side's hands is one more factor for superpower statesmen to worry about in times of international tension. Because of this, during a crisis, *any* space activity, even of non-hostile intent, such as the launching of satellites, changing satellite orbits and so on, might be misinterpreted as an ASAT move and trigger the pre-emptive first-strike.[51] In addition, Stafford's claim that military space superiority can be obtained 'at a relatively modest cost' is far from accurate. The sums necessary for such a purpose are so immense that some US officials are anxious to avoid drawing public attention to the matter. They fear that neither Congress nor the electorate would approve the enormous amounts involved without clear signs of an impending threat.[52] At the same time they fear a technological Pearl Harbour if funds are not made available. The two areas where fear of technological breakthrough by the other side is greatest are in 'directed energy weapons' — lasers and particle-beams — and in re-usable spacecraft or space shuttles.

THE LASER DIMENSION

The use of 'directed energy weapons', lasers and particle-beams in space is a major research area. It is being taken very seriously in both the USA and USSR and is seen as being a particularly useful prospect against high velocity and high priority targets.[53] In particular their uses as an ASAT weapon and as anti-ballistic missile weapons are receiving a great deal of attention. Once again this is an example of technological progress allowing the military to goad civilian administrations into funding. There are in fact serious doubts about the feasibility of directed energy weapons (DEWs) but these have done little to stem the enthusiams in military circles for weapons which conjure up visions of 'death rays travelling at the speed of light to destroy attacking missiles, beams of charged particles ripping through the atmosphere to cripple satellites'.[54] A recent study of laser weapons at the Massachusetts Institute of Technology concluded that 'any attempt to develop laser weapons and deploy them in space would be militarily impractical, prohibitively expensive and could trigger an all-out nuclear war'.[55] The report argued that space-based anti-satellite systems can easily be destroyed and that countermeasures can quickly be developed by the enemy.

A laser-satellite system would pose a threat to other nations' ballistic missile systems and 'therefore it is quite possible that the system will be attacked by one or more adversaries while it is vulnerable during the embryonic stages of its development'.[56] Once in orbit, laser weapons could easily be jammed, by blinding them with beams of laser light or by transmitting false instructions to them.[57]

Scepticism about the military potential of particle-beam research has been compared to the earnest attempts of alchemists during the Middle Ages to turn base metals into gold.[58] Particle-beam technology has many technical difficulties to overcome. Not least of these is the tendency of the beam to become weaker as range increases, limiting its useful range to a few hundred kilometres, the same as effective laser range. Therefore DEW satellites could not operate in geostationery orbit, yet at any lower altitude the satellites would be constantly moving in relation to the area of Earth they were supposed to be guarding.[59]

Even so, US intelligence reported in 1980 that the Soviet Union had developed a ground-based laser weapon capable of destroying American satellites. The same report, sent to President Carter in May 1980, gave evidence that the USSR is working on an anti-satellite laser weapon that could be deployed in space during the 1980s. This appeared to confirm a claim made three years earlier in *Aviation Week*, that the USSR was preparing to test a space-borne hydrogen fluoride laser designed for a satellite-killer role.[60] The American intelligence agencies had delayed presenting a formal report to the President on Soviet DEWs because of serious arguments within the intelligence community about the extent and feasibility of Soviet DEW efforts. There is little doubt within the US scientific and intelligence communities that the Soviets are involved in developing high-energy technology components that could be used to produce a charged particle-beam, but there is a serious difference of opinion over whether or not the Soviet Union is constructing a weapon based on this technology. Over the last few years opinion has been slowly moving over to the belief that they are, with attention focused on developments going on at Krasnaya Pahka near Moscow and Semipalatinsk in Soviet Central Asia.[61]

American beam weapons experiments were not a direct response to Soviet efforts however. Work began on the military applications of high-energy lasers at Kirtland Airforce Base, New Mexico in 1966. However, funding for such research was at a low level until the cooling of detente in the mid-1970s. Once again ASAT considerations provided a spur for the Pentagon. In 1977 President Carter told Georgia congressmen that the USA was working on a laser weapon designed to eliminate Soviet hunter-killer satellites before they could get close enough to destroy American satellites. George H. Heilmeier, director of the Defence Department Advanced Research Projects Agency, had already told a House Armed Services subcommittee that chemical lasers based in space provided a potential satellite defence system, but Carter was quoted as having described a weapon that could 'attack as well as defend'.[62] In tests carried out in 1978, the US Navy successfully shot down a TOW missile with a high-energy laser fired from a laboratory test bed.[63] At the 1980 Farnborough Air Show the USAF exhibited fragments of target aircraft 'shot down' by a laser beam. According to a 1979 report: 'there is a perceptible sense of cautious elation' among those in charge of the Pentagon's work on high-energy lasers.[64] The reason for this elation is the belief that lasers offer the promise of an effective defence against a full-scale ICBM attack.

In the last two years progress in this field has been marked. The US Defence Department now believes that high-energy lasers (HEL) technology has reached the point where chemical laser devices could destroy ICBMs during launch.[65] The USA has re-orientated its HEL development programme away from point defence systems for ships, aircraft and field armies and towards the development of a space-based system of ICBM interception using laser battle-stations.[66] It is estimated that it will be late in the 1980s before the USA will have the necessary technology, but this period could be shorter. It has been argued that the American DEW programme 'is not technology paced, it is paced by political consideration, and there is no reason why we cannot meet the USSR's schedule to fly laser weapons in space by 1984 to 1986'.[67] This money is being made available. In December 1980 a Senate committee called for a crash programme to develop a space-based laser system. They argued that the laser programme should be pursued with the urgency and thoroughness of the Manhattan Project which produced the atomic bomb during the Second World War, because the US had 'a unique opportunity to alter the strategic balance between the United States and the Soviet Union' through HEL technology.[68]

During the period immediately before President Reagan took office, his Defence Department transition team told key congressional Republicans that one of the new President's priorities was to increase spending on laser ABM technology.

President Reagan's personal commitment to the laser ABM concept culminated in his 'Star Wars' speech of 23 March 1983 in which he called for the establishment of a satellite-based defence system with 'the ability to intercept and destroy strategic ballistic missiles before they reached our own soil or that of our allies'.[69]

Space-based HEL weapons research is being carried out by the US Defense Advanced Research Projects Agency (DARPA) whose director declared in 1980 that testing of scaled systems had been highly encouraging.[70] The code name for DARPA's programme of tests on laser pointing, target acquisition and tracking is Talon Gold. The space shuttle will be used to test a promising device on one of its early missions. Even so, the Pentagon remains cautious about such weaponry. The cost would be phenomenal. For an ABM role between three and twenty laser battle-stations would be needed, depending on the orbit chosen, and each station would cost over $10 billion — and would be vulnerable to attack.[71] Just how vulnerable is debatable, a recent study concluded that space-based laser systems are inherently self-protecting.[72] Because of doubt about cost and vulnerability, it was the Pentagon itself which in 1979 was most critical of a proposal to mount 18 laser battle-stations in space. Even so, work on the technology that would be needed was speeded up. As Donald Snow has noted: 'new weapons systems gain momentum and support as they develop, and the history of abstinence from deploying new weapons is not encouraging'.[73] The history of abstinence from putting supposedly peaceful instruments to military purposes is hardly calculated to cheer either, which is why the advent of the space shuttle has caused concern in many quarters.

THE MILITARY IMPLICATIONS OF
SHUTTLE TECHNOLOGY

Although the USA has denied that the shuttle is intended for ASAT operations there is no denial that the shuttle is meant for military use. Former US Defence Secretary Harold Brown appearing before the Senate Committee on Commerce, Science and Transportation, testified in February 1980 that the shuttle was vital for the defence of the USA. 'Over the next five years our dependence on the Shuttle to support our space systems will become critical' he declared. Former President Carter had been lukewarm about the space shuttle programme until 14 November 1979 when Pentagon officials gave him a detailed briefing on the military aspects of the programme. He promptly approved an increase in NASA spending and requested an additional $300 million to help NASA overcome technical problems delaying the project. The shuttle's advantage is that it can place objects in orbit more cheaply and more frequently than is presently possible. This would allow the proliferation of US satellites so as to make it more difficult for an enemy to disable US space systems. The shuttle will also make possible the better defence of satellites. These will probably be made heavier by having shielding and by carrying extra fuel so that they can manoeuvre in space, and the shuttle can carry much heavier cargo than existing rockets can. In addition, some satellites will have to be placed in much higher orbits to escape the reach of ASAT attack — for example, one new US command and control satellite system will orbit 208,000 kilometres (130,000 miles) out in space. Though the shuttle itself can only operate in near-Earth orbit it can carry a 'space-tug', a smaller rocket capable of taking loads into high orbit once separated from the shuttle.[74]

In his Senate committee evidence, Harold Brown noted that the shuttle would enable America 'to recover our spacecraft from low orbit' and 'perform on-orbit servicing of spacecraft'.[75] It is this very flexibility of the shuttle system that causes the Soviet Union to view it with such concern. In 1979 the USSR caused a stir in Washington by demanding that the USA halt development of the shuttle. Specifically, the USSR was bothered by the fact that the shuttle had the capacity to manoeuvre close to Soviet satellites and inspect them in orbit. If so desired, the shuttle could sabotage or destroy Soviet satellites or even retrieve them for closer inspection back on Earth. The shuttle itself could become a weapons platform. The 60-foot-long cargo bay could in time carry a large and powerful chemical laser for ASAT purposes. Already the Pentagon has announced that one of the first missions of the space shuttle will be to test an aiming device for a space-based laser weapon.[76] The Pentagon's expenditure on space programmes now rivals that of NASA, the first time for 20 years that this has been the case. Over a third of all shuttle flights will be for purely military purposes and two of the fleet of five shuttles will be permanently stationed at Vandenberg Air Force Base in California. NASA officials are deeply concerned that the military will make a serious attempt to wrest full control of the shuttle programme away from civilian administration.[77] A recent study of US space policy carried out by a USAF team came to the ominous conclusion that separate civilian and military space programmes were 'expensive philosophical luxuries' which the US could not indefinitely afford.[78]

The Soviet Union is working on a shuttle of its own despite its moving complaints about the American version. An American reconnaissance satellite photographed the Soviet craft in 1978 as it was being drop-launched from a Tu-95 'Bear' bomber. The same satellite photographed a particularly long runway at the Tyuratam Cosmodrome suitable for shuttle-type landings. In October 1978 the USSR publicly announced that it had developed the prototype of such a vehicle.[79] The Soviet craft, designated 'Kosmolyot', incorporates many design concepts similar to those in the US space shuttle, and is planned to serve a similar role. Because of this, the Soviet craft threatens near-Earth American satellites in the same way that the shuttle threatens Soviet satellites. A US Senate staff study declared that 'Soviet military planners would be unimaginative if they did not think of the whole realm of possibilities and military consequences' of space warfare systems.[80] In fact it is obvious, both from their record of ASAT tests and from the nature of their criticisms of the US shuttle, that the Soviets have indeed thought very carefully about the possibilities for war in space.

This is what makes Kosmolyot potentially far more dangerous to the West than the Soviet hunter-killer satellite programme. For the Kosmolyot system possesses the flexibility which satellites lack. This flexibility derives from two features, its launching systems and its manoeuvrability in space. It can be launched vertically using an expendable booster, probably the SS-6, in the same way that the US shuttle is launched. However, a second launch technique is far more significant. The Kosmolyot can be launched horizontally, carried on the back of an aircraft until it could separate and accelerate into low orbit. The horizontal launch system would enable the Kosmolyot to be injected into far more varied orbital inclinations than is the case with current Soviet ballistic launches. However, to achieve this feat, Kolmolyot would have to be extremely small and require a larger aircraft than the USSR currently possesses. Even so Soviet cosmonaut Vladimir Shatalov has said 'the device can start from any airfield in the Soviet Union equipped for this purpose; this makes the system more flexible in mission operations'.[81] To change orbital plane in space, the Soviet shuttle will use the Earth's atmosphere to aid the operation. The crew will initiate re-entry manoeuvres, and as the vehicle dips into the atmosphere, aerodynamic forces can be used to accomplish course changes, as with a conventional aeroplane. When the new orbital angle has been achieved the Kosmolyot's chemical and electrical propulsion rocket motors can be fired to insert the craft into the new orbit. The Kosmolyot carries enough fuel to make several of these manoeuvres, giving it significantly more flexibility than the US space shuttle which is limited to a single orbital plane for each launch. Although still some way short of it, the advent of the Kosmolyot will bring the age of 'dogfights in space' that much nearer.

POSSIBILITIES FOR RESTRAINT IN SPACE

On 8 June 1978 the superpowers began negotiations on arms control measures for ASAT weapons. The leader of the American delegation, Paul Warnke, warned that: 'there is no question in my mind that we could have war in space within a decade unless we devise a treaty that will stop it'. Even so, by the time the third round of discussion had ended, the Soviet invasion of Afghanistan had driven ASAT talks from the superpower agenda. These talks were the latest of a long line of discussions. As far back as 1963, after the superpowers had reached a 'gentlemen's agreement' not to orbit weapons of mass destruction, Adlai E. Stevenson declared: 'there has been enough social progress to sustain the hope that outer space will not be chaotic'.[82] Stevenson was right not to be too optimistic. The years since have seen the superpowers apparently beset by schizophrenia — co-operating with each other in space to an encouraging degree, signing treaties in 1967 and 1972 limiting their military options in space, publicly recognizing the dangers of conflict in space — and yet at the same time pressing forward with the militarization of space, and seemingly unable to bring talks on controlling the use of space to a fruitful conclusion. There is no doubt that controls are urgently needed. In the absence of agreement, technological and political pressures will only intensify, making agreement even more difficult, even as it becomes more necessary. In the absence of agreement, technology will steadily increase the advantage of the offence over the defence. In this area of the arms race at least, the technological situation, if not the political, favours moving quickly to an agreement *now,* while the technological constraints on war-fighting in space still predominate, and while 'preventive' arms control still offers the possibility of averting the chaos that Adlai Stevenson and Paul Warnke foresaw.

5

Nuclear weapons in Europe

Europe is the most heavily armed region on Earth and the European theatre has been the key area in the East–West military confrontation since the end of the Second World War. Though both NATO and the Warsaw Pact (WTO) have had nuclear weapons deployed as essential elements in their deterrent strategies in Europe since the 1950s, the recent modernization programmes in both alliances, with regard to nuclear weapons, have generated fears in both East and West that a new and extremely dangerous 'Eurostrategic' arms race has begun.[1] The effect of such a development upon the global nuclear equation has also been criticized. SIPRI in 1980 declared that: 'the build-up of Eurostrategic systems is the most disturbing element in the global nuclear arms race in 1979–80. Whatever control SALT II might exert over the nuclear arms race is being undermined by the European developments.'[2]

THE EUROPEAN NUCLEAR BATTLEFIELD

There are large numbers of different types of nuclear weapons designed for use in Europe, but for convenience they can be divided into two classes: 'battlefield' or tactical nuclear weapons, and 'theatre' or intermediate-range nuclear weapons. Broadly speaking, battlefield weapons are designed purely with war-fighting in mind. Their purpose is to destroy an attacking army and its support facilities around the actual battlefield. The kinds of armaments which fall within this category are basically short-range weapons such as nuclear artillery shells, short-range missiles and bombs dropped by aircraft on battlefield missions.

108

Weapons of this sort would have many potential uses in wartime. They could be used to destroy units as they concentrated for an attack, thus denying the enemy the ability to build up forces large enough to break through at any one point. They could be used to destroy an attacking force's logistical support, its supply dumps, artillery and so on. Short-range nuclear weapons could also be used to modify terrain in such a way as to block the enemy's advance, or force him to move into narrow areas where he can be attacked more easily. Reinforcements and supplies *en route* to harassed enemy units could also be destroyed. Attacks of this sort would be accomplished using low-yield nuclear weapons to minimize the collateral damage and fall-out, particularly since the fighting would probably be going on in, or near, 'home' territory. It is in this context, the desire to reduce 'unintended' damage, that the enhanced radiation/reduced blast (ER/RB) weapon, or 'neutron bomb' was seen by many NATO strategists as a necessary addition to the NATO nuclear arsenal. However, because of the political controversy sparked off by this weapon, the USA, while going ahead with production, has decided to stockpile its ER/RB weapons in the USA rather than deploy them in Europe.[3] Since they would only be useful in the European context however, they would obviously be moved to Europe should the threat of war become serious.

Behind the enemy lines, nuclear weapons could be used to destroy airfields, supply depots, missile sites, troop concentrations and important choke-points in the enemy's communication network, such as railway junctions, bridges, ports, and so on. The centres for the enemy's electronic warfare activities would also be important targets.

In contrast to battlefield nuclear weapons, theatre weapons have a dual function. They too would have important uses for attacks on targets behind the front line such as airfields, missile sites and transport choke-points. More importantly, the range of theatre weapons gives them an important deterrent function. Because they can hit targets in the home territories of all the European states, the existence of theatre weapons means that a nuclear war in Europe could not simply be limited to an area on either side of the front line. By threatening *all* European states, and by extension the USA and Canada, with total disaster in the event of war, their existence acts as a deterrent against the initiation of such a war in a way that battlefield nuclear weapons do not. Weapons coming into this class would include the land-based and submarine-based missiles targeted on Europe by NATO and the USSR, and medium-range bomber aircraft.

Clearly some weapon systems do not fit neatly into either the tactical or theatre category. Aircraft such as the British Buccaneer and the Soviet Su-19 Fencer, both with a combat radius of around 1,000 miles, might be assigned short- or long-range missions, depending on circumstances. Similarly aircraft and artillery might or might not be given a nuclear role. A nuclear-capable aircraft such as the F-4 Phantom might in fact be assigned a non-nuclear role as an interceptor during wartime. Estimating the total number of delivery systems available to each side in Europe, is therefore complicated by the fact that not all weapons which *could* deliver nuclear payloads are intended to do so. Against this, some systems designed as 'strategic' weapons such as US Poseidon SLBMs and Soviet SS-11 ICBMs have been retargeted to perform Eurostrategic missions. However, some idea of how many of these nuclear-capable systems ought actually to be counted can be gathered by looking at the history of NATO and WTO nuclear deployments in Europe, and at the rationale behind those deployments.

NATO – THE NUCLEAR ALLIANCE

NATO is a nuclear alliance,[4] an alliance whose strategy, character and politics have been largely shaped by the distribution of nuclear weapons among its members. While the USA is not the only NATO state to possess its own nuclear weapons, the overwhelming reliance of NATO upon the American nuclear arsenal has profoundly affected NATO's history. Even so, NATO is more than the US nuclear umbrella, and in this sense it can be distinguished from the Warsaw Pact which is simply an alliance round a nuclear power.

In the early 1950s, NATO faced the problem of the overwhelming conventional superiority of the Soviet forces in Europe. The presence of American ground forces in large numbers was an important part of NATO's capacity to offset this threat. What made the NATO allies feel secure, however, was the American nuclear superiority over the USSR. In the early 1950s, the USSR did not have ICBMs or long-range bombers capable of inflicting massive damage on the USA. The USA by contrast, because it could bade its bombers in Europe, was able to threaten the USSR with nuclear devastation in the event of war. 'Massive retaliation' would be the NATO response to any Soviet attack on Western Europe.

Gradually, however, the Soviet Union increased the power and range of its own nuclear forces. It was inevitable that at some stage the USSR would bring the USA within range of its nuclear weapons. Once this occurred, at the end of the 1950s, it brought in its wake a crisis of confidence within European NATO countries. The reliability of the US nuclear guarantee was now brought into question. It simply did not seem credible that the USA would invite its own nuclear destruction by using its strategic nuclear forces to stop a Soviet conventional attack on Western Europe. The credibility of the deterrent had declined, not because of a question mark over the capacity of the USA to devastate the USSR, but because of the doubts about the likelihood of the USA doing so when the USSR could respond in kind. The advent of strategic parity was beneficial to the stability of the superpower balance, but seemed to undermine the concept of 'extended deterrence', of the USA's willingness to risk everything on behalf of its allies.[5]

NATO was therefore faced with the problem of how to restore deterrence in Europe. The USSR maintained a marked superiority in conventional forces and particularly in numbers of tanks. One possibility was for NATO to increase the size of its own conventional forces to match those of the USSR. In the early 1950s, NATO had produced grandiose plans for building up to a level of over 90 divisions. In fact NATO has never made a serious attempt to attain this objective. For the European governments in particular the costs of raising and maintaining huge peacetime armies were seen as being too great. Money spent on paying the extra soldiers and buying the additional equipment for a war which nobody really expected to break out, was money wasted — money which could be better spent on new schools, new hospitals, new houses. A further reason why NATO–Europe was not disposed to build-up to conventional equilibrium at a high level of armaments was that it might make European war *thinkable*. This is an option which has never appealed to NATO–Europe's leaders. The costs of the Second World War had been so great, and the costs of even a 'conventional' Third World War would be so much greater, that preventing war rather than winning it, became the European posture. This attitude has been particularly strong among the West Germans upon whose territory a war would necessarily take place, and in which millions of Germans, East and West, would be casualties. Chancellor Schmidt once remarked, *à propos* the 1979 Iranian crisis, that: 'Carter has to worry about 52 hostages in Iran, I have to worry about 17 million hostages in East Germany.'

The absence of massive conventional remarmament increased reliance on nuclear weapons. NATO strategists argued that if NATO armies were too small to cope with a Soviet offensive then the Soviet forces must be destroyed in wartime through the use of nuclear weapons in Europe. In the face of this reality the USSR would then have no incentive to launch such an invasion since all prospects of success would be removed. For this purpose 'small' nuclear devices would suffice — small in comparison to the warheads on ICBMs that is, though many of them would have an explosive yield well in excess of the 20 kiloton weapons used against Japan in 1945. It was felt that the threat to use nuclear weapons would be a far more effective deterrent, psychologically, than any equivalent conventional strategy, because the threat posed was infinitely greater.

However, if the threat was greater, so too were the attendant dangers of such a strategy. In 1955 NATO carried out a major exercise codenamed 'Carte Blanche' in which, as part of the defence of Western Europe, NATO exploded 375 nuclear warheads. The estimated German casualties from the initial release was over five times the total German casualties from air-raids in the Second World War. The exercise reinforced the European belief that Europe would not 'win' a nuclear war in any meaningful sense. For NATO–Europe therefore, the emphasis had to be on preventing such a war from breaking out in the first place, upon deterrence.

This dilemma of wanting to deter the USSR, yet fearing that the USA might not risk its own destruction in Europe's defence, produced a painful and protracted debate within NATO. In the early 1960s, the USA suggested a possible solution, a strategy which came to be known as 'flexible response'. The American reasoning was that in the face of an all-out Soviet invasion of Europe, the US strategic guarantee was still credible, since such an event would clearly affect American interests and overturn the global balance of power. While NATO–Europe reasoned that 'an attempt to deter conventional aggression in Europe with a nuclear arsenal controlled by a non-European power that is itself subject to nuclear retaliation' was hardly 'an example of political and military rationality',[6] the Americans looked at the problem from the Soviet perspective where *any* possibility that the USA would fulfil its nuclear commitment to Europe was a risk too great to contemplate.

The American's felt that the real danger lay in Soviet efforts to alter the European balance of power in a series of small-scale steps, each in itself insufficient to justify massive nuclear retaliation, but cumulatively acting to place the NATO allies in a position of inferiority *vis-à-vis* the USSR. The seizure of West Berlin or a small portion of Northern Norway were mentioned as examples in this regard. President Kennedy warned at the start of the 1960s that NATO faced the danger of being 'nibbled to death'. By paring their conventional forces to the bone, NATO governments would leave themselves no option but to use nuclear weapons to counter even small-scale Soviet incursions. Such a policy was neither credible nor morally defensible.

Flexible response was seen as the answer to this dilemma. By this policy NATO would develop the capacity to respond in kind to any level of Soviet aggression, whether conventional, battlefield nuclear, theatre nuclear, or strategic. For a number of reasons, however, the European members of NATO were unenthusiastic about the idea of flexible response. One drawback was the cost. To match the Warsaw

Pact at every level would require just the kind of massive increase in defence expenditure which the European allies had been resisting since the early 1950s. Moreover, once again it seemed to raise the possibility of a war-fighting strategy rather than one based simply on deterrence. To that extent it seemed to increase rather than reduce the danger of war. By acquiring the capacity to fight a conventional war in Europe NATO might be encouraging the USSR to believe that it could launch a conventional assault on Western Europe without having to fear a nuclear response. Yet it was just that fear which European leaders were determined to place firmly in the minds of Soviet leaders. Nor, to many Europeans, did flexible response seem to address the basic fear of abandonment by the USA in the event of war.

NUCLEAR WEAPONS AND TRANSATLANTIC 'COUPLING'

Flexible reponse seemed to some Europeans to reduce rather than increase the likelihood that the USA would fulfil its nuclear guarantee. According to American leaders, flexible response increased the credibility of the US guarantee by creating 'a seamless web of deterrence'. In the event that any particular level of response proved inadequate, NATO would escalate to a higher level of violence. Thus if NATO's conventional forces did not hold, after a suitable pause NATO would use first battlefield, and then theatre, nuclear weapons. Since the latter would eventually mean striking the USSR this would mean that any Soviet attack on Europe would lead inexorably to a superpower confrontation.

Yet, Europeans argued, if the final guarantee was still the US strategic arsenal, why bother with the intermediate steps? Why not simply reaffirm the policy of massive retaliation? It was, after all, still an American willingness to attack the USSR with nuclear weapons, at the ultimate risk to themselves, that would provide the deterrent. Increasingly France adopted the view that the USA could *not* be expected to commit suicide on Europe's behalf. Pursuing this logic to its obvious conclusion, she initiated her own nuclear defence programme, and by 1967 had withdrawn from NATO's integrated military structure. The doubts expressed by France were shared to a lesser extent by many of the other European NATO allies.

By the end of 1967, NATO had officially adopted flexible response as its defence posture. However, the doubts about the policy found in European capitals were reflected in a failure to implement the policy in the manner originally envisaged by the USA. For one thing, no serious effort was made to redress the conventional inferiority *vis-à-vis* the Warsaw Pact. Instead, by the 1967 compromise, Western Europe accepted the need for a serious conventional response while the USA reaffirmed its guarantee that continuing Soviet attacks would lead to an American nuclear response. The change in policy was declaratory, however, it did not lead to the reorganization of NATO forces necessary to give it effect.[7] Thus, to a large extent, flexible response remained a dead letter, and the NATO posture continued to rely upon 'an inadequate conventional defence backed by an incredible nuclear guarantee'.[8]

The obvious inconsistencies in NATO's nuclear doctrine have occasioned bouts of self-doubt at intervals since 1967. to some extent, however, the European leaders seem to have welcomed the ambiguity of the nuclear equation in Europe, and taken policy decisions which have had the effect, whether or not intended, of increasing the ambiguity of the situation. Whereas the USA has tended to see the nuclear weapons in Europe as supporting the conventional defence, Europeans have chosen to stress their existence as signifying the unbreakable nature of the link with the American strategic deterrent.[9]

In taking weapon-procurement decisions since 1967, NATO governments have increased this uncertainty. Large numbers of weapons have been deployed which are 'dual-capable'; that is, capable of carrying either conventional or nuclear warheads. This is the case with battlefield systems like the 155 mm artillery deployed by NATO, but it is even more evident at the level of theatre weapons with systems such as the F-111 fighter bomber.

Why has NATO pursued this policy? On the one hand it is obviously cheaper to buy a single weapon capable of performing more than one military function, rather than two specialized weapons. More importantly, however, reliance on dual-capable systems acts as a further reinforcement of the NATO nuclear deterrent against the Warsaw Pact's conventional forces.

In the early stages of any European war, NATO is committed by its flexible response policy to using conventional weapons to meet a conventional assault. Thus, in the first few days NATO's F-111s and Phantom F-4s would be used to attack bridges, troop concentrations, airfields and other targets, with conventional bombs. The F-4s would be performing their role as interceptors. If this failed, and NATO's defences began to crumble, the decision would be taken to escalate to the use of battlefield, or even theatre, nuclear weapons. The F-111s would be re-armed with nuclear weapons. However, after several days furious conventional fighting, it is a matter for speculation as to how many F-111s would be left to carry out a nuclear role. It has been calculated that 11 per cent of NATO's combat aircraft would be lost within the first three days, and that after four weeks, half of NATO's aircraft would have been lost.[10] Clearly well before that point had been reached, NATO'S ability to guarantee the effectiveness of theatre nuclear strikes would have been lost. Not enough aircraft would get through to guarantee the infliction of 'unacceptable' levels of destruction upon the USSR and its allies. Thus, in the event of war, the attrition-rate in dual-capable systems would oblige NATO to escalate to the nuclear level even before her conventional land forces began to waver. NATO would escalate early, while it still had the capacity to do so. The reality of the NATO posture is therefore not one of 'flexible response' but rather one of 'delayed massive retaliation', and given the reality of the situation in Europe, that delay would not be a long one. The military and political leaders of the Warsaw Pact are therefore obliged to take this reality into consideration, giving them overwhelming reasons to refrain from the offensive which would trigger such a holocaust. Far from reducing its dependence on nuclear weapons through a policy of flexible response, NATO has in fact maintained, or even increased that reliance.

The need for NATO to deploy nuclear weapons in Europe in the late 1950s and early 1960s was met by a number of systems. As early as 1953, the US Corporal missile with a range of 120 kilometres (70–80 miles) and a one kiloton warhead was deployed by the US Army. Several hundred of these weapons were issued to the American and British armies, the former including two battalion units in Italy. This missile remained in service until 1966.[11] In June 1959 the USA introduced an early cruise missile, the Mace, which equipped the 38th Tactical Missile Wing in West Germany. Mace carried a nuclear warhead and had a range in excess of 800 kilometres (500 miles). Another American missile introduced at this time was Honest John. This could deliver a nuclear warhead at a range of 37 kilometres (23 miles). As well as the US Army, Honest John equipped the forces of Belgium, Britain, Denmark, France, West Germany, Greece, Holland, Italy and Turkey.

Other American missile systems deployed in Europe in the early 1960s included Redstone with a range of 397 kilometres (249 miles); Sergeant (which equipped both American and German forces) with a range of between 45 and 139 kilometres; and the bizarre Davy Crockett, a nuclear missile so small that it could be fired by one man from the back of a jeep. In 1962 the US army and some Luftwaffe units were equipped with Pershing, a mobile nuclear missile with a range of between 160 and 736 kilometres. During the 1960s and 1970s this powerful missile was steadily improved. In 1967 the Pershing 1A became operational. Unlike its predecessor it could be moved on a single transporter and had a much shorter reaction time before it was ready for firing. In 1976 American and German units received the 'Automatic Azimuth Reference System/Sequential Launch Adapter'. This improved system enabled a Pershing 1A commander to fire three missiles in succession from a previously unsurveyed firing site. Each missile carries a 400 kiloton warhead.[12] All Pershing warheads have remained under American control. In 1981 some 180 Pershing 1A missiles were in service.

NATO's short-range systems also include her nuclear-capable artillery, of which some 1,400 pieces are available, though only about half of these have been assigned nuclear roles.[13] Short-range capabilities were enhanced after 1972 when the Lance missile was introduced. This can carry a ten kiloton warhead and is fully mobile with a maximum range of 120 kilometres. Lance is in service with the USA, West Germany, Belgium, Britain, Canada, Holland and Italy. The USA has produced and is stockpiling enhanced radiation/reduced blast (neutron) warheads capable of being fired by Lance.

In addition to these American weapons, from the early 1970s French intermediate range ballistic missiles were added to the arsenal. In 1974 France introduced Pluton, an all-French tactical missile. It is fully mobile, very accurate and can carry either a 25 kiloton warhead, for attacking rear areas, or a 15 kiloton warhead for attacking advancing troops. Pluton's range is 120 kilometres. By 1981, 30 Pluton units, equipped with reloads, had been deployed. France is now working on Hades, a successor system which would be even more accurate than Pluton and have twice the range.

TABLE 5.1
NATO battlefield nuclear systems[14]

System	Number deployed	Nuclear-dedicated	Warheads available
155 mm Artillery	1,081	540	1,081
203 mm Artillery	319	160	319
Lance missile	90	90	90
Honest John missile	91	91	91
Pluton missile	30	30	30
Pershing 1A	180	180	180
Total	1,791	1,091	1,791

Aircraft systems

NATO also possesses numbers of nuclear-capable aircraft which could be used in battlefield support roles, particularly the F-104 Starfighter, F-4 Phantom, Jaguar and Mirage aircraft. These capabilities blur into NATO's longer-range systems among which can be included the F-111 E/F and Buccaneer fighter-bombers and the A-6, A-7 and Super Etendard carrier-based aircraft. Britain has just phased out the Vulcan B-2 bomber force, but along with West Germany and Italy will be deploying large numbers of the powerful Tornado aircraft during the 1980s.

TABLE 5.2
NATO nuclear-capable aircraft in Europe[15]

Aircraft	Range (km)	First deployment	Inventory	Warheads per plane
Vulcan B-2	2,800	1960	57	2
F-111 E/F	1,900	1967	156	2
Mirage IV A	1,600	1964	33	1
Buccaneer	950	1962	60	2
F-104	800	1958	318	1
F-4	750	1962	364	1
Jaguar	720	1974	80	1
Mirage III	600	1964	30	1
A-6E	1,000	1963	20	2
A-7E	900	1966	40	2
Super Etendard	560	1980	12	2

THE MODERNIZATION DECISION OF 1979

From the early 1950s onwards NATO has relied upon aircraft for part of its theatre nuclear deterrent forces. It was American bombers stationed in Europe which initially provided this capability. During the 1960s more modern aircraft, such as the British Vulcan B-2 and American F-111 took over the role. NATO has *always* believed that it needed systems capable of hitting targets in the Soviet Union after being launched from Europe. It is, after all, the USSR that NATO has been primarily interested in deterring. The other Warsaw Pact countries would hardly start a war on their own initiative. Theatre systems were therefore needed so that the organ-grinder as well as the monkeys would be deterred.

NATO has not relied solely on aircraft systems. For a short while, at the end of the 1950s, Thor and Jupiter medium-range ballistic missiles performed the role. These were unreliable, however, and when President Kennedy phased them out they were not replaced by follow-on missile systems. In the 1970s a number of Poseidon submarine-launched ballistic missiles were allocated to perform a European theatre role. The idea of these weapons was to create an unambiguous link between European defence and US strategic deterrence. However, the Poseidon missiles, along with the British Polaris and French MSBS-M2 missiles were not seen as being wholly suited to NATO's flexible response strategy. Because the submarine-launched missiles were essentially strategic weapons, their use could raise conflict to a strategic rather than a theatre level, as NATO intended. For this reason aircraft, which were unambiguously theatre systems, were preferred.

During the 1970s, however, NATO became concerned about the credibility of its theatre nuclear deterrent. The NATO aircraft were becoming rather long in the tooth and the Soviet anti-aircraft defences had been steadily improved over the years. Doubts were expressed as to whether NATO's aircraft, or indeed any improved NATO aircraft would be able to penetrate the Soviet defences in sufficient numbers in time of war. NATO therefore established the High Level Group (HLG) to look into the problem of bringing the theatre deterrent up to date. A number of guidelines for the modernization programme soon emerged. It was felt that there should be no increase in the number of nuclear weapons possessed by NATO–Europe, nor should modernization entail any increase in NATO's reliance upon nuclear weapons. Although the new SS-20 Soviet missile was alarming European leaders, it was not felt that NATO needed a similar weapon, rather NATO needed an offsetting capability that provided a credible response. The weapons system chosen had to have the range to strike the USSR. A missile system was preferred because unlike aircraft it would be certain to reach its target.

It is important to note that NATO's intermediate nuclear force (INF) modernization decision was prompted by the recognition of a need to update an existing NATO capability.

It was not, as is sometimes thought, a simple response to the appearance of the SS-20 missile. In October 1977 German Chancellor Helmut Schmidt made a speech in London in which he expressed concern about the impact of the SALT process upon Europe. Schmidt argued that the recognition of strategic nuclear parity by the superpowers seemed to magnify the significance of the disparities between East and West in theatre nuclear and conventional forces. Foreign Minister Genscher stressed that the SS-20 was 'a strategic threat to Europe, and the West has nothing comparable with which to match it'. However, if the appearance of the SS-20 served to crystallize NATO's difficulties, it did not create them. NATO's need to modernize its theatre forces was the result of fears about the diminishing credibility of the theatre deterrent, not a result of the deployment of the SS-20. Even if the SS-20 had never been deployed, NATO would have wanted to deploy new missiles in order to modernize its theatre deterrent. The novelty of the SS-20 threat was stressed by NATO simply in order to gain the support of European public opinion for the modernization decision.

NATO decided in December 1979 to deploy 572 new missiles. Existing Pershing 1As, based in West Germany, would be replaced with 108 new Pershing II missiles. In addition, 464 Tomahawk ground-launched cruise missiles (GLCM), with a range of 2,500 kilometres, would be deployed in Britain, Italy, West Germany, Holland and Belgium. All the new missiles would be American-controlled, have single warheads and would replace 572 warheads already deployed in Europe.

As part of the overall modernization 'package' NATO also decided to withdraw 1,000 older warheads from Europe and to make a theatre-nuclear arms control offer to the USSR. The linking of the arms control offer to the modernization programme was probably responsible for the high level of deployments finally decided upon. The High Level Group (HLG) had operated with the guideline that between 200 and 600 missiles would be needed.[16] The number decided upon, 572, is so close to the upper limit that some of the new missiles are probably 'bargaining chips' to trade away in the arms talks, rather than an essential military requirement.

The number and mix of the new weapons chosen was produced by a curious interplay of military, political and arms control requirements. Chancellor Schmidt had argued in 1977 that if the Eurostrategic imbalance was not corrected, NATO might be self-deterred, might fear to take political stances unacceptable to the USSR. To demonstrate its resolve therefore NATO *had* to deploy some missiles. To make a meaningful gesture NATO would have to deploy more than a handful. The lower HLG figure of 200 represents the NATO assessment of the minimum number required to solve NATO's 'theatre deterrent' problem. To deploy more than 600 might create the idea that a separate Eurostrategic balance had come into being. That is an idea that NATO has no wish to foster. However, the ability to strike the USSR from Western Europe with land-based nuclear warheads was the most important change, and this ability does mark a significant upgrading of NATO's capabilities.[17] Nor will NATO allow this increased capability to be negotiated away. As one German minister has stated, while certain weapons may be negotiable, the theatre nuclear option is not.[18]

Choosing a mixture of Pershing II and Tomahawk cruise missiles had a number of advantages for NATO. Pershing II is a ballistic missile with guaranteed penetration ability and can reach its target in just over six minutes. It thus has utility as a first-strike weapon and for this reason the numbers deployed have been deliberately restricted to 108.

However Pershing II can only just reach the USSR when fired from positions well forward in West Germany. In wartime it would be vulnerable to being overrun by rapid WTO advances. The cruise missiles by contrast have much longer ranges and can therefore be deployed well back from the front line in sites in Britain, Italy, Belgium and Holland, enabling these states to share the risks involved in deployment with West Germany. Although cruise is slow and therefore less certain to penetrate Soviet air defences, the great numbers deployed enhance its credibility. In addition, its slow subsonic flight time means that it cannot by any stretch of the imagination be seen as a first-strike weapon. The Tomahawk GLCM will also be highly accurate. It is equipped with a TERCOM (terrain comparison) navigation system to supplement inertial guidance. TERCOM works by matching the ground passing beneath the missile with data contained in the missile's computer memory. The USA also plans to link the missile's navigation to the Navstar satellite system.[19]

It was only in the early 1960s that the USSR began to 'nuclearize' its European forces in the way that NATO had earlier done.[20] The Soviets operated on the basic assumption that both sides would be using nuclear weapons in a European war; that since NATO *possessed* nuclear weapons it would employ them at an early stage. As with NATO both ground launchers (primarily missile-firing) and aircraft were to be used to deliver the nuclear attacks. Soviet doctrine asserted that war in Europe would only break out if the NATO states attacked the USSR and her WTO allies. This NATO 'surprise' attack was invariably depicted as beginning with a strategic nuclear attack upon the USSR. In such circumstances the USSR would have no incentive to refrain from retaliating through the use of her own nuclear weapons. The purely conventional offensive, as expected by NATO doctrine, was therefore given no credence by the USSR.[21] However, a massive conventional counter-offensive against Western Europe would follow the initial Soviet nuclear retaliation. This offensive would begin with heavy Soviet theatre nuclear strikes against key NATO targets.[22]

This doctrine obviously ran counter to NATO's conception of the use of nuclear weapons as an escalation which should be postponed for as long as possible. The doctrinal difference matters little, however, since NATO had no intention of attacking the USSR and thereby precipitating a massive nuclear response. In other respects Soviet doctrine on the use of nuclear weapons in Europe dovetailed nicely with the deterrent posture adopted by NATO. Soviet military analysts believed that the use of nuclear weapons would produce all-out strategic nuclear war — and this was exactly the linking conception which the NATO deterrent strategy sought to foster. In the late 1950s and early 1960s, the USSR concentrated its efforts upon the production of medium range ballistic missiles (MRBMs) with Eurostrategic capability, rather than ICBM or tactical nuclear deployment. There were a number of reasons for this. One factor was technical. MRBMs were technologically less demanding to produce than longer-range ICBMs. The USSR therefore chose to make a virtue of necessity and attempt to solve its strategic problems by concentrating on MRBM production.

The USSR suffers from an immense strategic disadvantage *vis-à-vis* the West, one which is invariably ignored in NATO assessments of the overall balance of power. Even if the USSR can achieve a strategic nuclear balance with the USA, and a theatre balance with NATO, the fact remains that in the event of a full-scale war the USA might suffer ICBM attack and Europe medium-range attacks, but the USSR would suffer both. In other words, in any war the USSR would suffer far more devastating attacks than she could inflict in reply. Short of gaining *immense* superiority at *both* levels, which neither the USA nor NATO–Europe will allow, there is no way out of this dilemma for the Soviet Union.[23]

In the late 1950s the Soviet Union decided to address the problem of a European deterrent first, since her technology in that area of research was more advanced. By establishing some kind of Eurostrategic superiority she hoped to overawe Europe, so that NATO would not dare to attack her. Behind the security of this 'hostage Europe' strategy, the USSR could then devote its energies to redressing the strategic inferiority with the USA, without having to fear a two-pronged attack.[24]

In the event the strategy was undermined during the 1960s both by the rapid growth of the American strategic arsenal and by the development of NATO INF capabilities and independent British and French strategic deterrents. The Soviet problem has remained acute therefore. Even marginal superiority in either category, though producing cries of alarm in the West, can provide a real comfort for the Soviet leadership faced with the dilemma of being double-targeted by NATO.

In the 1960s NATO possessed a clear superiority over the Soviet battlefield nuclear weapons deployed in Europe. The main Soviet battlefield missiles were the weapons given the NATO code names of Scud-A, Scud-B, and Frog. Scud-A is a single-stage, liquid-fuelled missile, with a range of 93 miles. The missile is capable of carrying conventional chemical or nuclear warheads, but though it was used to equip most of the Warsaw Pact armies, only the Soviet missile units were given nuclear warheads.

The smaller Frog missile, of which seven versions have been identified, has a maximum range of some 45 miles. The early Scud-A and Frog missiles were rather inaccurate and unreliable. They also took a long time to prepare for firing, anything up to an hour.[25] Scud-B is an improved version of its predecessor, still liquid-fuelled but with greater accuracy thanks to an inertial guidance system and a range increased to 105 miles. The time taken to fire Scud-B is markedly less than the earlier version.[26]

During the 1970s the USSR began to deploy a new generation of more sophisticated battlefield nuclear delivery systems. The older Scud and Frog missiles were by the end of the decade beginning to be replaced by solid-fuelled, more accurate SS-23 and SS-21. In addition, the USSR for the first time began to deploy significant numbers of dual-capable artillery, such as the 203 mm and 240 mm guns. These weapons have not as yet been assigned to forward Soviet or WTO units, and remain deployed in the Western USSR, but they could be moved forward rapidly in time of crisis. In addition the Soviet Union has the SS-12 Scaleboard missile. This has a range of 800 kilometres, placing it almost into the theatre weapon class. Deployment began at the end of the 1960s. It carries a warhead in the megaton range, but like the Scud-B is liquid-fuelled and relatively inaccurate. By the end of the 1970s the USSR was starting to replace it with the solid-fuelled SS-22.

SOVIET THEATRE NUCLEAR MISSILES

The theatre nuclear systems of the USSR were also substantially upgraded during the 1970s. As with tactical weapons, NATO had a clear advantage in the early 1960s. The basic Soviet weapons were the SS-4 Sandal and SS-5 Skean. The SS-4 possesses a range of 1,789 kilometres and carries a one-megaton warhead. It is powered by a storable liquid propellant and has an inertial guidance system. A semi-mobile missile, it has the weakness of being very slow to prepare for firing. The SS-5 is basically a scaled-up version of the SS-4. Like the SS-4, it is liquid-fuelled, inertially guided and carries a one-megaton warhead. It has a range of 3,480 kilometres. It was this missile which was at the heart of the 1962 Cuban Missile Crisis. About 100 SS-5s are still deployed against Western Europe. The size of this missile force reached a peak in 1965 when there were 733 SS-4s and SS-5s deployed, of which 598 were semi-mobile and 135 were in hardened silos.[27]

In the late 1960s the USSR began to take steps to upgrade this force. From 1969 to 1971, 120 SS-11 Sego ICBMs were deployed in Intermediate-Range (IRBM) missile fields and were clearly targeted against Western Europe rather than the USA.[28] The SS-11, with a range of 10,440 kilometres, had by the mid-1970s become the main theatre threat to Western Europe, though in the context of the controversy over the SS-20 and TU-22M it is interesting to note that this development produced virtually no reaction in the West, possibly because NATO had no deployments of its own which needed the SS-11 as a justification at that time. In 1969 the USSR tested the SS-11 with a MIRVed warhead, and by 1978 at least 60 of the second version SS-11s had triple warheads.

From 1974 onwards the USSR began to supplement its SS-11 force with the more powerful SS-19. Sixty SS-19s are deployed in Soviet IRBM sites in such a way that they can target either the USA or Western Europe. There are strong indications that the SS-19 will be used to carry out the theatre role at present performed by the SS-11.[29] The SS-19 is a two-stage missile, capable of either hot-launch or cold-launch. The latter technique makes it possible to launch more than one missile consecutively from the same silo. Version I carries six MIRVs with yields estimated in the 800 kiloton to one megaton range. Version II has been tested with a single highly accurate warhead. The missile's range is over 9,942 kilometres.

A number of other Soviet missiles may have theatre functions. SIPRI believe that a certain number of the SS-14 Scamp-Scapegoat missiles deployed in the Eastern USSR are in fact targeted on Europe. They have a range of 4,000 kilometres.[30] At sea SIPRI include numbers of SS-N-3/12 missiles carried by Echo II and Juliet-class submarines and on Kiev, Kresta I and Kynda-class surface ships. There are also six Golf-class submarines permanently based in the Baltic Sea. These are armed with SS-N-4 (range 550 kilometres) and SS-N-5 (range 1,200 kilometres) nuclear missiles. These are not included in the SALT II totals.[31]

However, from the perspective of political visibility, the most dramatic improvement in the Soviet theatre nuclear forces in the 1970s was the introduction of the SS-20 IRBM. The SS-20 is a two-stage,[32] solid-fuelled missile with a range of 5,667 kilometres. Unlike the older SS-4s and SS-5s which it is replacing, it is fully mobile and carries three warheads. It is also far more accurate having a CEP of 750 metres when fired from a pre-surveyed launch site. The Soviet Union has argued, not unreasonably, that the SS-20 is simply a timely upgrading of the old, unreliable, inaccurate and increasingly vulnerable SS-4s and SS-5s. President Brezhnev, in November 1981, pointed out that:

> when deploying one new missile, we replace one or two old missiles and scrap the latter together with the launchers. It is true that the SS-20 can carry three warheads. But their overall yield is less than that of one old warhead. Consequently, in the process of replacement of obsolete missiles, the total number of our carriers has been decreasing, and simultaneously the aggregate yield of our medium-range nuclear potential has been growing less.[33]

Against this NATO argues that the SS-20, first deployed in 1976, marks a dramatic and destabilizing element in the European military equation. The French strategist General Pierre Gallois declared that, thanks to the advent of the SS-20, the USSR had acquired the ability to annihilate NATO's entire nuclear arsenal within ten minutes. About two-thirds of the deployed SS-20s are targeted against Western Europe. Because it is solid-fuelled and fully mobile, the SS-20 is very difficult to monitor and even harder to hit. Intelligence data also suggests that most SS-20s have a second missile available in reserve for re-loading — a potential doubling of the threat.[34]

TABLE 5.3
Soviet battlefield nuclear systems[35]

System	Number deployed	Nuclear-dedicated	Warheads available
203 mm artillery	—	150	300
240 mm artillery	—	150	300
Frog/SS-21 missiles	375	250	250
Scud-A	251	168	168
Scud-B/SS-23 SS-12/SS-22	506	506	506
SS-N-4	0	9	9
Total	1,141	1,233	1,533

TABLE 5.4
Soviet theatre nuclear systems[36]

System	Number deployed	Nuclear-dedicated	Warheads available
SS-4 (Sandal)	275	275	275
SS-5 (Skean)	16	16	16
SS-N-5 (Serb)	60	60	60
SS-20	315	315	945
SS-11	120	120	240
SS-19	60	60	360
Total	834	834	1,574

WTO AIRCRAFT SYSTEMS

Like NATO, the USSR also includes aircraft as part of its theatre-nuclear inventory. These include numbers of MiG-27, Su-24, Su-7 and Su-17 fighter-bombers, and Tu-16 Badger, Tu-22 Blinder and Tu-22M Backfire medium-bombers. The fighter-bombers would be used for essentially battlefield missions. The most effective of these aircraft is the Su-24A Fencer, the first aircraft specifically designed by the USSR for its fighter-bomber role. It has terrain-following radar and is capable of all-weather, low-altitude precision attacks.

TABLE 5.4
WTO nuclear-capable aircraft in Europe[37]

Aircraft	Range (km)	First deployment	Inventory	Warheads
Tu-22M Backfire-B	4,025	1974	65	4
Tu-16 Badger	2,800	1955	310	2
Tu-22 Blinder	3,100	1962	125	2
Su-24A Fencer	1,600	1974	480	2
MiG-27 Flogger-D	720	1971	500	1
Su-17 Fitter C/D	600	1974	700	1
Su-7 Fitter A	600	1959	165	1
MiG-21 Fishbed J-N	400	1970	750	1

Of the bombers, the Badgers and Blinders have done sterling service for the USSR, but they are ageing. The Badger entered squadron service in 1955, and since then has been the basic workhorse of Soviet Long Range Aviation and Naval Aviation. The Blinder became operational in 1962 and was the first operational Soviet supersonic bomber. But it is now over 20 years old. About 2,000 Badgers and 250 Blinders were produced, but less than half of these are still in service. Increasingly they are being replaced by the far more powerful Tu-22M Backfire. Backfire can fly at twice the speed of sound and has a range of up to 8,000 kilometres. Under the terms of a SALT II 'understanding' the USSR can produce 30 Backfires a year.

PROSPECTS FOR ARMS CONTROL

The opening, in November 1981, of the Geneva talks on limiting nuclear weapons in Europe seemed to evidence a desire on the part of the superpowers to control the nuclear arms

build-up in Europe (see map). President Reagan declared that
'with Soviet agreement, we could substantially reduce the
dread threat of nuclear war which hangs over the people of
Europe. This, like the first footstep on the moon, would be a
giant step for mankind.'[38] The Soviet delegation to the talks
also appeared to be in earnest. Yuli Kvitsinsky the delegation
leader spoke of their 'honest and constructive approach aimed
at achieving a mutually acceptable agreement with the United
States on radical reductions of medium-range nuclear armaments in Europe'.[39] Whether negotiations of this type can in
fact succeed depends upon a number of factors related to the
scope of the talks.

On the face of it, the prospects for successful negotiations
are reasonably good. Both NATO and the Warsaw Pact have
called for such talks several times since 1978. The NATO
modernization decision of 1979 was coupled with an arms
control offer suggesting that both sides limit their theatre
nuclear arsenals. At the same time, the 1979 decision led to
the reduction of the NATO stockpile by 1,000 older nuclear
warheads. This reduction can be seen as an American/NATO
response to the earlier withdrawal of 20,000 Soviet troops
and 1,000 tanks from East Germany in 1979.[40]

However, there are clear limits on NATO's willingness
to reduce the size of her nuclear arsenal. Certainly NATO
needs to make *some* gesture towards INF arms control. The
European anti-nuclear weapon movement has flowered since
1979, and while there are many factors behind that growth,
the basic reason was expressed on one of the banners carried
at a demonstration in West Germany in 1981 —"ICH HABE
ANGST' (I am afraid). NATO is therefore obliged to address
itself to the fears of its people that recent NATO and Warsaw
Pact INF developments have increased the danger of war.

However NATO is not going to give up its nuclear weapons.
For one thing it relies on tactical nuclear weapons to offset
its weaknesses at the conventional level, particularly in tank
numbers. It also needs these weapons as a vital rung in the
'ladder of escalation' implied in the theory of flexible response. Moreover the European NATO states want to keep
some theatre nuclear weapons to deter the USSR from using
its nuclear weapons. As one West German minister put it, 'as

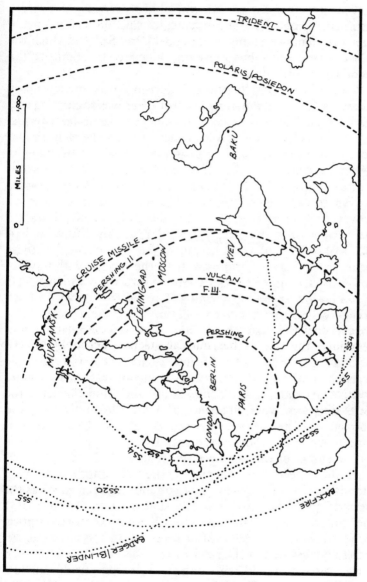

FIGURE 5.1: *The European INF balance, 1982*

long as no comprehensive Soviet renunciation of nuclear options against Western Europe is forthcoming, a comparable nuclear option must remain available to NATO'.[41] Since a significant part of her Eurostrategic capability comes from intercontinental systems such as SS-11 and SS19 — which the USSR is very unlikely to give up, there are clear limits to the negotiating possibilities.

When the 1979 'two-track' decision was made, many observers felt that the arms control offer was something of a dead letter, designed to convince unenthusiastic ministers in certain weak coalition governments, such as the Belgian and Dutch governments, and to satisfy the 'peace' movement in Western Europe. But the offer was not seen as being serious because it quite clearly ran completely counter to the reasoning which lay behind the parallel modernization decision. However, this scepticism was not shared by all. Willi Brandt, the former West German Chancellor, in an effort to halt the deployment of what he called 'das Teufelszeug' — these diabolical things — proposed that the USSR withdraw an unspecified number of its IRBMs, in return for which NATO would no longer deploy Pershing II or the Tomahawk GLCMs. Brandt called this his 'zero solution'.[42] In September 1981 *Pravda* declared that the USSR would contemplate 'considerable reductions' of medium-range missile stocks in INF negotiations. The growth of feeling against the Cruise/Pershing decision in Europe led the USA reluctantly to take a more positive attitude towards the arms control element in the 1979 decision. When Secretary of State Alexander Haig and Foreign Minister Andrei Gromyko met in New York in September 1981, they agreed that INF talks would begin on 30 November of the same year in Geneva.

As the date for the opening of the talks approached, Willi Brandt's zero solution, by now commonly referred to as the 'zero option' began to be widely canvassed. In October 1981 the London *Times* called for the USA to make a zero option in which America would 'offer to abandon the controversial plan to deploy 464 cruise missiles and 108 Pershing II missiles, if the Russians would relinquish all their own missiles, including the massive SS-20'.[43] Even while advocating the idea, *The Times* noted ruefully that it would make little sense militarily.

Nevertheless this was the offer which President Reagan unveiled on 18 November 1981. 'The United States', he declared, 'is prepared to cancel its deployment of Pershing II and ground-launched cruise missiles if the Soviets will dismantle their SS-20, SS-4 and SS-5 missiles.' The immediate Soviet reaction was to dismiss President Reagan's claims to sincerity. Tass declared that Reagan was only 'pretending' to renounce deployment of US medium-range missiles in order to curry favour with European public opinion. However, the USSR indicated that it did want serious talks to begin when Sergei Losev, director-general of Tass declared that the USSR hoped that the zero option was not President Reagan's final offer.[44]

The Reagan offer was in any case patently insincere. The leading military powers within NATO had absolutely no intention of agreeing to any treaty which included the cancellation of *all* the planned Pershing II and Tomahawk deployments. One defence analyst has recently argued that 'the central paradox of theatre nuclear arms control in Europe is that it is desirable but impossible'.[45] This is an exaggeration; INF *arms control* is possible, but major INF *disarmament* is very unlikely. There are a number of reasons why this is so, some technical, some political and some doctrinal.

The technical problems standing in the way of successful theatre nuclear arms control talks are formidable enough. The basic asymmetry of NATO and WTO force structures is one major problem. The two alliances face different military problems and have historically pursued different strategies and adopted different weapon systems in order to solve their problems. This makes arms control trade-offs difficult, for systems that to NATO are marginal and expendable are central to WTO plans, and vice versa.

There is also the perennial problem of scope. Long-range theatre nuclear systems blend into battlefield weapons at the shorter ranges. The American offer deals only with long-range missile systems, but many analysts would argue for the inclusion of shorter-range systems such as SS-N-4 and SS-22. There is also the vexed question of aircraft. The Soviet Union has rejected the simple missile-for-missile trade-off, arguing for the inclusion of aircraft, the so-called 'forward based systems' (FBS). They argue that the USA will not consider FBS inclusion because these aircraft contribute to a favourable INF level for NATO in Europe.[46] The USSR also argues that the British and French 'strategic' deterrents should be included in the theatre nuclear balance. When these systems together with certain Poseidon and SS-N-5 SLBMs are included, the balance, according to the USSR, is one in which NATO possesses 986 delivery vehicles while the WTO has 975.[47] According to the USSR, therefore, the addition of 572 'new' NATO systems would give the West a 50 per cent advantage in deliverable warheads.[48] This presumption overlooks the fact that the new NATO missiles replace older missiles on a one-for-one basis.

Against this, the USA argues that including FBS would impose almost insuperable verification problems related to the question of dual-capable systems. In addition, extending the scope of the talks would bring in not only the problem of how to deal with submarine systems, but also the question of the Soviet ICBMs targeted on Europe. If aircraft *were* brought in, NATO would want to exclude aircraft which are nuclear-capable but not assigned nuclear roles, for example NATO's F-4 Phantoms and carrier-based A-6s and A-7s, but would want to include Soviet aircraft in the Naval Airforce — which the USSR would see as being outside the Eurostrategic equation. The complexities of such talks would blight any hope of a reasonably quick agreement. Keeping the talks limited to a missile-for-missile trade-off offers greater hope of success, but such talks could not be based upon the zero option.

Why is the zero option such a non-starter? The basic reason is that neither side wants it. The USSR rejects it because it asks the USSR to give up systems already deployed in return for a promise by the USA not to deploy weapons not yet in existence. According to President Brezhnev 'not a single state that was concerned about the security of its people would agree to this if it were in our place'.[49] This reflects a traditional Soviet reluctance to accept the idea of planned deployments as bargaining chips. In their view only actual weapons can be traded for actual weapons.

Nor are the European members of NATO anxious to see

the zero option implemented. It was, after all, they who appealed to the USA to upgrade its Eurostrategic weapons in the first place. The appearance of the SS-20 and the Backfire bomber were not the whole explanation for this demand.

INF modernization was the result of technical advances in Soviet anti-aircraft defences. The removal of the SS-20 would not eliminate these defences, so the question mark over the deterrent value of NATO's nuclear-capable aircraft would remain.

The importance of the SS-20 to NATO is rather that it is a visible example of a growing Soviet 'threat', and therefore a way to 'sell' long-range INF modernization to a sceptical European public who would be unlikely to enthuse about the strategy of 'escalation dominance' if it was explained to them as a rationale for NATO missile deployments. Europeans in general would prefer to see arms control rather than arms deployments. It was NATO's recognition of this that led to the decision, in December 1979, that the modernization programme should be explicitly linked to an arms control initiative.

The zero option as such is not a genuine offer. It is a propaganda ploy designed to put the USSR on the defensive diplomatically, and to ward off the challenge posed by the European Nuclear Disarmament movement. Had the USSR promptly accepted the zero option it would have thrown NATO into total disarray. For political and military reasons NATO needs some missile deployments. However, it does not need the whole package, so scope for reductions is available.

The Soviet Union also has reasons for wanting a deal. It is profoundly hostile to the NATO modernization programme. The Soviets see the programme as the devious American way of getting around the ICBM constraints imposed in the SALT treaties, by targeting Soviet ICBMs from Western Europe. As one Soviet commentator has noted: 'the snag here is that the USSR cannot reply in kind. The best it can do is to create a counter-balance in Europe, but for all this it will not be able to deliver a single extra strike against targets in the USA proper.'[50]

Even so, anything the USSR can do via negotiation to reduce the threat posed by the NATO deployments is clearly to its advantage. Since NATO has the British and French deterrents, Poseidon SLBMs and aircraft, to supplement its ground-launched missile force, it can afford to negotiate away many of the planned deployments without threatening the requirements of its 'flexible response' doctrine. The USSR, which planned to replace all its SS-4s and SS-5s with SS-20s, but stopped withdrawing them once negotiations became imminent, can cheerfully negotiate these away. Moreover, since it has spare capacity in the SS-11, SS-14 and SS-19s targeted on Western Europe, and has almost certainly deployed more SS-20s than it originally planned, it can also afford to dismantle a significant number of SS-20s as part of an arms control treaty.

Although the zero option is not really negotiable it is a worthy objective, since, if it were achieved, it removes an entire class of nuclear weaponry from the European theatre. It was, therefore, quite legitimate for the American negotiators to aim for this in the initial talks and the fact that the USSR felt unable to accept it demonstrates the extent to which their proposals too contain a strong element of propaganda.

With the accession of Mr Andropov to the Soviet leadership a new Soviet offer was made: to reduce the size of the Soviet INF forces aimed at Western Europe to a number equivalent to the British and French submarine-launched ballistic missiles. This offer was worthy of greater consideration than it was given. It would have offered an opportunity for NATO to reduce the Soviet INF threat to its lowest level since the early 1960s. Phased reductions in the Anglo-French forces (rejected swiftly by France) could then have eliminated the threat entirely. Had progress been made at the START talks, the USSR would have been left with a considerably smaller ICBM force, and would have had less scope to target some of the ICBMs on Europe.

This would not have overcome NATO's problem of relying on aircraft to penetrate Soviet airspace carrying nuclear weapons, but in the absence of a Soviet missile monopoly the airborne NATO deterrent would have provided a far more credible linkage to American strategic systems than it does at present. Certainly, such an option should have been given far greater consideration than it achieved, for politics, as Bismarck said, is not only 'the art of the possible, it is also the art of bringing into the realm of the possible that which is necessary'.

What this episode demonstrated is the need for greater interplay between concurrent arms control negotiations. Global equilibrium must be the aim, and to this end account must be taken of the 'grey-area' systems which currently bedevil negotiations, because they do not fit neatly into any one set of talks. Thus weapons such as the Anglo-French nuclear deterrents must be dealt with in either START or the INF talks. They cannot simply be ignored. Nor, increasingly, can the small, but growing Chinese nuclear inventory. Only if the problem of the *totality* of nuclear weapons is addressed can the particular problems of areas such as Europe be dealt with satisfactorily.

6

The European central balance

> The numerical balance over the last 20 years has slowly but steadily moved in favour of the East. At the same time the West has largely lost the technological edge which allowed NATO to believe that quality could substitute for numbers.[1]

The statement above is an accurate generalization. It is one that most military analysts, even Soviet ones would accept, though the latter would probably refer to 'changes in the correlation of forces beneficial to international peace'. However, the statement is essentially a lowest common denominator. To discuss the *ways* in which things have changed, and the implications of such change, is to find almost as many opinions as there are analysts.

Certainly NATO's technological edge is narrower and the number of men and machines in the Warsaw Pact (WTO) have increased. The problem is to determine by how many and to what extent NATO's own force improvements over the same period offset these Soviet/WTO gains. To do this with confidence is difficult because one is not comparing like with like. In some areas NATO is ahead, in others the WTO has the advantage and these asymmetrical advantages are difficult to compare. There is also the question of what to include. How reliable are the Soviet Union's allies? Should French forces be included in the NATO figures? Should weaponry kept in storage be counted? Even more difficult are the unquantifiable variables such as morale, training, tactical initiative, deployment patterns, weapon quality and geographical factors.

It is possible to create quite different pictures of the

military balance in central Europe, depending upon which elements are included and which ones excluded. Thus, in the words of the former American Defense Secretary Harold Brown, 'the simple comparisons you hear so much about rarely illuminate more than the idiosyncrasies of their authors'.[2] A large element of subjectivity will always be present. It is necessary therefore to examine the approximate strengths of NATO and the WTO and the processes of change at work in each alliance, but also to be aware of the difficulties involved in comparing NATO and WTO force levels.

THE SHIFTING BALANCE SINCE 1965

In the past 15 years the Warsaw Pact has improved its forces considerably. Just how considerably is not clear, since even the estimates of the various NATO allies differ markedly. For example, whereas in 1977 Britain noted an increase since the mid-1960s of 31 per cent in Soviet tanks and 20 per cent in tactical aircraft,[3] American sources put the increases at 40[4] and 200[5] per cent respectively. Similarly, estimates of the increases in Soviet manpower over the same period vary from 100,000[6] to 154,000.[7]

If one looks at the European picture as a whole, there is a rough equality in numbers of men and equipment between the WTO and NATO, and in certain areas NATO still maintains an advantage. However, when those forces in the Western and Southern military districts of the USSR are added, the balance, in equipment terms, tilts fairly sharply in the Warsaw Pact's favour.

The figures given in table 6.1 indicate a picture of essential equilibrium. However one should note that they are for the whole of Europe and therefore include factors such as large numbers of Turkish infantry divisions who would be of little help in countering any Soviet thrust in central Europe. On the other hand, NATO divisions are generally much larger than WTO divisions. A US division in wartime would have 48,000 men in it, whereas a Soviet division would have 21,000. The real imbalance illustrated in the figures is in reserve divisions and equipment normally positioned in the Western USSR.

The whereabouts of those reserve divisions in time of crisis is therefore the crucial element in European security, and this will be examined later.

TABLE 6.1
NATO and WTO forces in Europe, 1981[8]

	NATO	WTO	Western and Southern USSR included
Manpower[9]			
Total manpower	4,933,000	4,788,000	–
Reserves (all services)	4,646,000	7,118,000	–
Total ground forces	2,713,000	2,613,000	–
Total ground forces Europe	2,123,000	1,669,000	–
Divisions			
Manned and in Europe	89	78	–
Available for immediate reinforcement	8	10	–
Mobilizable reserves	19	89	–
Equipment			
Tanks	17,053	26,300	45,500
Artillery, MRL	9,502	9,980	19,446
SSM launchers	355	620	1,224
Anti-tank guns	964	1,868	3,614
ATGW launchers	5,784	1,437	1,822
Anti-aircraft guns	5,273	3,586	6,486
SAM launchers	1,768	3,151	6,293
Aircraft			
Bombers	81	365	365
Ground attack	2,293	1,755	3,255
Fighters	204	665	1,565
Interceptors	572	1,490	1,490
Reconnaissance	397	524	899
Armed helicopters[10]	733	156	806

Since the key element of the European theatre is the central front, another way of looking at the military balance is in terms of who has what in place. The nature of the military balance depends upon the danger that is envisaged. Thus, because of her large mobilizable reserves, the USSR might want to move these forward before attempting an offensive. However, such movements could not be completed without NATO becoming aware of their significance and triggering its own mobilization.

Although NATO's immediate mobilizable reserves are fewer, given warning time of this sort, NATO would be able to blunt the Soviet offensive and in time (and assuming the fighting did not escalate rapidly to nuclear levels — a big 'if') her superior resources in terms of manpower and industrial muscle would enable her to match or surpass the Soviet war effort.

An alternative policy would be for the WTO to exploit the advantages of a surprise attack, using only the forces normally stationed in Eastern Europe. This would mean relying on a sudden breakthrough to precipitate the collapse of NATO, before the latter could produce a coherent political and military response. In this scenario, the sudden 'blitzkreig', the relevant balance would be as set out in tables 6.2 and 6.3.

The assumptions involved here are that Soviet forces based in Hungary would not be moved north, but that the French forces in Baden-Wurtemburg and Alsace-Lorraine would be committed to NATO's support. The figures once again show an approximate balance, all the more so when the much larger size of NATO divisions is taken into account, plus the fact that a further 5,000 NATO tanks would be available in West Germany, made up of prepositioned US weapons and NATO reserves.[13] Moreover, some analysts believe that up to eight of the WTO divisions are kept in such a low state of readiness in peacetime that they would be of little or no use in a sudden attack without prior mobilization of reserves.[14]

A surprise attack would allow NATO other advantages. For example the Soviet navy is normally based in the Baltic, Barents and Black Seas. Yet to support a WTO offensive they would need to move to the Mediterranean and Atlantic where they could attack NATO reinforcements *en route* to Europe, otherwise NATO would rapidly build-up a local superiority. Yet any major fleet movements of this sort would be a clear warning of attack to NATO.[15] Even major naval exercises put NATO on its guard.

TABLE 6.2
Warsaw Pact forces in Central Europe[11]

	Tank	Mechan-ized	Other	Total	Man	Tanks	Aircraft
East Germany	2	4	—	6	70,000	1,400	300
Czechoslovakia	5	2	3	10	100,000	2,800	400
Poland	5	5	5	15	150,000	2,600	800
Total	12	11	8	31	320,000	6,800	1,500
Soviet Union	14	13	—	27	460,000	8,000	1,300
Total	26	24	8	58	780,000	14,800	2,800

TABLE 6.3
NATO forces in Central Europe[12]

	Divisions	Men	Tanks	Aircraft
Belgium	2	40,000	220	180
Britain	3	50,000	580	400
Canada	—	4,000	40	60
Denmark	$\frac{2}{3}$	20,000	90	130
West Germany	12	235,000	2,800	750
France	4	147,000	640	485
Netherlands	3	45,000	470	230
USA	5	185,000	1,250	550
Total	$29\frac{2}{3}$	725,000	6,090	2,785

A NATO surprise attack against Eastern Europe might be more successful since it would be so unexpected. However the likelihood of such an attack is zero. It requires a certain amount of wishful thinking even to see some NATO members defend themselves against attack, never mind attack anybody else. In any case, Europe is not an area of resource or territorial competitions likely to provoke war. One reason for this which is worth noting, is the existence of NATO and the Warsaw Pact. Although in the West, Soviet hegemony in Eastern Europe is routinely condemned and the WTO regularly denounced, the existence of both serves to keep a lid on the pressure-cooker of East European nationalisms which would otherwise have led to endemic border disputes since 1945. And the existence of the two blocs, mirror-imaging each other's fears, tends to override lesser nationalistic rivalries, such as those between Germany and France or Hungary and Romania.

Given this situation, of a Europe weighed down with weaponry but with a tacitly accepted status-quo and an approximate military balance between the two dominant blocs, are there actually any arms race elements or causes of serious concern present? The answer to this question is by no means clear-cut. In some areas of technological development, an 'arms race' is clearly developing — one such area, chemical weapons, is looked at in the next chapter. Other areas present a picture of stability. This mixed picture is important if Europe is to develop arms control mechanisms appropriate to the situation. Before examining this question, the military momentum in the two alliances must be assessed.

THE WTO BUILD-UP: 1965–80

The Warsaw Pact forces have expanded quite considerably since 1960, but this growth has slowed markedly since 1970. Although the Soviet Union increased its army from 140 to 170 divisions, much of this effort was the result of increasing tension with China, and most of these new forces went to the

TABLE 6.4
Changes in ground forces of USSR 1964–76[16]

Type of force	Eastern Europe		Western USSR		Far East		Central USSR	
	1964	1976	1964	1976	1964	1976	1964	1976
Armoured	13	14	20	23	3	7	14	4
Motorized	13	17	34	35	13	38	23	25
Airborne	0	0	6	6	1	1	0	0
Total*	26	31	60	64	17	46	37	29

*Another 20 divisions are kept understrength but fully equipped.

Chinese border. The other main increase in Soviet ground forces was related to the redeployment of forces to Czechoslovakia following the 1968 invasion. Thus the number of Soviet divisions in Eastern Europe has increased from 26 to 31 divisions since 1964, but their presence is aimed more at 'deterring' the Czechs than the NATO allies.

The number of Soviet divisions has not expanded dramatically therefore, except in response to a newly-perceived Chinese threat. However, the *quality* of these divisions has improved. For example, the élite of the Soviet ground forces are those divisions in the Group of Soviet Forces in Germany (GSFG). The size of each GSFG division has increased by 20 per cent in the last 15 years. The number of artillery pieces with this force has doubled, while the number of tanks in each motorized rifle division has gone up by 40 per cent.[17] Since the GSFG is the prime danger to NATO, the units that would provide the cutting edge of any Soviet offensive, this build-up has alarmed NATO leaders. So heavily equipped are some GSFG units, in fact, that some observers see this as a potential weakness. Many Soviet divisions are now relatively thinly manned and can therefore scarcely operate all the equipment they possess. Because of this, in wartime, losses which would hardly affect a NATO division could immobilize their undermanned Soviet counterparts, depending upon how much time elapsed before they were replaced.[18]

Outside the GSFG, the changes in tank strengths have not been dramatic, increasing from 6,600 Soviet main battle tanks in 1967 to 9,250 in 1980.[19] Again, however, most of those, 1,800 out of 2,650, went to the Soviet forces occupying Czechoslovakia after 1968. These still of course pose a threat to NATO, but their presence in Central Europe was, and is, only indirectly related to the balance of power with NATO.

It took the USSR 15 years to develop a successor to the T-62 battle tank. The successor, the T-72, was little more than a slightly improved version of the T-62. This came as a surprise to NATO analysts, who had expected the 1970s and 1980s to see continuing major Soviet efforts to increase the quality and quantity of their tank holdings in central Europe. This did not happen. However NATO could draw little comfort from this, for while Soviet tank stocks levelled-off, the supporting hardware of any armoured offensive was dramatically improved. Thus, while the number of tanks in GSFG increased during the 1970s, the number of artillery, anti-tank and anti-aircraft pieces increased by a far greater margin, as did logistic support.[20]

The most dramatic improvement in Soviet ground offensive capabilities has been in the development of armoured personnel carriers. Since 1970 the Soviets have given steadily increasing importance to moving infantry quickly across the battlefield in well-armed APCs. Two vehicles in particular alarm western strategists. The BMP, first seen in 1967, is far more than a 'battlefield taxi'. The vehicle is designed to operate in a nuclear, chemical or biological environment, and in addition to a crew of three carries eight infantrymen. However the BMP has the firepower of a light tank, including a 73 mm anti-tank gun, an AT-3 'Sagger' anti-tank guided missile, and a coaxially mounted 7.62 mm machine-gun. In addition it has firing ports for its passengers to use their weapons if necessary. The BMP is fully amphibious. The 20 new divisions deployed by the USSR since 1964 were *all* motorized rifle divisions, equipped with the BMP to enable the Soviet infantry to keep up with their tanks in a rapid offensive.

Even more ominous in many respects is the BMD. This is the airborne version of the BMP. The BMD first appeared in 1973. In addition to the weapons mounted by the BMP, the BMD carries a further two 7.62 mm machine-guns mounted in the bow. Whereas NATO armies have tended to view paratroops as increasingly anachronistic because, armed only with light weapons they could not, as the Arnhem operation during the Second World War showed, resist armoured counterattacks, the USSR has armoured its paratroops. Soviet airborne units, mounted in the swift, heavily-armed BMD, could create havoc in NATO's rear areas. In addition, Soviet airborne forces also have the ASU-85 self-propelled anti-tank gun. Each Soviet airborne division has 220 BMDs and 18 ASU-85s,[21] dramatically reducing the vulnerability of airborne units to armoured counter-attack. ASU-85s figured prominently in the Czechoslovak and Afghanistan operations.

The USSR has transferred 6,430 BMPs to the other Warsaw Pact countries, primarily to Poland (5,500 BMPs).[22] In addition, the other WTO states possess about 5,500 earlier model APCs, especially the BTR-60. The BTR-60 carries 12 soldiers and mounts a turreted 14.5 mm machine-gun and a coaxial 7.62 mm machine-gun. This is in fact one area where the much-vaunted standardization of WTO equipment is not much in evidence. There are, for example, eight different types of personnel carrier in service with WTO armies using four different track systems and seven different engine types.[23]

The manpower levels and tank holdings of the WTO have stabilized during the 1970s and the major momentum during the 1980s is likely to be qualitative rather than quantitative, particularly in areas such as command, communication and control, electromagnetic warfare and combat engineering.[24]

WTO AIR FORCE DEVELOPMENTS

A land battle is fought not only with ground forces but with these forces supported by air forces (and on occasion naval units). In the European context, the balance of air forces is as important as that of the ground units, particularly since the 1970s saw rapid developments in airborne anti-tank weapons.

Between 1964 and 1976 Soviet 'frontal aviation' the tactical air forces of the USSR, which are designed to support the

TABLE 6.5
Composition of Soviet air force, 1964 and 1976[25]

	1964		1976	
	Fixed wing	Heli-copters	Fixed wing	Heli-copters
Air defence command	4,040	—	2,590	—
Naval aviation	800	200	950	250
Long-range aviation	1,100	—	849	—
Frontal aviation	3,360	—	4,600	2,950
Military transport	1,700	790	1,550	320

ground forces, increased in size by a third, and the USSR's capacity to move war material and soldiers by air was doubled.

Tactical aircraft, such as those of Soviet frontal aviation, have several functions, with specific types of aircraft performing each task. Obtaining air-superiority using fighters and interceptors such as the MiG-21 Fishbed and MiG-23 Flogger would be a primary role. These aircraft would seek to dominate airspace in and around the battlefield. Secondly, frontal aviation would supply close support to the ground forces, attacking NATO units which were blocking the WTO advance, and concentrating particularly against NATO armoured formations. For this role, aircraft like the Sukhoi Su-17 Fitter C and Su-20 Fitter D ground attack planes would be used. Further behind the battle, interdiction strikes against NATO bases, bridges, railway yards, ammunition dumps, ports and so on would be carried out using the Sukhoi Su-24 Fencer, of which some 750 are expected to enter service. Fencer is an extremely good Soviet aircraft capable of long-range penetration raids deep into NATO territory. Medium bombers such as the Tu-16, Tu-22 and Tu-22M (Backfire) might also be used to carry out long-range bombing raids.

Helicopters as well as aircraft now play an important ground support role. The most formidable of these is the Mi-24 Hind range of attack helicopters. The Hind-D is armed with a four-barrelled gatling gun in a chin turret, two anti-tank guided missile (ATGM) launchers and four rocket pods. It has a combat radius of 62 miles (100 kilometres). Less advanced, but even more heavily armed is the older HipE attack helicopter of which the WTO states possess some 1,800.[26] HipE mounts a 12.7 mm machine-gun in the nose, four anti-tank missiles and 192.57 mm rockets.

The 1970s in fact witnessed a major transformation in Warsaw Pact air power. As the Nunn-Bartlett Report of 1977 declared:

In 1968, Soviet tactical air forces were oriented primarily toward the defense of air space over Pact territory, and accordingly were composed largely of short-range, low-payload aircraft possessing only incidental ground-attack capabilities. Since then, Soviet tactical air forces have been fundamentally restructured with the apparent objective of acquiring a powerful offensive force for both close air-support along the entire breadth of the battle area and deep interdiction throughout NATO Europe.[27]

NATO has relied upon aircraft to control airspace, whereas the WTO has always given a high priority to ground-launched anti-aircraft weapons. The Soviet army has in fact tried to become self-sufficient in this respect, so as not to rely on air support. The losses sustained by the Israeli air force at the start of the 1973 war show how effective these weapons can be. Weapon systems available to the WTO include the ZSU-23/4 radar- or optically-guided missile, with a range of two and a half kilometres, the SA-7 Grail, a heat-seeking missile with a range of over two kilometres, the SA-9 (range eight kilometres), SA-8 Gecko (range eight to sixteen kilometres), SA-4 Ganef (range 68 kilometres) and SA-6 Gainful (range 35 kilometres). With the exception of the man-portable SA-7 Grail, all these weapons are self-propelled.[28]

THE NATO BUILD-UP DURING THE 1970s

The balance of power in central Europe has not altered dramatically in the past 15 years, although perceptions have changed considerably. In the 1950s and 1960s NATO was convinced that it stood little or no chance in a conventional war with the USSR and its allies because of the tremendous numerical advantage of the WTO. This gloomy assessment led to NATO adopting a nuclear-based defensive strategy relying upon the use of tactical nuclear weapons to offset its conventional weakness. During the mid-1960s, however, the figures on which these assumptions were based were re-assessed in Washington and Secretary of Defence, Robert McNamara, announced that things were not, after all, as bad as they had seemed. On the contrary, NATO and the WTO possessed a rough equivalence in ground forces, while NATO was marginally superior in tactical airpower[29] and clearly ahead in naval power, and this even without the inclusion of French forces in the total.

In this regard those who cried 'wolf' too soon in the early 1960s did NATO a grave disservice by shackling her to the incredible nuclear strategy discussed in chapter 5 and by inducing a climate of political defeatism which was not justified by the facts. During the late 1960s, however, NATO's relative position *did* worsen as the USA struggled to cope with the strains of the Vietnam War while the USSR strengthened its forces in Eastern Europe as a result of the Czechoslovak crisis. However, in the middle 1970s NATO responded by accelerating its own force improvement programmes, which have largely regained the earlier parity. For most of the 1970s NATO was modernizing and expanding at a rate comparable to that of the WTO.

Like the WTO, NATO modernized its tank forces during the 1970s. The German Leopard II tank went into full-scale production in 1979. West Germany plans to acquire 1,800 Leopard IIs, while the Dutch will purchase 445.[30] Other NATO forces such as the Belgian, Danish, Norwegian and Italian armies which operate the Leopard I, may follow suit. The Leopard II is more than a match for the Soviet T-72. By the middle 1980s the still more powerful Leopard III is due to be deployed. The USA is also modernizing. The M-1 Abrams tank, of which 7,000 are to come into service by 1987, is also a match for the T-72, though not perhaps for the T-80 which will be in Soviet service in some numbers by the end of the 1980s. British Chieftain tanks are now being replaced by Challenger while France is upgrading its AMX-30s. As well as improving the quality of its tanks, NATO has been making efforts to close the numerical gap with the WTO. While the WTO continues to have somewhere in the region of three times as many tanks as NATO, NATO has managed to cut the gap in tank production rates from 4:1 to 2:1.[31]

NATO's anti-tank capabilities consist of more than its tank inventory however. Soviet Marshall Grechko noted in 1975 'the continuing process of perfecting the anti-tank Weapon'[32] which had threatened the viability of tank forces. Although the Soviets have been aware of the potential of anti-tank guided missiles since the early 1960s, it was the apparent 'lessons' of the 1973 Arab–Israeli war which stimulated

Grechko's concern. Heavy Israeli tank losses at the hands of Egyptian infantrymen using ATGMs seemed to indicate a new era of warfare. In fact, the Sinai experience should not be exaggerated. Most of the Israeli tanks knocked out in the 1973 war were destroyed by other tanks. The Egyptian infantry in barren desert terrain proved very vulnerable to Israeli fire as they aimed their ATGMs. Even so, the 1973 war demonstrated clearly that tanks can be destroyed by appropriately armed infantry, and this is encouraging to NATO which places a high reliance upon the effectiveness of infantry-launched ATGMs. NATO also has high performance aircraft and attack helicopters to carry out the anti-tank role. In general NATO's infantry ATGMs are superior to those of the WTO because they are easier to operate and have shorter flight times. This latter factor gives the user a greater chance of survival. Against this, however, a much higher proportion of WTO gunners would be firing their missiles from the relative security of armoured fighting vehicles.[33]

Attack helicopters (AHs) would play a vital role for NATO, and are being increasingly emphasized within the alliance. So far seven NATO states deploy AHs including the British Lynx, German PAH-1, Italian Mangusta, French Puma and US Cobra series. The Italian Mangusta (Mongoose) is the first European AH which can operate in any weather, in daylight or at night. It is armed with eight TOW anti-tank guided missiles and a 7.52 mm machine-gun. The middle 1980s will see NATO deploy an even more powerful helicopter, the Hughes AH-64 gunship. This helicopter is the most well protected ever designed and carries the powerful Hellfire anti-tank missile, as well as 76 rockets and a 30 mm cannon.[34] As well as helicopters, NATO would use the Fairchild A-10A Thunderbolt II tankbuster to attack WTO armoured columns.

Other technological developments have also added to NATO's growing confidence that it could halt a WTO armoured offensive. During the 1970s, while the Warsaw Pact was doubling the number of its artillery pieces, NATO concentrated on improving the quality of its artillery. One example of this is the 'Copperhead' precision-guided missile, which most NATO armies are likely to adopt. Copperhead is a cross between a shell and a missile. It is fired like an ordinary artillery round, but once in flight wing and tail fins deploy. The missile is then guided onto its target by a laser tracking beam. Exotic systems like the American 'Aquila' may be used to guide Copperhead. Aquila is a remotely piloted vehicle which sends television pictures back to its operator. Using Aquila, Copperhead's laser target-designator could be operated without exposing the operator to enemy fire.[35]

NATO'S LONG-TERM DEFENCE PROGRAMME

During the 1970s NATO took two related major initiatives designed to increase its military power. Two central problems for the alliance were identified: first, that the NATO states were not spending enough on defence; and second, that the available money was not being used in the best way. As one defence specialist has noted in this respect: '*how* you spend your money is at least as important as *how much* you spend.[36]

To meet these difficulties the NATO states made two major commitments. One was to increase defence spending *in real terms* (that is, allowing for the effects of inflation) by 3 per cent per year.[37] Secondly, in order that the increased NATO expenditure should meet the Alliance's real military needs, NATO committed itself to a 'Long-Term Defence Programme' (LTDP) setting out medium-term goals in ten areas where NATO seemed inadequately prepared.

The NATO commitment to a 3 per cent increase in defence spending per year was in practice more of a political act than anything else. Many NATO states were already making such an increase during the 1970s, and those countries which for economic reasons were not able to reach the target invariably, by 'creative book-keeping', juggled the figures to make it appear as if they had. Even Britain, generally regarded as a state which honoured the 3 per cent commitment, was prone to do this. Thus the period 1979–81 was portrayed as one in which Britain averaged a 3 per cent increase because the rise was 5 per cent one year and zero the next.[38] In fact, much of that increase went on factors, such as wages, that contributed little to Britain's military capability, whereas the cuts of

1980–81 weakened the UK forces. Thus maintaining the increase has not necessarily added to NATO's capabilities.

The LTDP is therefore a more important factor in the NATO build-up, and the military value of that build-up, than is the financial commitment. In all, some 1,300 goals were laid down by NATO in the LTDP, with most NATO states being asked to respond to over 100 improvement suggestions.[39] The LTDP established ten areas of special concern—readiness, reinforcement capabilities, reserve mobilization, maritime posture, air defence, command control and communications, electronic warfare, standardization and interoperability, logistics, and theatre nuclear force modernization. This programme has been called 'the boldest and most far-reaching step taken by NATO since the inception of the Alliance itself.[40]

TABLE 6.6
*NATO defence spending as percentages of GDP
in purchaser's values, 1970–79*

Country	Average 1970–74	1975	1976	1977	1978	1979
Belgium	2.8	3.1	3.1	3.1	3.3	3.3
Denmark	2.2	2.4	2.2	2.2	2.3	2.3
France	3.9	3.8	3.8	3.9	3.9	3.9
Greece	4.4	6.5	5.9	6.8	6.6	5.8
Italy	2.7	2.5	2.3	2.4	2.4	2.4
Luxembourg	0.8	1.0	1.0	1.0	1.1	1.0
Netherlands	3.3	3.4	3.2	3.5	3.2	3.4
Norway	3.2	3.2	3.1	3.1	3.2	3.1
Portugal	6.9	5.3	4.0	3.5	3.5	3.5
Turkey	4.2	5.8	6.2	5.8	5.2	4.6
United Kingdom	5.0	5.0	5.0	4.8	4.7	4.8
West Germany	3.5	3.6	3.5	3.4	3.4	3.3
NATO–Europe	3.7	3.8	3.7	3.6	3.6	3.6
Canada	2.1	1.9	1.9	1.9	2.0	1.8
USA	6.7	6.0	5.4	5.3	5.2	5.2
Total NATO	5.2	4.7	4.4	4.4	4.3	4.3

Source: *NATO Review*, Vol. 29, No. 1 (Feb. 1981), p. 33.

It is one of the paradoxes of the arms race that although arms races as such are to be condemned there are circumstances in which a build-up may be a good thing. Thus it was noted in the chapter on nuclear proliferation that it may be better to supply a state with sophisticated conventional weapons if this will reduce the need for it to acquire nuclear weapons. Similarly the current NATO conventional weapons build-up offers hope as much as it arouses fears; the hope being that NATO reliance upon battlefield nuclear weapons will be significantly reduced. The better the conventional balance in Europe the higher the nuclear threshold becomes, and the stronger the overall deterrent. Should deterrence falter or fail, and defence becomes necessary, then it is far better that that defence be carried out using conventional weapons, for once nuclear weapons, however limited their yield, were employed, a threshold would be crossed from which it is unlikely there would be any turning back and the possibility of negotiation would be one of the earliest casualties.

PROSPECTS FOR ARMS CONTROL

The question of arms control in Central Europe is currently dominated by the fate of the Mutual Force Reduction (MFR) talks going on in Vienna. When these talks opened in October 1973 Leonid Brezhnev remarked that they would still be going on when our grandchildren grew up.[41] What Brezhnev meant was that there should be a continuing commitment to conventional disarmament, but in fact his words seem quite likely to come true even in the obvious sense. By October 1982, the MFR talks had been going on for nine years and the two sides were not much nearer to an agreement than they were in 1973.

There are a number of reasons why the MFR talks have produced so little progress. One clear reason is that neither side is really determined that the talks succeed. The main political incentive for the NATO States was the Mansfield Amendment. In 1966 US Senate Majority Leader Mike Mansfield introduced a senate resolution calling for 'a substantial reduction of US forces permanently stationed in Europe'. Forty-three Senators (out of 100) voted in favour. The amendment was resubmitted at intervals, and as the cost of the Vietnam War mounted, political pressure in favour of European troop cuts mounted also. NATO attempted to head off the threat of unilateral American withdrawals by calling for arms control talks with the Warsaw Pact in which American force reductions would be matched by WTO cutbacks. The pressure came to a head in 1971 when Senator Mansfield forced a debate on the subject of halving the number of American troops in Europe. President Nixon was forced to call upon 'virtually every living major figure in the making of US defence and foreign policy since 1945' in favour of keeping the troops there. Perhaps even more importantly, President Brezhnev had indirectly testified on Nixon's behalf when, the day before the crucial Senate vote, he had accepted the Western offer of MFR talks.[42]

President Brezhnev's motives in agreeing to MFR were equally tangential. The USSR agreed to discuss MFR purely as a quid pro quo for NATO participation in a Conference on Security and Co-operation in Europe, which the Soviet Union was determined should take place.[43]

Thus, by the end of 1975, when the Helsinki Conference on Security and Co-operation in Europe had taken place and the American participation in the Vietnam War was over, with a consequent reduction in domestic political pressure, neither side any longer had a powerful incentive to negotiate.

However, because the MFR talks were seen as a symbol of European detente they were not allowed to collapse, but the will to succeed was lacking and in the absence of a political commitment to success, the technical obstacles assumed major proportions. The objectives of the MFR talks were, according to the WTO, reductions which would not 'disturb the existing balance of power in central Europe and in the European continent in general',[44] and, according to NATO, the achievement of 'a more stable military balance at lower levels of forces with undiminished security for all participants at the talks'.[45]

These approaches revealed a clear disparity in objectives from the beginning. According to the USSR, a balance of power existed in Europe, therefore reduction should be symmetrical so that the prevailing balance of forces remained unaltered. According to NATO, an imbalance, in the WTO's favour, existed, therefore reductions would have to be asymmetrical, so that the two sides would be brought to parity. Thus NATO called for a phased reduction to a common ceiling of 700,000 ground forces, beginning with a cut of 29,000 American and 68,000 Soviet troops.[46] The WTO called for a phased reduction of forces by 15 per cent, preceded by a cut of 20,000 men from each side.[47]

However, the symmetry/asymmetry problem has not proved the central stumbling block as was originally feared. By 1978 the Warsaw Pact had come round to accepting the original NATO proposals for equal ceilings of 700,000 in ground forces, and equal common ceilings of 900,000 for ground and airforce personnel.[48] This did not open the way for the rapid conclusion of an agreement however, because the central issue of *data* had not been resolved. For the first three years of the MFR talks, the Warsaw Pact refused to give any figures for the size of its forces in the central European area. When in 1976 they finally submitted figures, these were dramatically lower than NATO intelligence estimates.

TABLE 6.7
Discrepancy between NATO and WTO estimates of WTO forces[49]

	Western estimates	Eastern estimates	Difference
Ground	962,000	805,000	157,000
Air	200,000	182,000	17,700
Total	1,162,000	987,000	174,000

The differences between the figures for air force personnel are small enough to be ignored. This is not the case with the figures for ground forces however. According to the Pact, the WTO allies would have to reduce their forces by 105,000 men to reach the ground force ceiling of 700,000. However by NATO's estimation, the WTO must lose over 260,000 men to reach the agreed ceiling. Thus if NATO's estimate is correct and the two sides reduced to 700,000, the WTO in

reality would have achieved an advantage of 155,000 men —
a distinct military gain. Although NATO estimates invariably
inflate the size of WTO forces, the discrepancy in MFR figures
is too large to be a statistical quirk. Even when allowance for
Polish marine forces and some border units is made, the discrepancy is over 125,000 men. If these troops were Polish
and Czech, many of whom are used for labour, rather than
military tasks, the problem would be less alarming, but half
the total, 60,000 men, is made up of Soviet troops whom the
USSR insists are not there.[50]

The inability to agree on the number of men each side has,
has left the MFR talks immobilized. Only if the WTO explains
exactly how it has arrived at its figure of 805,000, so that the
source(s) of the discrepancy can be identified, can the MFR
talks be expected to progress. Without agreement on data,
neither the size of the reductions necessary, nor an effective
means of verifying that they have taken place, can be agreed
upon.

The uncertainty which surrounds the MFR talks may not,
however, be altogether damaging. A number of observers
have come to believe that the whole *approach* to conventional
arms control in Europe, as embodied in the MFR negotiations, may be ill-conceived. If this is so, then the failure of
the talks is not so much to be feared as welcomed if it leads
to a more productive approach.

Even the military confrontation of the superpowers in
central Europe is not without redeeming features, for as
Selwyn Lloyd noted in 1958:

> The world is a much safer place if in critical areas there
> is a direct confrontation of the major parties and not an
> area of uncertainty. In Central Europe the two great
> nuclear powers do confront each other directly. As long
> as this situation prevails, a war triggered off by chance
> border incidents will be unlikely.[51]

The confrontation in central Europe is, nevertheless, a
matter for great concern. The problem lies not so much in the
sheer numbers of soldiers and weapons (with which MFR has
been concerned), but rather in the *deployment patterns* of

those forces, which is where an alternative to the 'bean-count' approach of MFR may lie, through 'confidence building'.

Confidence building measures (CBMs) are a particular form of arms control which do not directly affect the size, weaponry and structure of military forces and weapons of war. Instead CMBs aim at increasing trust and confidence between two hostile sides, making the intentions and actions of each clearer and more predictable to the other. This usually involves restrictions on the availability of armed forces, their actions, and their deployment in certain areas.[52]

Certain CBMs have already been applied to Europe. They were mentioned in the first part of the Final Act of the 1975 Helsinki Conference on Security and Co-operation in Europe (CSCE). This comprised prior notification of military manoeuvres involving more than 25,000 men, and notification of smaller manoeuvres involving significant numbers of amphibious or airborne troops. Twenty-one days' notice of such manoeuvres was to be given, and details provided of the number and type of forces involved, the area affected, and the duration of the exercise.[53]

Smaller scale exercises, especially those held in sensitive border areas were also to be notified. The CSCE document encouraged states to invite observers to attend their manoeuvres. The document also urged states 'at their own discretion' to give notice of any significant movements of troops outside their garrison or base areas.[54]

These CBMs, while useful, are extremely tame. They are nowhere near comprehensive enough to produce a real increase in mutual confidence. The area of confidence which needs strengthening is that relating to fear of a devastating surprise attack. Thus US Congressman Les Aspin urged in 1977 that NATO worry less about numbers and more about warning time, proposing that 'instead of using the MBFR talks to negotiate a reduction in troops, we use it to negotiate measures to increase warning time and reduce the chance of a surprise attack'.[55]

The sort of measure that would be useful in this respect would be a 'system constraint' on primarily offensive weapons such as that proposed by Alton Frye in 1978.[56] Frye proprosed a mutual tank disengagement of about 100 miles on either side of the iron curtain. Within this zone only light infantry armed with anti-tank weapons would be allowed. Moving armoured divisions to the rear in this way would have a number of advantages. Any movement of enemy tanks into the border zone would be a signal of intent, available well before they crossed the border. By the time they did reach the border, the direction of the offensive would be clear. The defending side would be enabled to move their mobile reserves towards the area under threat, where anti-armour defences in the shape of anti-tank gun and guided-missiles would already be in place. By moving armour to the rear, while the offensive threat was reduced, the defensive flexibility of each side would be correspondingly increased. Moreover, in NATO's case, such a move, while politically painful for any West German government, would force NATO out of its current militarily unsound 'layer cake' cordon defence and give it what it needs, an echelon defence based on reserves of armoured divisions.

CBMs to supplement such a move could include a complete ban on military manoeuvres within the limitation zone. Though this would reduce the ability of the defenders to familiarize themselves with the battlefield, after nearly 40 years of static confrontation each side now knows its own side of the border fairly well! Other measures could include notification of all out-of-garrison movements, notification of smaller military manoeuvres, an upper limit on the size of manoeuvres to 40,000 or 60,000 men, limitations on naval and aerial manoeuvres, the banning of offensive support elements such as bridge-building equipment within the border zone, and extension of the date of prior notification of manoeuvres to sixty days.

Restructuring forces in this way would address both the subjective and objective elements of threat perception in the European balance. The approach offers a way out of the immobilism that has come to characterize MFR. CBMs can serve as 'an underpinning for more conventional types of arms control agreement and as alternatives when traditional types of agreements prove impossible to negotiate or sustain . . .'[57] Their advantage is that by increasing confidence and reducing mistrust, they create the essential preconditions for more substantive action to produce genuine reductions.

7

The chemical arms race

One of the central problems of the struggle for ending the arms race and reducing the threat of war is the problem of banning chemical weapons.[1]

In February 1982 the United States announced its intentions of resuming the manufacture of chemical offensive agents for the first time since 1969, rejoining a chemical arms race from which the Soviet Union had never withdrawn.[2]

THE RENEWAL OF CONCERN

Chemical weaponry is an area in which an arms race seemed to have ended in the early 1970s. At that time a convention banning biological weapons had been concluded,[3] and the convention committed the signatories to pursue negotiations towards a treaty banning chemical weapons as well. Although it was recognized that a chemical warfare treaty would be more difficult to negotiate than the biological weapons convention, in the atmosphere of detente the omens appeared favourable. For once the superpowers made no great effort to hinder such talks by their actions. The USA suspended live testing and further production of chemical warfare (CW) agents in 1969, and what little evidence that came from the USSR seemed to indicate that they too were not adding to their chemical weapon stocks. At the Moscow summit of June 1974, President Nixon and Mr Brezhnev agreed that the USA and USSR would present a joint initiative on chemical weapons to the United Nations' Committee on Disarmament.

The thinking behind this was that if the superpowers could agree upon what they would accept, other states should have little difficulty in acceding to it, and that conversely there was little point in the UN producing a treaty that satisfied everyone *except* the superpowers.

The bilateral talks opened in Geneva in August 1976. Although arms control talks are not always pursued seriously, the chemical disarmament negotiations were pursued in a serious and purposeful manner. Adrian Fisher, the US delegation leader, reported to the UN in 1977 that the chemical talks were making 'measurable progress'.[4] On 7 August 1979 the USA and USSR gave a detailed report on the progress of the talks to the Committee on Disarmament. The report laid out those areas in which the two sides had reached broad agreement, those areas where difficult problems remained and those actions which they felt could be taken to build mutual confidence in this field before a chemical disarmament convention came into effect.[5]

This report indicated that the talks, while obviously, and predictably, difficult, were showing progress. Already, however, warning signs of danger were appearing. In January 1979 the US Joint Chiefs of Staff had reported that 'progress in the US/Soviet chemical weapons talks during the past year and a half has not been substantive'.[6]

What was happening was that the USA was beginning to reconsider its attitude towards chemical warfare. For a number of reasons, discussed later in this chapter, the opinion was gaining ground within the US Government that the decline in emphasis on chemical warfare capability should be reversed.

Why has this happened? Why has a class of weaponry seemingly on the verge of abolition returned to occupy a central position in the contemporary arms race? The explanations are many, but before going on to look at them it is worth putting the present situation in perspective by taking a brief look at the history of chemical warfare and chemical arms control.

THE HISTORY OF CHEMICAL WARFARE

Chemical warfare is not a twentieth-century invention. The first recorded gas attack occurred not in 1914 but during the Peloponnesian War (431–04 BC) in Greece. Spartan forces besieging the cities of Platea and Delium used giant bellows to blow the smoke from a concoction of pitch, charcoal and sulphur into the besieged cities 'in hopes of choking the defenders and rendering the assault less difficult'. In later centuries the Byzantine Empire perfected a weapon known to others as 'Greek fire', a flame-throwing device whose flame jet produced a blinding, asphyxiating smoke (sulphurous dioxide).[7]

Two further examples are worth mentioning because they predate the attitudes of this century. In 1456 Belgrade was besieged by the Turks. The defenders used arsenical gas clouds to drive back the attackers. An Austrian observer, von Senfftenberg, said of this: 'it was a sad business. Christians must never use so murderous a weapon against other Christians. Still, it is quite in place against Turks and other miscreants.'[8]

This attitude, that some weapons are too horrible to be used except against 'barbarians' of one's choice, has lingered on into this century as will be noted later. One other element worth noting is the venerable tradition of American attachment to chemical weapons as an essentially 'humane' form of warfare. In the early stages of the American Civil War, John W. Doughty of New York recommended the firing of chlorine gas shells against the Confederate forces, arguing in his letter to the Secretary of War:

> As to the moral question involved in its introduction, I have, after watching the progress of events during the last eight months . . . arrived at the somewhat paradoxical conclusion, that its introduction would very much lessen the sanguinary character of the battlefield, and at the same time render conflicts more decisive in their results.[9]

Again, we shall have cause to return to this theme later. As has been seen, however, chemical warfare predates the Great War of 1914–18, with which it is usually associated in the public mind. Equally, efforts to ban the use of chemical weapons occurred before 1914.

In 1899 the First Hague Conference met to consider arms limitation and the peaceful settlement of international disputes. The Conference, a Russian initiative, discussed among other things, a ban on projectiles containing 'asphyxiating and deleterious gases'. All the powers represented on the subcommittee discussing gas weapons were in favour of supporting the Russian call to ban them — all except one. The American Government had issued instructions to its delegates urging them not to support any disarmament measures which the Conference might propose.[10] Accordingly, Mahan, the American representative on the chemical weapons subcommittee, while admitting he knew little about the subject, echoed the ideas of Doughty in 1861 and declared that gases were probably more humane killers than bullets or shells and could produce more decisive results.[11] Other American delegates wished to support the ban, but Mahan prevailed and the proposal failed. Thus when war broke out in Europe in 1914 there was no legal requirement upon the warring powers to refrain from using chemical weapons.

THE FIRST WORLD WAR AND ITS AFTERMATH

The first use of chemical weapons in the First World War was actually by French troops, policemen who, when joining their reserve units, had brought their tear-gas rifles with them. These had little military effect, but did enable Germany to claim subsequently that it was not *they* who had initiated gas warfare on the Western Front. On 31 January 1915 the Germans used shells carrying irritant gas to attack Russian artillery positions at Bolimov, severely reducing the Russian fire. But it was the battle of Ypres in 1915 which gave gas its deadly reputation.

Ypres could have been the decisive battle of the First World War. The German High Command had decided to use gas on a large scale in order to win a victory that would break the trench stalemate that had developed on the Western Front. However Ypres was essentially a large-scale field test for gas attacks, because the High Command had such little confidence in the new weapon that they did not commit the huge reserves to the attack that could have made it a decisive victory.[12] Even so the effects were devastating.

British intelligence actually knew the attack was coming, but ignored the warning because they assumed a large-scale gas attack to be 'technically impossible'. On 22 April 1915 a concentrated cloud of chlorine gas began rolling towards the allied lines on a six kilometre front. As it reached the allied lines they simply disintegrated. Total panic broke out as casualties mounted. The gas attack produced a peculiar reaction of horror which it has never really lost. As one British survivor noted:

> The first poison gas sufferers. This horror was too monstrous to believe at first . . . Far as we had travelled from our civilised world of a few months back, the savagery of it, of the sight of men choking to death with yellow froth, lying on the floor and out in the fields, made me rage with an anger which no cruelty of men, not even the degradation of our kind by the hideous concentration camps in later Germany, ever quite rekindled; for then we still thought all men were human . . .[13]

The Ypres attack was devastating because it was against unprepared troops. Five thousand allied soldiers were killed, and a further 10,000 wounded. The Germans took 5,000 prisoners and, had they had the reserves, could have broken through to the channel. A few weeks later a similar attack was made on the Eastern Front. At Bolimov on 2 May 1915 the Russian army lost 9,100 casualties including 6,000 dead and the 53rd and 54th Siberian Regiments were wiped out.[14]

As the war continued so did the refinement of chemical weapons. In 1917 the Germans introduced mustard gas, which rendered respirators an inadequate defence because it attacked the skin directly. Although the number of casualties went up, the number of deaths caused by gas declined as a proportion of total casualties because mustard gas was rarely fatal. One British expert has speculated that the American view of poison gas as a relatively humane weapon was due to the late entry of America into the war which meant that most of its gas casualties were non-fatal mustard gas victims.[15] However, as we have seen, to some extent the American attitude predates the First World War.

The public revulsion against gas weapons was marked after the end of the First World War. By that time, over 100,000 soldiers had been killed in gas attacks and over a million more had suffered injury.[16] The revulsion encouraged international efforts to have chemical weapons banned and these led to the signing on 17 June 1925 of the Geneva Protocol.[17]

The Geneva Protocol, though of some value, suffered from a number of weaknesses. The text is riddled with ambiguities which enabled states to avoid submitting to the spirit of the proposal. The treaty forbade the use of chemical weaponry, but only against signatories of the protocol, thus leaving the way open for states to use chemical weapons against non-signatories, including both other states and non-state actors such as guerrilla fighters. In addition, most of those states that did sign the protocol inserted a caveat reserving the right to retaliate in kind against a chemical attack. Because of this the protocol became essentially a 'no-first-use' agreement rather than a ban, and allowed states to continue to develop and stockpile chemical weapons as deterrents against chemical attack.[18] Even this restraint was too much for some. The American Government, having encouraged the conference and drafted the protocol, was unable to convince the US Senate of the value of ratifying it. Because of this, half a century passed before finally, in 1974, the USA became a full signatory.

The protocol did not, however, bring an end to chemical warfare. During the 1920s and 1930s Britain used gas against unprotected Afghan tribesmen; Italy used it against the Abyssinians; and Japan against the Chinese. Why was this? Britain and Italy had both suffered from gas warfare in the First World War. In one action in 1916 a gas attack produced Italian losses of 6,000 men while the attacking Austrians lost 36. Casualties of this sort seemed to have produced a deep revulsion against chemical weapons in both countries.

Revulsion against the use of poisons in war seems deeply ingrained in human nature. It has been suggested that this is because they cross the boundary between the warrior who injures by assault and the doctor who heals by giving medicine to take. Because the poisoner uses the doctor's methods to take life, rather than save it, he has always been seen as a particularly foul murderer.[19]

One attitude helping to undermine this cultural taboo was undoubtedly racialism or, more broadly, the separation of groups into those who were 'civilized' and those who were not. Thus in 1456 an Austrian could approve of the use of gas against 'Turks and other miscreants',[20] while in 1936 Mussolini allowed the use of mustard gas against Ethiopian tribesmen, justifying it on the grounds that the latter were barbarians guilty of atrocities and not covered by the laws of war as practised in Europe. In 1982 the *Wall Street Journal* in an editorial warned that 'No one should assume that the Russians would never use against European white people the deadly mycotoxins and other poisons they are testing in Asia.'[21] Again, this is racialism; the suggestion being that to use chemicals against whites is somehow worse than its use against Laos, and the assumption that the readers of the *Wall Street Journal* are counting on this shared belief to inhibit Russian chemical warfare in Europe.

Because they were used during the 1920s and 1930s, there was a widespread expectation in 1939 that chemical weapons would figure prominently in the impending war. In practice, however, gas was hardly used at all during the Second World War, largely because of the fear of retaliation. However, both Germany and Britain came close to using chemical weapons. As early as 1939 there were plans to seal off the Franco-German border if Britain and France went on the offensive.[22] Hitler at this stage was dubious about using chemical warfare, because German cities were so vulnerable to retaliation. By 1945, however, he felt that Germany had 'failed' him and orders were given to use new nerve gases in a final holocaust as the Reich fell. Only the unexpected speed with which the Reich collapsed prevented their use.[23]

Britain was well aware of the danger of gas attack. In particular it was feared that Germany would place chemical warheads on the V-2 rockets with which they were bombarding Britain in 1944 and 1945. Accordingly Churchill told his service chiefs:

> If the bombardment really became a serious nuisance and great rockets with far-reaching and devastating effect fell on many centres of government and labour, I should be prepared to do anything that would hit the enemy in a murderous place. I may certainly have to ask you to support me in using poison gas. We could drench the cities of the Ruhr and many other cities in Germany in such a way that most of the population would be requiring constant medical attention.[24]

Even on the Eastern Front, where the conflict was in most respects unlimited, neither side used chemical weapons. It is particularly noteworthy that the Soviet Union did not, even *in extremis*, resort to chemical warfare. The horrendous experience of gas attacks in the First World War had caused the USSR to press for chemical disarmament while at the same time developing her own chemical forces. Thus, the USSR was an early signatory of the Geneva Protocol, yet at the outbreak of the Second World War the Germans 'considered the Soviet Union to be the best equipped and trained army in the world for chemical warfare'.[25] However, since the Germans did not initiate gas warfare the USSR abided by its commitments under the Geneva Protocol.

Although gas was not used during the war, the pace of research into chemical warfare accelerated dramatically during the years 1939–45. A number of breakthroughs were made, the most important of which was the discovery of 'nerve' gases.

The gases used during the First World War were fairly simple. Some like chlorine were simply the products of standard industrial processes. Most of them killed by asphyxiation. Hydrogen cyanide, a blood gas,[26] caused convulsions before the victim choked to death. Phosgene attacked the lungs so that the victim drowned in his own blood plasma. The other agent frequently used, mustard gas, rarely caused death but was painful and incapacitating, producing hideous skin blisters.

Compared to nerve gases, the gas weapons of the First World War were primitive. The first nerve gases were developed in Germany, and large quantities were captured by the allies at the end of the war. The deadly German nerve gases called 'Tabun', 'Sarin' and 'Soman' were coded as GA, GB and GD by the allies.

Nerve gases work by affecting a chemical in the body called cholinesterase. This causes the victim's muscles to contract uncontrollably until he asphyxiates, drowning in his own mucus. It is not a 'humane' death. Nerve agents are colourless, odourless and tasteless, and therefore extremely difficult to detect except with special equipment. After the Second World War the Soviet Union chose to base its CW production on two of the nerve agents captured from the Germans, Tabun (GA) and Soman (GD), whereas the West concentrated upon production of the third agent, Sarin (GB).[27]

The new 'G' agents as they were known were fifty times more deadly than the 1914–18 blood agents. During the 1950s nerve agents more deadly still were discovered. Britain had established a chemical warfare research establishment at Porton Down, Wiltshire in January 1916, and it was at Porton during the 1950s that the new 'V' agents were discovered. These were five times more deadly even than the German 'G' agents.

Before going on to look in more detail at the chemical weapon stocks held by the Warsaw Pact and NATO it is necessary to ask why they are there. After the initial successes with gas in surprise attacks in the First World War, the use of the weapon faded. Successful chemical warfare is highly dependent upon the vagaries of the weather, and many other factors, thus so far as the infliction of casualties is concerned, it is somewhat unpredictable. The use of gas during the First World War made command and control problems difficult, and in the last 18 months of the war it became evident that the trench deadlock could be broken using weapons other than gas, such as the tank. During the 1920s, General George Patton envisaged the next war as being one in which battlefields would be dominated by masses of tanks advancing through clouds of poison gas. However, the prediction did not come true and chemical weapons were not used in the Second World War. Yet Patton's vision is exactly the kind of scenario which NATO planners see occurring in a future European war. So why have chemical weapons come back into fashion, and what are their military advantages?

TABLE 7.1
Selected chemical agents[28]

Code-name	Common name	Class	Persist-ance	Dissemina-tion form	Type/symptoms	Remarks
AC	Hydrogen cyanide	Blood	NP	Vapour	Lethal: asphyxia	Common Soviet agents
CG	Phosgene	Choking	NP	Gas	Lethal: coughing, foaming, asphyxia	80 per cent of First World War gas deaths
HD	Distilled mustard	Blister	P	Vapour/liquid	Harassing: inflammation, blindness	Kills if reaches lungs
GA	Tabun	Nerve	NP	Vapour/liquid/aerosol	Symptoms immediate, lasting ten minutes.	
GB	Sarin	Nerve	NP	Vapour/liquid	For skin absorption, a few minutes to half an hour	
GD	Soman	Nerve	P	Vapour/liquid/aerosol	Harassing: vision blurs	Soviets use thickened form
GP	CMPF	Nerve	?	Liquid/vapour/aerosol	Difficulty in breathing	New agent
VX		Nerve	P	Liquid/aerosol	Lethal: drooling, sweating, nausea, vomiting, cramps, spasms, convulsions, coma, asphyxia	V Agent: in US and USSR arsenals
CX	Phosgene oxime	Blister	P	Liquid	Skin: destroys skin tissue completely	Irritant: in Soviet arsenal
CK	Cyanogen chloride	Blood	NP	Gas/vapour	Lethal: convulsions, choking	Irritant: First World War agent

THE MILITARY USEFULNESS OF CHEMICAL WARFARE

Although chemical and biological warfare are frequently spoken of in the same breath, the powers have agreed to ban the latter, but not yet the former. The simple reason why one is banned and the other not is that, largely because of their unpredictability, the superpowers see no military advantage in biological weapons, but still see a large number of reasons for retaining a chemical warfare capability.

Many of the uses of chemical warfare are based almost entirely upon the experience gained between 1914–18, since there has been no comparable chemical conflict since then. The advantages of using chemical weapons to support offensive operations were seen as being the following.[29]

(1) Softening up an enemy position prior to assault.
(2) Neutralizing enemy artillery batteries.
(3) Using persistent agents, such as mustard gas, to tie down an enemy-held area that was not to be attacked.
(4) Protecting the flanks of an advance with barriers of persistent agent.
(5) Using persistent agents to seal off reserves held in the enemy's rear, or to restrict their movement forward.
(6) Using persistent agents to block enemy lines of retreat.

Similarly, in defence chemicals were useful to:

(1) Engage enemy troop concentrations massing for an assault.
(2) Neutralize enemy artillery.
(3) Contaminate evacuated terrain.

These advantages are still held to obtain, and a number of others have been added to them since 1945. The great advances which have occurred since 1918 are in the technology of delivery systems which mean that chemical munitions can be delivered with great accuracy over long distances, and in the nature of the chemicals themselves, the 'nerve' agents in particular being both extremely difficult to detect and extremely rapid in their effects.

Thus, while the essential advantage of chemical over

conventional munitions, in terms of being able to attack very large areas, has been maintained, the areas subject to assaults of this sort have been greatly extended. Moreover, in the era of mechanized warfare, vehicles can be contaminated as effectively as troops.

In rear areas chemical attacks could be even more effective than they would be near the front-line. Defending troops and their civilian support are less likely to have received chemical warfare training, or to have been issued with protective clothing. Casualties would therefore probably be far higher. Storage sites, communication centres, airfields and ports would all be high priority targets. Ports in the rear areas, such as Britain's, could be attacked with persistent agents so that they would become inoperative for long periods.

As noted earlier, chemical warfare arouses a particular horror. This very reputation contributes to its effectiveness. Even the *possibility* of chemical weapons being used weakens a defending force's ability to fight. Defence against chemical warfare (CW) requires special protective equipment and the ability to cope in a highly toxic environment. Wearing the protective NBC clothing is extremely tiring and no soldier can perform his tasks as quickly or efficiently wearing such clothing as he can without it. Even the ordinary bodily functions become major problems in these circumstances. For example it has been estimated that in the 70°F heat of combat operations in an NBC suit, a soldier can operate only for about an hour.[30] In this respect Warsaw Pact troops would be at a disadvantage. Their suits are inferior to NATO's and overheating would occur more rapidly.[31]

Thus, even if chemical attacks did not kill enemy soldiers in large numbers, such attacks, or even the serious possibility of such attacks, by forcing the defender to wear protective clothing, would seriously impair their efficiency. Once CW agents had been employed the whole pace of the ground fighting would slow down and become more difficult as troops were forced to wear, or at the very least remain close to, protective equipment.

Elaborate arrangements would be needed for the servicing of these equipments, for decontamination and for the resting of combat troops. Careful reconnaissance by chemical detection patrols would be necessary before moving positions. Special medical supplies and decontaminants would have to be moved up to all forward areas, and sufficient time for their use would have to be fitted into the scheduling of operations. The latter would also have to take into account the likelihood of reserves being needed earlier than usual, for in a chemical environment the length of time for which a given combat unit can operate effectively will be shortened.[32]

The effectiveness of CW attacks in terms of casualties would depend upon the preparedness of those under attack. It has been estimated that even with troops wearing protective equipment, a unit could expect 5–15 per cent casualties simply because of mistakes, oversights and leaky suits.[33] Even this assumes that the troops are well-equipped and well trained. Against unprepared or poorly trained troops casualties could be between 70 per cent and 90 per cent, with 25 per cent of these fatal. Gas attacks can also be carried out using time-delay bombs and mines. If these were set to go off at night when troops were asleep and not wearing protective clothing, the effects would be devastating.[34]

Despite the effectiveness of this kind of warfare, the major armed forces did not retain a tremendous enthusiasm for chemical weapons between the wars. The innate conservatism of military establishments may have played a part in this, but probably more important was the belief that CW was outmoded by other developments, that on balance it was more trouble than it was worth.

What kept the chemical warfare establishments alive in this period was the feeling that chemical weaponry was needed as a deterrent. 'The situation was that senior military personnel were unwilling to see merit in gas as a weapon, but were prepared to believe that potential or actual enemies did – or at least were prepared to – concede that use of gas might be sufficiently advantageous to an enemy to demand the preparation of defensive countermeasures and possibly even some sort of retaliatory capability.'[35] This essentially has remained the situation. Both sides claim that they have no desire to use CW and that their training is defensive and their weapon stocks are a deterrent. Yet the situation in 1982 is alarming because NATO in particular now feels that a major build-up of new weapon stocks is needed to restore this deterrent capability.

The Soviet Union began a major refurbishment of its chemical warfare capabilities between 1945 and 1950. This was almost certainly prompted by the American atomic monopoly which existed until 1949. Because chemical weapons could be seen as weapons of mass destruction, particularly if used against civilian concentrations, the USSR probably felt that a credible chemical retaliatory capacity would serve as something of a deterrent against an American nuclear attack. Soviet research was also stimulated by the German scientists and 'G' nerve agents which fell into their hands in the closing stages of the war. A further acceleration in munitions production occurred in the period 1958–62 (when the last major American build-up took place), but since then emphasis seems to have been upon coping with a chemical environment, in training and in the production of protective equipment.

The basic Soviet chemical forces are the Chemical Troops (BKhV) which make up a separate arm of the Soviet Ground Forces. Units exist at all levels of the Soviet forces. Each Soviet 'Front' includes one chemical brigade, each army has a chemical battalion. Divisions have attached chemical companies and each regiment has a chemical platoon. Generally speaking, the smaller units carry out major decontamination exercises.[36] If every unit was at full strength the chemical specialists would number 130,000 in all, but actual numbers are probably nearer 80,000.

The function of these troops is essentially defensive, that is, their jobs are to detect chemicals and decontaminate Soviet troops and material that have been contaminated.[37] The large number of troops involved is explained partly by the fact that Soviet decontamination techniques are extremely labour-intensive. The American Defence Department, despite pushing for larger CW effort, has stated that it has no desire to create anything like what it sees as the 'giant janitorial force' of BKhV.[38]

Decontamination equipment ranges from the personal decontamination kit issued to each soldier, to the TMS-65. The latter is a truck-mounted, modified turbo-jet aircraft engine which tows its own trailer full of decontaminant. At their most dramatic these can be positioned one on each side of the road to act like a car wash. In this way a Soviet tank battalion could be decontaminated in 70 minutes, allowing the pace of a fast armoured assault to be maintained.[39]

Soviet troops also exercise regularly in toxic environments. In 1967 they allegedly carried out an operation in which two parachute battalions were dropped into a zone contaminated with mustard agents. However, the Soviet military press frequently complains about the lack of realism in Soviet chemical exercises, and about the laxity of troops involved.[40]

These exercises, and the protective equipment that go with them do not 'prove' that the Warsaw Pact intends to attack Western Europe with chemical weapons. All they prove is that the Warsaw Pact expects to fight in a chemical environment, which could be NATO-produced. In fact, Soviet exercises do not even prove *that,* since NBC suits are designed to cope with nuclear as well as chemical poisoning, and the USSR has long maintained that nuclear weapons would inevitably come into play in any future European war.

More alarming for the West is the scope for *offensive* chemical warfare possessed by the Pact. Chemical warheads could be delivered by a range of systems including mortars, rockets, artillery and aircraft. The Soviet Union could use these systems for offensive operations in four main ways.[41]

(1) Long-range bombardment with a 'drizzle' of persistent nerve agents GD, or VX, designed to contaminate NATO airfields, supply depots or areas where NATO reserves were building up. This would be done using sprays or bombs from aircraft, or a high-burst Scud B warhead.
(2) To protect the flanks of an armoured offensive, the Warsaw Pact could use persistent agents (GD, VX, HD), probably fired from artillery.

(3) Persistent and non-persistent agents could be used to harass NATO troops, forcing them to wear protective clothing, with consequent loss of efficiency.
(4) Direct attacks with non-persistent agents would probably involve the use of the blood gas AC delivered by the BM-21 multiple rocket launcher. The BM-21 in a battalion group of 20 launchers is capable of firing off 480 rounds over a range of 15–20 kilometres.[42]

FIGURE 7.1
Soviet chemical warfare

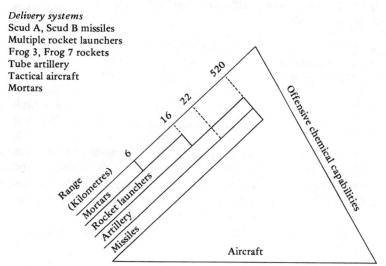

Delivery systems
Scud A, Scud B missiles
Multiple rocket launchers
Frog 3, Frog 7 rockets
Tube artillery
Tactical aircraft
Mortars

Source: US Dept of the Army

As to how much chemical agent the Soviet Union has stockpiled, or is capable of producing, this is very hard to estimate given the total lack of information on the subject divulged by the USSR. Estimates appearing in Western sources in the past ten years have varied wildly, with an upper estimate that as much as 50 per cent of all munitions in East–Central Europe are chemical warheads.[43] A figure between 15 and 30 per cent seems most likely.

TABLE 7.2
Soviet chemical delivery systems[44]

System	Chemical warhead	Range (km)	
Scud B	GD, persistent agents	160–180	Theatre missile
Frog 7	GD, VX	70	
BM-21	AC, GD	15	Tactical
M-1965	AC, GD	10	rockets
BM-24	AC, GD	11	
D-30 122 mm Howitz.	HD,GD,GB,AC,VX	15	
D-74 122 mm Howitz.	HD,GD,GB,AC,VX	22	
SAU 122 mm SP	?	20	Tube artillery
M-46 130 mm	HD,GD,GB,AC,VX	27	
D-1 152 mm Howitz.	HD,GD,VX	17	
M-1953 240 mm	HD,VX?	10	Mortar
KhF	VX,HD,GD		Bounding chemical mine

Soviet chemical agent production is estimated at some 30,000 tons a year, and production occurs within closed areas of ordinary civilian chemical complexes.[45] Most of the USSR's CW stocks consist of mustard and nerve gases, the latter including Tabun, Soman and VR-55, which is probably a thickened form of Soman. Total Soviet stocks are around 300,000 tons.

NATO CHEMICAL WARFARE CAPABILITIES

The early 1980s have witnessed a major effort by the NATO nations to improve their chemical defences. In 1979 a NATO subcommittee noted that 'The Pact forces are equipped and trained to fight in a chemical environment. NATO forces are not.'[46] Since then NATO has included chemical warfare in its field training exercises, and Britain plays host to NATO units in special CW exercises on Salisbury Plain. In addition, whereas in 1979 protective equipment was in short supply, this deficiency has now been rectified. By 1980, 5,000 NBC protective suits and casualty evacuation bags were being produced by British factories each week,[47] and some 200,000 had been acquired by the USA for issue to their forces stationed in Europe. Again, while in 1979 NATO vehicles lacked NBC protection,[48] by late 1981 all the new NATO aircraft and vehicles had been given NBC protective systems 'equal to or superior to Soviet technology'.[49]

The largest NATO CW units are in the US army. In 1975 their number had fallen to 2,000, but has since been rising steadily.[50] When the programme is complete, each US division will have an attached CW company and cavalry regiments will have chemical reconnaissance teams. Forth-three NBC reconnaissance and decontamination teams were active in 1980.

The American chemical forces are larger than the numbers in specific CW units would indicate. Each army company includes soldiers who have been assigned chemical defence duties, as many as 34 men out of 130 in some units, of which three will have had training at a specialist CW school.[51] Thus, in total, between 90,000 and 250,000 army personnel have some degree of CW training, a number similar to the Soviet total, though most will have had less training than their Soviet counterparts.

Training for CW defence has been considerably stepped up in the US army in recent years. In September 1980, for example, during the annual NATO 'reforger' exercises in Germany, US troops simulated attacks by liquid nerve agents to see how well their decontamination techniques worked and how quickly soldiers could return to the front line after such an attack.[52] A five-year $1,500 million programme of equipment procuring and increased training has been under way for some years, and the US Air Force has spent $234 million on anti-chemical defences for its airfields.

A number of other NATO nations are prominent in this field, especially France, West Germany, which has ABC-Abwehrtruppe units analogous to the Soviet BKhV, and Britain which produces the best NBC protective suits in the world. British troops train regularly for chemical warfare.

However, Britain has no *offensive* chemical capability of its own. During his time as British Defence Minister, Francis

Pym made a personal effort to change this position by acquiring British nerve gas stocks and using them as chemical deterrents.[53] However, although Mrs Thatcher showed some interest, the matter was not pursued by Pym's successor, John Nott. The assumption in British defence circles has always been that if chemical warfare did become a very strong possibility, then the USA would make some of its stocks available to its NATO allies. However, according to a Congressional Research Service report released in July 1981, the USA has no plans to release nerve gas weapons to its allies even in time of war.[54]

This would not alarm all NATO's members, several of them, including Denmark, West Germany, Italy and Norway have already declared that they would not use chemical weapons even in retaliation.[55] Whether such restraint would hold in reality is open to question, and a number of NATO nations have weapon systems compatible with American chemical munitions which could be used to deliver chemical retaliation.

TABLE 7.3
*US chemical warfare delivery systems
common to NATO states*[56]

	US delivery system			
	4.2 inch Mortar	*105 mm Howitz.*	*155 mm Howitz.*	*8 inch Howitz.*
Belgium	X	X	X	X
Canada		X	X	
Denmark	X	X	X	X
France		X	X	
Britain		X	X	X
Italy		X	X	X
West Germany		X	X	X
Greece	X	X	X	X
Netherlands	X	X	X	X
Norway	X	X	X	
Portugal	X	X		
Turkey	X	X	X	X

Essentially, however, NATO's offensive chemical capabilities are those possessed by the USA. The USA possesses about 38,000 tons of CW agent, of which half is mustard gas, and half nerve gas. Of the latter, most is VX and the rest Sarin.[57] About a third of the total supply is stored in munitions, the rest is in bulk storage. If the bulk-stored agent were loaded into munitions the total US stock would rise to 400,000 tons, more than the Soviet total. At present, however, less than 200,000 tons are held in munitions,[58] though even this is enough in theory to kill the world's population 4,000 times over.[59] The American CW munitions stocks include three million CW artillery shells filled with GB and VX nerve agents, hundreds of thousands of VX-filled land-mines, and several thousand GB bombs.[60]

For most of the 1970s, the USA did not add to its chemical munitions stocks. Over time, some of these, such as the M34 1000-16 Sarin Cluster bombs have become obsolete and have been discarded. Much of the mustard gas supply will by now also be of dubious reliability. As far as immediately available stocks are concerned, the USA maintains about 10,000 tons of CW munitions in West Germany,[61] and has 1,500 2,000 lb VX-filled aircraft spray-tanks which could be fitted to US tactical bombers.

The only other NATO state to possess its own supplies of chemical munitions is France. France has never released any details about the size of its stocks, but US estimates put the stockpile at about 10,000 tons of munitions, that is, about 1,000 tons of chemical agents.[62]

As has already been noted, during the 1970s neither the USA nor the USSR appear to have added to their stocks of chemical munitions. However, in the second half of the decade, increasing concern was voiced in America about the apparent continuing Soviet efforts in the CW field. Essentially these efforts were defensive, a continuing build-up of chemical protection capabilities. However, weapons capable of firing chemical munitions were also deployed in larger numbers. These weapons were also of course capable of firing conventional munitions, and this may in fact be their sole function, but their so-called 'dual capability' kept NATO fears alive. Moreover, some training exercises produced alarm.

For example, Soviet CW units monitored on manoeuvres have been seen 'marking out the limits within which the advancing columns should pass'.[63] Again, this could be simulating reaction to NATO bombardment, but it is ambiguous, and therefore alarming.

The most dramatic sign of the renewed American interest in chemical warfare is the binary munitions programme. In February 1982, the Reagan administration asked Congress to approve a huge increase in funds for chemical weapons, most of which would be spent on binary chemical munitions. The CW budget will therefore have doubled in each year of the Reagan administration and is expected to keep doubling. Congress had already approved the $23 million for a binary munitions plant to be built at Pine Bluffs, Arkansas,[64] producing 155 mm artillery shells.

Binary weapons are safer to handle and store than present chemical munitions because the ingredients which go to form the agent are kept separate in a reasonably safe form until the weapon is charged, or in actual flight, after the weapon has been fired.[65]

What is unusual about the binary programme is that the weapons planned are less efficient than those they are to replace. Although safer to store they are less efficient than present stocks. A greater volume is needed to produce the same effect, and performance is less predictable because the chemical reaction only takes place as the warhead is *en route*.[66] Thus, at best, binaries would only be as efficient weapons as the agents they are replacing, and in all probability, they will be *less* efficient. Yet binaries have been presented as the most cost-effective way to 'modernize the current deterrent/retaliatory capability'.[67]

It is quite possible that the binary programme is an example of technology driving policy. The technology for binary weapons is now available and the US Chemical Corps would find such new technology difficult to resist, irrespective of an increased Soviet threat.

THE SOVIET THREAT – RECENT ALLEGATIONS OF SOVIET CW

Although the pace of American build-up in chemical munitions in the early 1980s was slow, it was accelerating rapidly, with funding annually doubled. Moreover, it was quite clear that a major public relations campaign was being mounted in support of American chemical rearmament. In the late 1950s, when the US Chemical Corps was suffering comparative neglect, it launched a publicity drive 'Operation Blue Skies' in an attempt to project itself as a humane agency using painless weapons.[68] In the 1970s, with American images of nerve-gas leaks in the 1960s and the record of American chemical warfare in Vietnam still fresh, the CW supporters seem to have adopted the alternative strategy of stressing the existence of the Soviet CW threat. As well as emphasizing an alleged Soviet CW build-up in Europe, reports have drawn attention to alleged chemical warfare by the Soviet Union in Afghanistan, and by its allies in Laos and Cambodia.

What is remarkable about these allegations is the total lack of evidence. Given the frantic desire of the USA to prove the guilt of the USSR, one would expect every effort would be made to find concrete evidence to support the American claims. None has appeared. Western diplomats have become more and more puzzled by the single-minded determination of Reagan officials to be convinced on the basis of a total lack of information, even to the point where an infatuation with unsubstantiated CW allegations serves to direct attention away from the very real suffering which Soviet conventional munitions have been inflicting in Afghanistan.

A recent British study which examined the Soviet CW allegations and showed their lack of substance, concluded:

> the fact remains that, whatever the motivations under-lying them when they were made, the different allega-tions have since taken on a life of their own, sustaining one another to the point where, despite their lack of evident substantiation, they have set a deeply menacing impression of Soviet CW capabilities and intentions into the public consciousness.[69]

The reasons for this are not hard to find since they have created the environment in which the appropriate NATO 'response', an accelerated chemical arms build-up has been made possible. The last major Soviet CW build-up occurred in the early 1960s, in tandem with a well-publicized American CW build-up. In the 1970s, both the USA and USSR refrained from adding to their CW stocks. In the chemical warfare area at least, the action–reaction explanation of arms race dynamics (referred to in chapter 1) seems to operate almost mechanistically. Given this, the likely Soviet response to the current US chemical weapons build-up is easy to predict.

PROSPECTS FOR CHEMICAL ARMS CONTROL

There are two major problems standing in the way of a chemical disarmament treaty. The first, and probably most important, is that leading military powers still see chemical weapons as useful tactical military instruments, capable of achieving certain military objectives without the massive levels of destruction that the use of nuclear or conventional weaponry would involve. The second problem is the important question of how a chemical weapons treaty could be adequately monitored.

Although most diplomatic activity centres around the resolution of the second problem, no advance is likely until the first is addressed. This can only occur if the military value of CW is undermined, that is, if states decide that the disadvantages of CW on balance outweigh the advantages, or if at the highest level of political leadership the decision is taken to pursue the arms control route to security rather than the arms building route. If both sides possess such weapons, the concept of 'like deterred with like' promises some security, but if neither side possesses such weapons, security is clearly enhanced. Once this political commitment were achieved, as with biological weapons in the early 1970s, the question of verification would become a genuine, but not insuperable, stumbling block.

The difficulty with CW verification is that it must, of necessity, be intrusive. It is possible to verify a treaty like SALT with 'national technical means', especially satellites. This is because ICBMs are too big to hide and are quite different from anything else. They are therefore comparatively easy to count. Chemical weapons, however, can be produced in facilities that are essentially indistinguishable from innocent industrial plants. For example, as noted earlier, Soviet CW production occurs in special areas of ordinary chemical works.[70] It would, therefore, be impossible for US satellites to verify that CW production had ended. They would see only the factories, but would have no way of determining what was going on inside them. The only way that chemical disarmament could be adequately verified and monitored would be if investigators were allowed *into* chemical works to check that no weapon material was being produced.

American sources have in the past expressed fears that such intrusive verification 'on-site' would allow the investigators to discover other secrets, perhaps industrial or economic. However, recent exercises in which Britain, West Germany and the USA have allowed scientists to carry out such investigations seem to have laid these fears to rest. The onus is therefore on the Soviet Union in this instance. It is the paranoid obsession of the USSR with security, and their objection to 'on-site' inspection, which stands in the way of agreement.

Binary chemical weapons pose extra verification problems, because innocuous elements could be produced which, only when combined in the warhead, constitute a chemical weapon in the true sense. There is also the problem of industrial gases, such as chlorine and phosgene, which can be used (and have been) as crude but effective chemical weapons. However, production levels can be monitored. Any unusual increase in chemical production would then arouse alarm unless there were an adequate explanation for it.

Monitoring can also be conducted of CW logistics. To carry out chemical warfare requires more than just a supply of chemicals. The vehicles and systems to transport and store them safely for military use have to exist. Weaponry capable of delivering them must be available. Troops must have clothing, vehicles and buildings which offer defence against chemical attack. Back-up decontamination materials are necessary. Chemical Weapons units and ordinary soldiers must have adequate training in how to fight in a chemical environment, manoeuvres must involve practice in the techniques necessary to co-ordinate attacks successfully in a chemical environment. All these kinds of activities *can* be monitored by national technical means.

Because of this, while recognizing that verification could never guarantee 100 per cent certainty, British Government advisers have been convinced for some time that a chemical disarmament convention can be achieved. Shortly before President Reagan suspended the CW talks, the Soviet Union had begun making encouraging concessions on the question of verification. These should be pursued, for it is certainly in nobody's interest that the chemical weapons talks be abandoned. The current justified concern about nuclear weapons has tended to overshadow the danger of a new chemical arms race, but this should not be allowed to happen. The draft CW treaty put forward by Britain in 1976, which provides for a complete ban on the possession or use of lethal chemical agents, includes adequate verification proposals and could form the basis of an effective chemical disarment treaty. This is urgently required if a new chemical arms race is not to disfigure the 1980s.

8

Arms control and disarmament

The world today is at a crossroads. One road leads to
utter hopelessness and despair; the other road leads
to utter destruction and extinction. God grant us the
wisdom to choose the right road.

Woody Allen

Cynicism about the prospects for arms control, exemplified
by the remark by Woody Allen, cited above, is widespread.
On the one hand, conservatives criticize arms control because
they perceive it as having a major detrimental impact on their
own country's arms build-up without having a corresponding
affect on their adversary. Radicals criticize arms control
because they believe it has had no impact upon the arms
build-up of *any* state. At the same time, there is a generally-
held belief that the arms control *process* is so laborious,
requiring negotiations spanning a decade, that the pace of
technological advance leaves it behind. Thus it is argued,
while the SALT treaties eventually produced an upper limit
on launcher totals, by the time they did so, advances in
warhead technology meant that the number of warheads was
greater at the end of the process than it had been at the start.
  The explanation for these widely divergent views of the
effectiveness of arms control since 1960 lies in a basic misunderstanding about the meaning and function of arms
control and the differences between the concepts of arms
control and disarmament.

THE MEANING OF DISARMAMENT

Disarmament has a long and venerable history as an approach

185

to international security. As early as 546 BC a conference of four major and ten minor Chinese powers produced a disarmament agreement which ended a period of 72 years of warfare.[1] The virtues of disarmament have been revived at regular intervals since then. However, the term 'disarmament' itself can in fact apply to either of two processes.

Disarmament can mean total disarmament, often referred to as GCD, 'general and complete disarmament'. This approach aims for a reduction of armaments down to the bare minimum required for domestic policing purposes.

Secondly, disarmament can refer to partial disarmament, in which certain classes of weapons are abolished, while others are not. In other words, in this sense disarmament is being used to refer significant reductions, rather than abolition. Generally speaking, when most proponents of disarmament use the term they are using it in its second meaning, though they see such reductions as a step towards the utopian goal of total disarmament. Critics of disarmament invariably interpret it in the first sense, because as a straw man it is easier to knock down.

What these two meanings have in common is a commitment to *reduction.* In Hedley Bull's definition, 'disarmament is the reduction or abolition of armaments. It may be unilateral or multilateral; general or local, comprehensive or partial, controlled or uncontrolled.'[2] But the key element is *reduction.* Thus, in Ken Booth's paraphrasing of Clausewitz, 'disarmament is a continuation of politics by a reduction of military means'.[3]

The disarmament approach is rooted in the belief that armaments are an independent source of tension, that the weapons themselves are a cause of war because of the mutual fear and hostility they instill into inter-state relations. Thus, in Lord Grey's words: 'the enormous growth of armaments in Europe, the sense of insecurity and fear caused by them — it was these that made war inevitable'.[4] The disarmers' solution to this is to treat the root cause, remove the source of the tension, the weapons themselves. Thus 'they shall beat their swords into ploughshares, and their spears into pruning hooks'.[5]

Unfortunately although the armaments *per se* are a source

of tension they are also symptomatic of deeper tensions. The accumulation of armaments reflects both a craving for security and a search for a flexible instrument of foreign policy (as noted in chapter 1). Thus even if armaments *are* an independent source of tension, states would be reluctant to disarm, and since such tensions exist, states lack the confidence to disarm. As one French diplomat put it during the 1930s: 'the verb "to disarm" is an imperfect verb: it contains no first person single'.[6] The idea that armaments are a reflection, rather than a cause of tension gives rise to the 'disarmament paradox', which is that when it is possible to disarm, it is unnecessary. In other words if so little tension exists that disarmament is possible then there is so little likelihood of the weapons being used that disarmament becomes unnecessary — though it should be noted here that even if this were true, such a situation would make the *economic* benefits of disarmament all the more attractive. The alarming corollary of the disarmament paradox is that when disarmament is most needed, it is least likely.

This dilemma has only served to reinforce the conviction of disarmers. Thus, as Jeremy Bentham argued in putting forward a proposal for general disarmament in 1789:

> What can be better suited to the preparing of men's minds for the reception of such a proposal than the proposal itself? Let it not be objected that the age is not ripe for such a proposal; the more it wants of being ripe, the sooner we should begin to do what can be done to ripen it: the more we should do to ripen it. A proposal of this sort, is one of those things that can never come too early nor too late.[7]

The last two hundred years have therefore seen no shortage of disarmament proposals. As the power of man's capacity for destruction has increased so have the efforts to counteract this development through disarmament. The horrors of the First World War brought these efforts to a head and the inter-war years were marked by a number of disarmament efforts, some of which, for example the 1925 Geneva Protocol on chemical weapons[8] and the naval disarmament agreements of

1922 and 1930, were in their own terms, fairly successful. But the rise of fascism and Japanese militarism destroyed the hopes of the disarmers in the holocaust of the Second World War.

The years after the Second World War were characterized by the 'Cold War' between the former allies of 1941–45. This period also saw disarmament proposals put forward by the major powers, but these were largely propaganda ploys rather than genuine efforts to disarm. To a large extent these disarmament initiatives were aimed not at the other power or powers, but at the domestic populations of the states proposing the initiative. Their purpose was to contain the political impact of domestic disarmament movements rather than to affect the military strength of other states. To a great extent the revival of Cold War politics by President Reagan's administration has produced a revival of Cold War disarmament. The American INF and START proposals have not been put forward in the serious expectation that they will be accepted by the USSR, rather they have been put forward to create an impression of US desire for arms control and thereby to undercut the political impact of the European Nuclear Disarmament and American 'freeze' movements. Similarly, the parallel Soviet proposals have been designed to give encouragement to groups such as END rather than to impress the NATO governments.

During the 1950s both superpowers used this method to pose as champions of disarmament. In practice each was careful to insert into their proposals at least one suggestion which they knew in advance would be unacceptable to the other side, a 'joker in the pack' designed to ensure that there was no danger of the offer being accepted.[9] One of the great Soviet propaganda coups of the post-war era occurred in 1955 when the USSR suddenly decided to accept a Western proposal for sweeping cuts in force levels put forward three years earlier.[10] NATO had been exploiting its advantage by pressing the USSR to agree to 'genuine disarmament', secure in the belief that the USSR would refuse. When the Soviet Union suddenly accepted, the NATO response was to call for a recess in the current negotiations while the Soviet concessions were analysed. When the talks reconvened the US delegate announced that:

> The United States does now place a reservation upon all of its pre-Geneva substantive positions taken in this Sub-Committee or in the Disarmament Commission or in the UN on these questions in relationship to levels of armament.[11]

In other words because the Soviet Union had *accepted* the American plan for substantial disarmament, the USA was withdrawing it, and just in case the Soviets were tempted to agree to any of the earlier disarmament proposals put forward by America, the USA was withdrawing them also.

In the face of such patent cynicism the myth of the major powers' commitment to disarmament was exposed. The Emperor quite clearly had no clothes. Since it was obvious that the governments of the major powers were not going to disarm substantially, disarmament as such was dead.

THE MEANING OF ARMS CONTROL

If disarmament, in the sense of large-scale reductions, had perforce been abandoned by the end of the 1950s, the pursuit of security at a lower level of armaments could not be. The problems which made disarmament appealing — economic difficulties, the existence of potential 'flash-points' for a major war in many areas, and above all the terrible 'shapeless fears'[12] induced by the existence of growing arsenals of nuclear weapons, were becoming more potent with every passing year.

The deep-rooted political antagonism existing between the superpowers ruled out large-scale disarmament because the essential element of trust was not present. States who see in military power the final guarantor of their existence in sovereign independence are unwilling to consider schemes that compromise their ability to resort to the military instrument.

However, the long debates over disarmament during the twentieth century had left their mark. While statesmen were not prepared to accept that weapons were dangerous *per se*, they were prepared to accept that some held peculiar dangers, and to accept that an entirely unconstrained arms race was more likely to undermine the balance of power and national security than to guarantee it. Thus while the relationship between the superpowers was characterized by a large degree of conflict, it also contained significant incentives to co-operate. Most important of these was the need to avoid a nuclear war in which both sides would be destroyed. Therefore, while it was recognized that arms competition would continue to be a significant feature of the competition between the major alliance systems, because of the shared danger of nuclear holocaust, a degree of control, which could only be exercised through explicit diplomacy, was clearly necessary.

The clearest definition of arms control remains that of Schelling and Halperin:

> We mean to include all the forms of military co-operation between potential enemies in the interest of reducing the likelihood of war, its scope and violence if it occurs and the political and economic costs of being prepared for it. The essential feature of arms control is the recognition of the common interest, of the possibility of the reciprocation and co-operation even between potential enemies with respect to their military establishments.[13]

Unlike disarmament, the essential element in arms control is *restraint* rather than reduction. Arms control is based upon the idea that security is a shared value, something that states in rivalry can pursue together, that it is not something they can only acquire at each other's expense. Whereas disarmament always refers to a reduction, arms control is concerned only with stability and restraint. Because of this arms control can refer to an *increase* in the level of armaments without any paradox being involved, the critical issue is simply whether or not the increase is *consciously restrained*. Thus Ken Booth refers to arms control as 'a continuation of politics by a mutual restraint on military means'.[14]

This crucial distinction has been largely responsible for the disillusion regarding the achievements of arms control which prevailed by the beginning of the 1980s. Critics who argued that the decade of SALT negotiations had left the number of warheads greater than ever missed the essential promise of arms control, which was not that negotiations would always lead to reductions but simply that the balance of military power would be maintained by channelling effort into certain directions rather than others, by exercising control. Controlled growth is still control.

Arms control sought to avoid the trap of fruitlessly seeking the best at the expense of the attainable good. The arms control approach had certain advantages over the disarmament approach with regard to negotiability. Because arms control agreements were limited in scope and only affected a small proportion of a state's armoury, they did not require the same degree of trust as disarmament agreements, and therefore were more likely to overcome the 'disarmament paradox'. For the same reasons the problems of verifying adherence to agreement was much reduced in scale, bringing it down to manageable proportions.

The arms control approach appealed to radicals and conservatives alike. For radicals it offered a way out of the diplomatic impasse of the 1950s. John Stuart Mill in the nineteenth century declared that 'against a great evil, a small remedy does not produce a small result, it produces no result at all', but it is hard for human beings to do nothing simply because they cannot do everything. Arms control, while less promising than disarmament, at least offered hope, and if successful might increase trust to the point where disarmament became feasible. Thus during the 1960s and 1970s many of those who had supported disarmanent came to support arms control. But in doing so they gradually forgot the distinction between the two approaches, coming to see arms control as partial disarmament and thereby becoming disillusioned when the disarmament impact of 20 years of arms control proved so meagre.

For conservatives, arms control was equally attractive, initially. It enabled politicians to outflank and neutralize the disarmament movements that had grown large during the 1950s. In addition, because it supported growth, if 'controlled' growth in weapon totals, conservatives were appeased. In any case, arms control is a fundamentally conservative undertaking. It is concerned with *managing* the arms race, not with ending it. It is rooted in support for the hallowed concept of the military balance of power, and does not seek to challenge the established conception of military power as a functional tool of policy. Thus arms control is essentially a mechanism for defending the status quo, whereas disarmament threatens it.

The essentially conservative nature of arms control is reflected in the negotiations that have exemplified it to date. Agreements like SALT have not been efforts to substantially interfere with the force structures of the major powers, rather they have been ratification of existing structures and efforts to affect possible *future* deployment decisions. SALT, for example, has been described as 'a photograph of the situation which has arisen from the programmes of the two super-powers, of their respective scientific, technological and economic capacities'.[15]

VARIETIES OF ARMS CONTROL

Arms control, unlike disarmament, does not proceed from the assumption that weapons themselves are a cause of war, they are simply seen as being symptomatic of deeper tension. However this does not detract from the catastrophe which war represents, and therefore arms control efforts are designed with a view to structuring and constraining military forces in such a way as to make their use less likely. In particular, arms control is traditionally associated with measures designed:

(1) to reduce the probability of war;
(2) to reduce the cost of preparation for war;
(3) to reduce the death and destruction involved if war should occur.

A state may pursue these objectives through unilateral action, tacit agreements or formal agreements. Unilateral action has the advantage that it sidesteps the drawbacks involved in negotiating arms control agreements (discussed later in this chapter) and can therefore be carried out quickly.

The drawback of unilateralism is that because it involves no binding international commitment, it can be reversed by an incoming government just as easily.

Tacit agreements also avoid the disadvantages inherent in the negotiating *process*. A tacit agreement is an unwritten understanding. For example, during the Korean War there was a tacit agreement between the warring powers not to widen the conflict by attacking strategic supply lines. Thus the UN forces did not attack China or the Soviet Union, while the North Koreans did not attack UN shipping *en route* for South Korea. The advantage of tacit understandings is that they do not have to be 'sold' to the domestic political audience and therefore no bribing of the legislature by policy concessions or 'pork-barrel' politics is required. Secondly, because the limits of the agreement are unclear, states are unwilling to risk pushing to the limit of the understanding, as they tend to do with treaties, in case they inadvertently go too far and bring about the collapse of the understanding. The major disadvantage of tacit agreements is that precisely because the limitations are not spelled out, there is ample room for misunderstanding and miscalculation.

Finally states may pursue the goal of arms control through formal negotiations. Treaties are much less likely to encourage misunderstanding than tacit agreements, because the restraints are 'spelt out' on paper, with agreed interpretations. Formal agreements are often easier to justify domestically than unilateral actions, because a government can point to the terms of the treaty to show exactly what benefits have been obtained in return for the concessions that have been made. Formal agreements also have an important domestic political effect in that they can settle a controversy in a way that a unilateral gesture cannot. Although a treaty may be bitterly opposed and signed amid self-doubt, once signed it tends to become sacrosanct. This effect may be even more important to Soviet leaders than to Western leaders since treaties enable the Soviet leadership to exert genuine political control over specific military programmes.

The *kind* of arms control agreements a state may pursue also vary. One kind of approach which has witnessed a lot of activity, and some success, since the 1950s, is the effort to prevent the spread of certain kinds of weaponry to new geo-graphical areas, the so-called 'Non-Armament Treaties'. The breakthrough in this regard was undoubtedly the Antarctic Treaty of 1959. Other small areas, such as Spitzbergen, had been demilitarized before this date,[16] but the Antarctic Treaty marked the first successful effort to demilitarize a major portion of the Earth's surface. The irony that the South Pole should be the first region to be excluded from the 'Cold' War has not gone unremarked.[17]

The Antarctic Treaty demilitarized the region by prohibit-ing the establishment of military bases, the use of Antarctica to carry out military manoeuvres or the testing of any kind of weapon there. However, the treaty did not prohibit the use of military personnel and equipment for carrying out peaceful scientific research. The treaty is interesting in that the Soviet Union agreed to verification by on-site inspection. The USA exercised its right in this regard in 1964, 1967 and 1971, and inspected the Soviet Antarctic bases, finding nothing that violated the 1959 treaty.

Although it was recognized that Antarctica was not an area of great strategic importance to the superpowers, the treaty was valuable. There had been some discussion of using Antarctica for military bases during the 1950s, and SSBNs might have used the area to hide themselves in. The treaty banned such activities *before* they became fact, and one area of the globe remained free of the deadly embrace of cold war politics.

The Antarctic Treaty was also important in setting the precedent for similar treaties covering other areas. In 1961 the United Nations General Assembly passed a resolution calling for Africa to be made a nuclear-free zone. In 1967 the Treaty of Tlatelolco established a Latin American nuclear-free zone. Also in 1967 came the Outer Space Treaty which prohibited military installations and activities in outer space, and in 1971 the Sea-bed Treaty was signed which prohibited the emplacement of nuclear weapons on the sea-bed.

Commendable as these efforts were, all of them were flawed to a greater or lesser extent. The most damning criti-cism levelled against them is that they were essentially meaningless. To the cynic, the mere fact that the treaties were signed by the major powers raises doubt as to their likely value. To a large extent, the non-armament treaties seem to be purely cosmetic, understandings to refrain from doing what no state seriously considered doing in the first place. With Antarctica, for example, why should NATO or the USSR worry about carrying out manoeuvres on the other side of the globe when Canada, Norway and Russia themselves fulfilled their training requirements? Nor was Antarctica really suitable for naval or airbases. Similar objections could be raised about the Sea-bed Treaty which prohibits 'The Emplacement of Nuclear Weapons and Other Weapons of Mass Destruction on the Sea-bed and the Ocean Floor and in the Subsoil thereof'. Again, no major power would fix nuclear weapons on the sea-bed where they could be targeted and destroyed in war. But the treaty does *not* forbid placing such weapons on the sea-bed within one's own territorial waters, nor the temporary resting of nuclear-missile submarines on the sea-bed.

Even so, it could be argued that such treaties, if they do no real good, do no harm, and may contribute to an atmosphere of detente which could be conducive to the achievement of more significant restraints. In addition, strategic and technological developments may mean that an area once free of great power interest, may become significant later, in which case the treaty obligations regarding it *would* be of significance.

Unfortunately this is exactly where the non-armament treaties seem to fail again. The classic example is the 1967 Outer Space Treaty.[18] The treaty bans the placing of 'weapons of mass destruction' in orbit or on celestial bodies, and bans also the establishment of military bases, training of troops or testing of weapons on celestial bodies. It is quite clear that the spirit of the treaty, whose preamble refers to the 'common interest of all mankind' in the use of outer space 'for peaceful purposes', was that space should not become an arena of military competition or warfare. When the treaty was signed, various schemes for the emplacement of weaponry in orbit had been shown to be of little, if any, military value, so that space, like Antarctica could be easily excluded from the Cold War.

However, as noted in chapter 4, while 'weapons of mass destruction' are not being placed in orbit, weapons, in the form of anti-satellite weapons of various kinds *are*. It can be argued that such activity does not break the letter of the 1967 Treaty, and this is true, but it is a legalistic interpretation designed to obscure the fact that the value of the treaty is being undermined. In other words, once a military value for the area appeared, the superpowers were able to prove that they were not in fact constrained by their earlier treaty commitment. If this were to be the attitude taken towards all the non-armament treaties then their real value is non-existent.

Arms control also encompasses efforts to limit the destructiveness of wars. Examples of this kind include the 1924 Geneva Protocol on chemical weapons, discussed in chapter 7, the 1972 Biological Weapons Convention,[19] which dealt with the prohibition of biological weapons and the destruction of existing stocks, the 1977 Environmental Modification Treaty,[20] designed to prevent the manipulation of the weather as a weapon of war and the 1981 Convention on Excessively Injurious Conventional Weapons,[21] which gave new rules for the protection of civilians and their possessions from attacks by 'incendiary weapons, land-mines, booby-traps and fragments that cannot readily be detected in the human body'.[22] The latter convention was the first international arms regulation agreement to be negotiated at a UN conference.

How effective agreements of this sort would actually be in wartime is open to question. Chemical weapons were not used on any great scale during the Second World War, it is true, but this seems to have been due to the mutual deterrence situation which existed rather than to an overriding devotion to the Geneva Protocol of 1924. States on the verge of defeat in wartime are likely to lose many of their inhibitions about use of certain weapons. A study of this subject concluded by arguing that the best that could be hoped for was that such agreements would cause states to 'pause and reflect' before escalating the violence.[23]

Because of the emphasis which arms control places upon *stability*, much of the energy devoted by governments towards arms control since 1960 has been aimed at limiting the development or deployment of new types of weapons which are felt to increase the risk of war. The SALT I Treaty was of this type, banning the deployment of anti-ballistic missiles which, by threatening each side's ability to retaliate against nuclear attack, would reduce stability. The essential criterion is stability. Some technological advances are opposed because they threaten stability, others supported because they seem to enhance it. Thus arms control treaties have limited the testing of nuclear weapons in the 1963 Partial Test Ban Treaty and 1974 Threshold Test Ban Treaty. However, arms controllers have welcomed advances in silo-hardening and SSBN technology which have made the superpowers' retaliatory forces less vulnerable to surprise attack, since these make for a more stable deterrent balance.

The pursuit of balances has, in fact, loomed large in the arms control effort since 1960. Reductions are sought only if they can be achieved in a balanced and co-ordinated manner. An obvious example of this kind of activity is the negotiations on mutual and balanced force reductions being carried on between NATO and the WTO.

A concern with balance and stability is what animates the anti-proliferation efforts such as the 1968 Non-Proliferation Treaty and the negotiations on limiting the sale of conventional weapons which the superpowers discussed in the late 1970s.

Not all arms control efforts, however, are directly concerned with limiting weaponry. The broad heading of 'arms control' also encompasses efforts to increase the ability of states to communicate during times of crisis, to reduce the chance of 'accidental' war or a war arising from misunderstanding. Examples of this kind of agreement are the 'hot-line' agreements between the superpowers of 1963 and 1971, a similar 'hot-line' agreement between Britain and the USSR in 1967, the US–Soviet agreement on 'measures to reduce the risk of outbreak of nuclear war (1971), the US–Soviet agreement on the prevention of military incidents on and over the high seas (1972), and the French–Soviet agreement on the accidental or unauthorized use of nuclear weapons (1976).

Arms control also includes efforts to reduce misunderstanding and increase trust through the use of 'confidence building measures' (CBMs); this 'involves the communication of credible evidence of the absence of feared threats'.[24] A large number of such measures have been discussed, over 60 proposals covering Europe alone have been put forward in the last 25 years,[25] and they concentrate upon 'continuous public demonstration of non-aggressive postures' and measures related to 'a reduction of the danger of surprise attack'.[26]

Arms control therefore embraces a wide variety of effort, yet despite all the bilateral and multilateral effort devoted to arms control since the early 1960s, the results have been meagre. They have not been insignificant, but they have been inadequate to satisfy the hopes of the disarmament constituency which had come to see arms control as the means to their desired end. In part, as was noted earlier, this disillusion is the inevitable result of the failure to bear in mind the very real differences between disarmament and arms control as approaches to international security, but it has been accentuated by a number of drawbacks related to the arms control negotiating process which themselves tend to increase, rather than decrease, the level of weaponry possessed by the protagonists.

DRAWBACKS OF THE ARMS CONTROL PROCESS

It is a truism that 'jaw, jaw is better than war, war' but it does not follow from this that negotiated settlements are always the best course to pursue, or that negotiations themselves have no arms control side-effects. On the contrary, it is possible that certain sets of negotiations have worsened rather than improved the situations to which they were addressed. A number of factors have contributed to this situation.

The microscope effect

Opening a set of arms control negotiations tends to highlight every sub-element of that particular arms competition. The number of planes, tanks, missiles, or whatever, belonging to each state is tabulated prior to serious negotiations. The obsession with parity means that each side begins to aim at equality in every form of weaponry, whereas prior to the talks, an overall balance might have existed which consisted of off-setting asymmetries, one side leading in one indicator, lagging in another, but an overall balance of *capabilities* existing. Putting everything under the microscope thereby encourages build-ups in all areas where one's own side is lagging.

Levelling-up effects

The arms control approach has concentrated upon the achievements of numerical balance, of 'optical parity' (to use Colin Gray's phrase). However, the drawback to this approach is that it is much easier to set equal high ceilings than equal low ceilings. Whichever state is behind is simply allowed to build up to the level already attained by the leading state, as happened with warhead totals in the SALT Agreements.

Displacement effects

Negotiations and any agreements reached, can encourage the displacement of resources into new channels, those not covered by the agreement. For example, the Treaty of Versailles after the First World War forbade Germany warships with a displacement over 10,000 tons. This was designed to prevent the Germans from building battleships. In practice, however, the Germans produced the so-called 'pocket battleships', ships that were within the Versailles tonnage limit but which carried far more powerful guns than other ships of their size, and in this way Germany defeated the spirit of the Versailles limitation. Any restraint in one area of military spending can release resources to develop other avenues, which may eventually produce weapons far more dangerous than those which have had limits placed upon them.

'Bargaining chip' effects

A fourth way in which negotiations themselves might encourage the acquisition of new weapons is through the so-called 'bargaining chip' phenomenon. A 'bargaining chip' is a weapon, plan or intention that the other side fears so much that they would be willing to make concessions in order to prevent it being adopted. The term can also be used to describe some idea that one side merely *pretends* interest in because they feel that the other side will be sufficiently concerned about it to want to trade concessions in order to prevent it.

The negotiations on intermediate-range nuclear weapons (INF) in Europe offer classic examples of the bargaining chip in action. When NATO took its 'dual-track' decision in 1979, the intention of many of the NATO states who approved the decision was clearly to use the new missiles as bargaining chips. The argument was that the new Western missiles, cruise and Pershing II, were needed to offset the new Soviet SS-20. Therefore, if the USSR dismantled its SS-20s, NATO would not need to deploy cruise and Pershing II. The bargaining chip tactic can be played by both sides however. Until 1979 the USSR had been using its new SS-20s to replace older SS-4s and SS-5s, but once negotiations loomed in prospect, the Soviets stopped taking the older missiles out of service, clearly hoping to keep them to throw into the scale as bargaining chips.

The obvious question that arises from this description is, Why are so few 'bargaining chips' actually bargained out of existence? The answer lies in the technological and political processes that lead to weapon production. New weapons are deployed only after a long period of research and development, a period that is rarely less than ten years. Bargaining chips, however, are selected 'off the shelf' as it were, from weapons that are either in production, or very close to being so. Weapon research programmes are initiated some 15 years before they are likely to come into service, so that the strategic environment in which they will operate is not clearly known. Thus, the decision to initiate research into cruise came long before NATO knew that a weapon called the SS-20 was about to be deployed against it.

No administration can tell the taxpayer that the government is spending a fortune on designing a weapon that is being developed to give away. Other forces impel the development of such weapons, and as the weapon moves off the drawing-board into early prototype stage, various forces line up in support of it — strategists who see it as valuable, the companies involved in its production, the politicians who represent areas where those companies are based, the branch of the armed service that is most likely to operate the new weapon, and so on.

As these bases of support strengthen over time, the weapon is portrayed as more and more vital, and therefore less and less negotiable. The weapons are normally selected as bargaining chips at a stage in their development process when the point of no return has already been passed so that whatever negotiators might say at the talks, it is most unlikely that a decision not to employ *any* examples of the new weapon would be taken.

Domestic bargaining effects

The impact of domestic politics is extremely important in this regard. In the arms control arena each government is carrying out parallel sets of negotiations, bargaining with its own domestic critics, as well as with the diplomats of the adversary state. If a powerful coalition of domestic forces develops which is opposed to the new treaty, a government will generally try to buy off its critics in some way. The most common method is to compensate for the restrictions in one area of defence spending by increasing spending in other areas.

For example, in 1963 President Kennedy wanted Congress to approve the Partial Test Ban Treaty, which ended atmospheric nuclear testing. In response to Congressional opposition to this measure he sent a letter to the Senate promising:

(1) a continuing 'aggressive' programme of underground tests;
(2) the maintenance of all testing laboratories;
(3) the maintenance of the facilities necessary to resume atmospheric testing at short notice, if this became necessary;
(4) the improvement of American verification techniques.

As a result of all this activity, the number of American nuclear test explosions per year actually *increased* after the partial test ban, to reach a level double that of the average during the 1950s.

Similarly, in order to secure support for the SALT I Treaty, President Nixon needed to have the Chiefs of the American Armed Forces testify to Congress that the Treaty was valuable and posed no danger to American security. The Joint Chiefs of Staff did so, but at a price. They asked for 'assurances'. These 'assurances' were new weapons programmes. To maintain their support for SALT therefore, President Nixon had to accelerate the Trident and B-1 programmes and initiate the MX missile programme.

Arms control effects

As noted earlier, arms control concerns itself with stability and restraint, and not with the pursuit of reductions for their own sake. In fact, the preoccupation with balance and stability inclines the arms control approach towards a preference for balances at a high rather than a low level of weaponry. This is because a small advantage to one side is more significant at a low level than at a high level. If one state has 155 tanks and another 150, there is little real difference. But if one state has ten tanks and another 15, that same difference of five represents a 50 per cent advantage.

Similarly, arms control takes a benign attitude towards high levels of strategic weaponry, because the key element is the 'surviving second strike capability' and the more missiles each superpower has, the more are likely to survive any sudden attack.

Bargaining effects

Arms control negotiations have also been marred by problems that can beset any international negotiations. A long series of negotiations such as SALT or MBFR can produce very cautious bargaining sequences. The reductions seen as possible by statesmen are merely those which the other side will reciprocate, so that cuts are made because they are *negotiable*, rather than because they are necessarily valuable. Even if a state knows that it could safely make greater reductions, it may not do so because this would weaken its negotiating position in the next round of talks by throwing away bargaining chips.

Technological effects

If an arms control agreement is to be accepted by domestic political audiences it must be seen as being *fair*. However, the great pace of current technological change can make this perception of fairness difficult to sustain. In the SALT I Treaty, the USSR was allowed more launchers than its rival to compensate for the fact that the USA could deploy more warheads. The rapid pace of Soviet MIRVing undermined this agreement so quickly that a new 'interim' agreement had to be signed a mere two years later, providing for equality of both warheads and launch platforms. If this perception of fairness is lost, arms control agreements can consume trust rather than increase it.

An important element in this trust is the efficiency of verification procedures. Arms control agreements must be adequately verifiable. During the 1960s, technological change was beneficial to arms control. Improvements in the sensitivity of satellite reconnaissance and seismic monitoring equipment meant that agreements such as the Threshold Test Ban and SALT I Treaties could be signed, which could not have been concluded earlier because verification techniques were inadequate. Technological change in the 1970s has not been so helpful. Verification depends upon observation, and significant weapon improvements have taken place since the early 1970s which are very difficult to monitor. For example, it is easy to count the *numbers* of missiles and increases in numbers, but it is far less simple to monitor and measure increases in the accuracy of those missiles. The less certain verification techniques are, the more strain is put on the limited supply of trust existing between the two sides.

Verification limitations can actually stimulate weapon procurement. In SALT II for example, the problem arose of verifying the limits placed on MIRVing, that is the limits on the number of warheads allowed per delivery vehicle. Since it is impossible to tell a MIRVed missile from a single warhead missile, the verification adopted was known as 'counting as if'. If a missile was test-fired and released a certain number of warheads, then from the moment of that test all missiles of that type would be counted as if they carried that number of warheads — whether they did or not. In these circumstances there was not much incentive to retain single warhead missiles when the other side already counted them as being MIRVed.

Verification by observation is also being increasingly hindered by 'grey area' technology and multi-mission weapons. Aircraft such as F-111 or Tu-22M, which can carry conventional *or* nuclear warheads, and look the same whatever their mission, defy current verification techniques. Similarly, missiles such as the SS-20 and cruise, which can carry nuclear or conventional warheads, pose enormous verification problems making the achievement of arms control agreements increasingly difficult.

THE POLITICAL DIMENSION

The future is not what it was. — *Anon.*

Arms control has essentially failed. Three decades of US–Soviet negotiations to limit arms competition have done little more than to codify the arms race.[27]

Has arms control failed? Is there no alternative to unrestrained arms racing? It is easy to become disillusioned with the lack of substantive progress of the past two decades, but total despair is not justified.

There is no doubt that arms control has disappointed its supporters. The difficulties involved in producing workable arms control agreements are, as has been shown, almost immeasurable. However, if arms control has disappointed, it has at least been attempted. The grandiose and impractical schemes of the 1950s have been superseded by serious negotiations aimed at producing worthwhile agreements. It is precisely *because* the negotiations of the last 20 years have been serious that it has not been possible to sidestep the difficulties involved, but this should be recognized for the progress that it represents.

It is easy for those not involved in the policy process to make light of the difficulties involved. But governments must contend with widely differing interests and must do so in a dangerous and largely unpredictable environment. It is one thing to recognize what *ought* to be the ideal world, quite another to try and inch towards it while coping with the present, far from ideal reality. The truism that 'ideal treaties can be drafted unilaterally, but they cannot be negotiated' is nowhere more applicable than to the field of arms control and disarmament.

For much of the 1970s, public concern about the dangers of the arms race and the value of arms control, was at a low ebb. Public perception of the period as one of *decreasing* danger, despite the growth in armaments, was the result of belief in the value of the detente process, and a broad assumption that detente had come to stay. The deterioration of the superpower relationship in the late 1970s has undermined confidence in the ability of statesmen to 'manage' the arms competition successfully. Detente was not seen by European populations as a device for freezing the status quo, but as a mechanism for recognizing political realities, while instituting a *process* which would ameliorate the least attractive of those realities — the arms race. Detente was a way to manage a gradual and painless evolution in great power relationships.

Thus, now that the dangers inherent in the total abandonment of detente have been belatedly realized, Western public opinion has manifested an unmistakable desire to preserve the arms control process intact, despite the general antagonisms between the superpowers. But as the question of arms control and disarmament has moved to the centre of political debate, so the nature of debate has tended to simplify the issues. The alternatives are starkly, far too starkly, posed. The protagonists, it often seems, are on the one hand those who not only defend the concept of nuclear deterrence, but go further and defend the idea of nuclear war.[28] On the other hand are the disarmers who will accept nothing less than total success and for whom anything less underlines what they see as a plunge to barbarism.

Between these two standpoints the multilateralist arms control community has been forced very much onto the defensive, assailed from all sides. Yet the tumult of the current debate cannot obscure the fundamental point that, however uncomfortable the arms controllers' position at present, it is they who reflect the reality with which the world will have to deal in the remaining years of this century. The superpowers are *not* about to exterminate each other and everyone else in a mindless armageddon. Nor is the marvellous idealism of the disarmament movement about to produce a world in which all the swords have been beaten into ploughshares.

There are innumerable areas where arms control and disarmament efforts can contribute to a safer and better world, and many such areas have been highlighted in this book. But the nation-state, the insecurity of the anarchic international state-system, and the recourse to the military instrument where it can serve as a functional political tool, are realities which are not about to disappear either in conflagration or concord. It is not the best of all possible worlds, but change will be slow and halting, human beings are neither lemmings nor sheep. Those who deify the balance of terror concept and those who point to the alarming dangers posed by the arms race are both right to a large extent, and the true challenge for statesmen and national populations in the 1980s is to devise and support measures which reverse the direction of the arms race, while preserving the essential stability of the balance of power system, thereby providing adequate security at lower levels of expenditure of precious human resources.

Notes and references

1
ARMS RACES AND MILITARY POWER

1 George H. Quester, *Offense and Defense in the International System* (John Wiley & Sons, New York, 1977), p. 191.
2 Robert L. Wendzel, *International Relations: A Policymaker Focus* (John Wiley & Sons, New York, 1977), p. 44.
3 Thomas C. Schelling, *Arms and Influence* (Yale University Press, New Haven, 1966), pp. 2–3.
4 Du Plessig-Marley, 'Discours au roi Henri III, sur les moyens de diminuer l'Espagnol', 14 Apr. 1584, in J. Daille (ed.), *Memoires de Messire de Mornay*, Vol. I (Amsterdam, 1624), p. 357. Quoted in M. Wight, *Power Politics* (Pelican, London, 1979), p. 239.
5 Quoted in J. Baylis, *et al.*, *Contemporary Strategic Thought* (Croom Helm, London, 1975), p. 51.
6 Robert Purnell, *The Society of States* (Weidenfeld & Nicolson, London, 1973), p. 98.
7 Michael Howard, 'Military power and international order', in J. Garnett (ed.), *Theories of Peace and Security* (Macmillan, London, 1970), pp. 46–7.
8 Cited in Correlli Barnett, *Britain and Her Army* (London, 1974), p. 168.
9 D. Hume, 'Of the balance of power', in T. Green and T. Grose (eds), *Essays: Moral, Political and Literary*, Vol. I (Longmans, London, 1829), p. 352.
10 Quoted in Martin Wight, 'The balance of power and international order', in Alan James (ed.), *The Bases of International Order* (London, 1973), p. 101.
11 An excellent work on this subject is G. Blainey, *The Causes of War* (Sun Books, Melbourne, 1973).
12 Henry St John, Viscount Bolingbroke, *Works*, Vol. I (London, 1754), p. 427.
13 Some writers, such as Charles P. Schleicher, *Introduction to International Relations* (New York, 1954), and A. F. K. Organski, *World*

Politics (2nd edn, New York, 1968) have argued that it was designed to preserve peace. Most writers, including E. V. Gulick, *Europe's Classical Balance of Power* (Ithaca, New York, 1955), George Liska, *International Equilibrium* (Cambridge, Massachusetts, 1957), and Martin Wight, 'The balance of power and international order', *op. cit.*, argue that peace is incidental.

14 Montesquieu, *De L'Esprit des Lois* (Garnier, Paris, no date), Book XIII, Ch. 27, p. 203.

15 A. F. Pollard, 'The balance of power', *Journal of the British Institute of International Affairs*, Vol. 2 (Mar. 1923), p. 59.

16 Pollard, p. 59.

17 Wight, *Power Politics*, p. 239.

18 Colin S. Gray, 'The arms race phenomenon', *World Politics*, Vol. 24 (1972), p. 41.

19 M. D. Wallace, 'Arms races and escalation', *Journal of Conflict Resolution* (Vol. 23, No. 1, Mar. 1979), pp. 3–4.

20 John Keegan, *Six Armies in Normandy* (London, 1982), p. 330.

21 Hedley Bull, *The Control of the Arms Race* (London, 1961), p. 5.

22 Robert S. McNamara, *The Essence of Security* (London, 1968), pp. 58–9.

23 J. Barton and L. D. Weiler (eds), *International Arms Control* (Stanford, California, Stanford University Press, 1976), p. 32.

24 Sir Harold Macmillan, *Pointing the Way* (London, Macmillan, 1972). Cited in S. Zuckerman, *Nuclear Illusion and Reality* (London, Collins, 1982), p. 122.

25 Lord Zuckerman, *The Guardian*, 9 Oct. 1980.

26 Philip Noel-Baker, *The Arms Race* (London, 1958), p. 74.

27 *Ibid.*

28 Colin S. Gray, 'The arms race and arms control', *Journal of International Relations*, Vol. 2 (1977).

29 Johan Jurgen Holst, 'Is there a strategic arms race', *Foreign Policy*, No. 19 (1975), p. 160.

30 G. Blainey, *op. cit.*, p. 138.

31 Blainey, *op. cit.*, pp. 138–9.

32 *Ibid.*, p. 138.

33 For example, J. David Singer, 'Threat perception and the armament-tension dilemma', *Journal of Conflict Resolution*, Vol. 2, No. 1 (1958), *passim*.

34 H. W. Koch, *The Rise of Modern Warfare 1618–1815* (Hamlyn, London, 1981), p. 10.

35 Kosta Tsipis, 'The arms race as posturing', in D. Carlton and C. Schaerf (eds), *The Dynamics of The Arms Race* (Croom Helm, London, 1975), pp. 78–81.

2
THE SUPERPOWER STRATEGIC BALANCE

1 Philip Noel-Baker, *The Arms Race* (London, 1958), p. 5.
2 IISS. *The Military Balance 1961–62* (London, 1961), p. 2.
3 M. Heylin, 'Nuclear arms race gearing for speed-up', *Chemical and Engineering News*, 16 Mar. 1981.
4 A. Wohlstetter, 'The delicate balance of terror', *Foreign Affairs*, Vol. 32, No. 2.
5 R. McNamara, *The Essence of Security* (London, 1968), p. 76.
6 H. Brown, *Annual Report, Department of Defense, Fiscal Year 1979* (Washington, 1978), p. 55.
7 D. Ball, *Politics and Force Levels: The Strategic Missile Programme of the Kennedy Administration* (University of California Press, 1981).
8 B. Tuchman, *The Guns of August* (New York, 1962).
9 Stephen M. Millett, 'Soviet perceptions of nuclear strategy and implications for US deterrence', *Economics and Policy Analysis Occasional Paper No. 18* (Columbus, Ohio, 1981), p. 4.
10 *Ibid.*, p. 5.
11 Millett, *op. cit.*, p. 6.
12 Raymond Garthoff, 'Mutual deterrence and strategic arms limitation in Soviet policy', *International Security* (Summer 1978), pp. 117–24.
13 Quoted in Robert L. Arnett, 'Soviet views on nuclear war' in W. Kincade and J. D. Porro, *Negotiating Security* (Washington, 1979), p. 116.
14 US Military Posture, F. Y. 1981 (Washington, 1980). Cited in William H. Kincade, 'Missile vulnerability reconsidered', *Arms Control Today* (May 1981), p. 6.
15 Millett, *op. cit.*, p. 10.
16 A good discussion of MIRV technology is contained in Herbert York, 'Multiple-warhead missiles', *Scientific American* (Nov. 1973), in *Progress in Arms Control: Readings from Scientific American* (San Francisco, 1979), pp. 122–31.
17 D. M. O. Miller, W. V. Kennedy, J. Jordan & D. Richardson, *The Balance of Military Power* (London, 1981), p. 24.
18 D. M. O. Miller, *et al.*, *op. cit.*, p. 25.
19 Alain Enthoven and K. Wayne Smith, *How Much is Enough?* (New York, 1971), p. 210.
20 Kosta Tsipis, 'Precision and accuracy', *Arms Control Today*, Vol. II, No. 5 (May 1981), p. 3.
21 Herbert York, *op. cit.*, pp. 124–5.

22 William H. Kincade, 'Missile vulnerability reconsidered', *Arms Control Today*, Vol. II, No. 5 (May 1981), p. 5.

23 Fred M. Kaplan, *Dubious Spectre* (Washington, 1980), p. 43–4.

24 Cited in Kosta Tsipis, *op. cit.*, p. 4.

25 Pierre Spey, cited in Kaplan, *op. cit.*, p. 41. Although extrapolating results in a data-free environment has its drawbacks, one would hope that the conditions never occur which would provide the missing data in superabundance.

26 Strobe Talbott, *Endgame* (Harper and Row, New York, 1979).

27 Quoted in Robert Bell and Mark M. Lowenthal, 'SALT-II: major issues', *Congressional Research Service, Washington*, 1978, p. 9.

28 Wayne Biddle, 'The silo busters', *Harpers Magazine* (Vol. 254, No. 1555).

29 *Ibid.*

30 *Ibid.*

31 Defense Secretary Harold Brown, Hearings, Senate Foreign Relations Committee, *The SALT II Treaty, Part I* (Washington, 1979), p. 301.

32 Department of Defense, *Selected Statements* (Washington, Oct. 1978), p. 23.

33 Edgar Ulsamer, 'A solid case for MX', *Airforce Magazine* (Apr. 1980), p. 28.

34 Biddle, *op. cit.*

35 Desmond Ball, 'The MX basing decision', *Survival*, Vol. XXII (Mar.–Apr. 1980), p. 58.

36 *The Economist* (31 May 1980), p. 114.

37 *International Defense Review* (Aug. 1979), p. 1284.

38 *Detroit News*, 11 May 1980.

39 *Washington Post*, 23 Nov. 1982.

40 R. Jeffrey Smith, 'Dense-pack — moving target for arms control', *Arms Control Today*, Vol. 12, No. 9 (Oct. 1982), p. 1.

41 *Ibid.*

42 *Long Island Newsday*, 4 Feb. 1980.

43 *The Times*, 5 Oct. 1981.

44 *Nevada State Journal*, 22 Apr. 1980; *Deseret News*, 10–11 Apr. 1980.

45 Out of a total of 316 aircraft. *The Military Balance 1981–82* (IISS, London, 1981), p. 5.

46 *The Times*, 5 Dec. 1981.

47 *Ibid.*

48 *The Guardian*, 11 Sept. 1980.

49 *The Military Balance 1981–82* (IISS, London, 1981), pp. 10–11.

50 It is symptomatic of the hypocrisy surrounding these matters that

American military specialists, while objecting to ratification of SALT II and describing the treaty as 'totally unsatisfactory', should at the same time denounce the USSR for alleged 'violations of the treaty', a claim refuted by the US Government itself. *The Guardian*, 10 Apr. 1982.

51 *The Military Balance 1981–82*, p. 11.

52 W. Gunston, *Rockets and Missiles* (London, 1979), p. 56.

53 Peter D. Zimmerman, 'Will MX solve the problem?', *Arms Control Today*, (Jan. 1980), p. 6.

54 Sources: *Aviation Week and Space Technology*, 16 June 1980; *The Military Balance 1981–82, op. cit.*

55 *Aviation Week and Space Technology*, 3 Nov. 1980, p. 28.

56 H. Legault and G. Lindsey, *The Dynamics of The Nuclear Balance*, (revised edn, London, 1976), p. 101.

57 SIPRI, *The Arms Race and Arms Control* (Taylor and Francis, London, 1982), p. 84.

58 *The Military Balance 1981–82*, (International Institute for Strategic Studies, London), pp. 106–7.

59 *The Arms Race and Arms Control, op. cit.*, p. 93.

60 *Ibid.*

61 Harry L. Wren, *SALT II: Major Policy Issues* (Congressional Research Service IB79074, Washington DC, 1980), p. 1.

62 US State Department, *The SALT Process* (Document No. 8947, Washington DC, 1978) p. 2.

63 Secretary for Defense, Harold Brown. Quoted in *SALT II: Senate Testimony*, US State Department publication No. 72A (Washington DC, 1979), p.10.

64 Alexei Kosygin, quoted in *New York Times*, 16 Feb. 1967.

65 Kulikov, Izvestia, 24 Aug. 1972. Quoted by Raymond L. Garthoff in 'ABM revisited: promise or peril?', *Washington Quarterly*, Vol. 4, No. 4 (Autumn 1981), p. 70.

66 William R. Van Cleave in 'ABM revisited', *op. cit.*, p. 77. Other proponents of this view include Colin S. Gray of the Hudson Institute, see C. Gray, 'A new debate on ballistic missile defence', *Survival*, Vol. 23, No. 3 (London, 1981), pp. 60–71, and former Defense Secretary James R. Schlesinger, see 'ABM revisited', *op. cit.*, p. 56.

67 Adam Yarmolinsky, 'ABM revisited', *op. cit.*, p. 83.

68 *The Times*, 20 June 1982.

3

THE SPREAD OF NUCLEAR WEAPONS

1 William Epstein, 'Why states go — and don't go — nuclear', *Annals*

of the American Academy of Political and Social Science, 430 (Mar. 1977), p. 18. Hereafter cited as Epstein, *Annals*.

2 Epstein, *Annals*, p.19.

3 George H. Quester, 'Nuclear proliferation: linkages and solutions', *International Organisation*, Vol. 33, No. 4 (Autumn 1979), p. 546.

4 Quoted by Trevor Fishlock, 'National pride could push General Zia to Islamic bomb', *The Times*, 13 August 1980.

5 Ashok Kapur, 'Nuclear proliferation in the 1980s', *International Journal*, Vol. 36, No. 3 (1982), p. 546.

6 Fishlock, *op. cit.*

7 Ashok Kapur, 'The nuclear spread: a Third World view', *Third World Quarterly*, Vol. 2, No. 1 (1980), p. 64.

8 Ashok Kapur, 'Nuclear proliferation', p. 547.

9 Ian Smart, 'Future conditional: the prospect for Anglo-French nuclear co-operation', *Adelphi Paper No. 78* (IISS, London, 1971), p. 5.

10 Judith Young 'The French strategic missile programme', *Adelphi Paper*, No. 38 (IISS, London, 1967), p. 7.

11 *The Guardian*, 11 July 1981.

12 Ernest W. Lefever, *Nuclear Arms in the Third World: US Policy Dilemma* (Washington, 1979), p. 43.

13 Lefever, p. 109.

14 *Ibid.*, p. 210.

15 Lefever, p. 109.

16 *Ibid.*

17 Document A/35/402.

18 For example, ITV's *World in Action* programme, 20 Oct. 1980.

19 *Washington Post*, 9 Mar. 1980.

20 Richard K. Betts, 'A diplomatic bomb for South Africa?', *International Security*, Autumn 1979, pp. 92–3.

21 *The Times*, 15 Aug. 1980.

22 Betts, *op. cit.*, p. 115.

23 Memorandum, US Central Intelligence Agency, 'Prospects for Further Proliferation of Nuclear Weapons', 4 Sept. 1974, p. 1.

24 Russell W. Howe, *Weapons* (London, 1981), pp. xvi–xix.

25 *The Times*, 18 June 1981.

26 *The Guardian*, 22 June 1981.

27 *The Observer*, 9 Nov. 1980.

28 William Epstein, 'The proliferation of nuclear weapons', *Scientific American*, Vol. 232, No. 4, (Apr. 1975), p. 24.

29 *Ibid.*, p. 27.

30 Stephen J. Baker, 'The international political economy of proliferation', in D. Carlton and C. Schaerf (eds), *Arms Control and Tech-*

nological Innovation (London, 1977), p. 87.
31 Robert F. Kennedy, quoted in Arthur M. Schlesinger Jr, *Robert Kennedy and His Times* (London, 1978), p. 692.
32 Kenneth Waltz, 'The spread of nuclear weapons: more may be better', *Adelphi Paper*, No. 171 (IISS, London, 1981), p. 30.
33 Winston S. Churchill, House of Commons, 1 Mar. 1955. Quoted in *Churchill Speaks 1897–1963, Collected Speeches in Peace and War*, ed. Robert Rhodes James (London, 1980), p. 969.
34 Sir John Hill, 'The driving forces of proliferation', *Arms Control*, Vol. 1, No. 1 (1980), p. 54.
35 Stephen J. Baker, p. 95.
36 John Maddox, 'Prospects for nuclear proliferation', *Adelphi Paper 113* (IISS, London, 1975), p. 11.
37 *Ibid.*, p. 10.
38 Stephen J. Baker, *op. cit.*, p. 97.
39 Amory B. Lovins, L. Hunter Lovins and R. Leonard Ross, 'Nuclear power and nuclear bombs', *Foreign Affairs* (Summer 1980), p. 1147.
40 *The Guardian*, 7 Apr. 1980.
41 Lovins, *et al.*, p. 1149.
42 Ashok Kapur, 'The nuclear spread: a Third World view', *Third World Quarterly*, Vol. 2, No. 1 (Jan. 1980), p. 60.
43 Lefever, p. 119.
44 John F. Kennedy, Commencement address at The American University, Washington, 10 June 1963.

4

THE ARMS RACE IN SPACE

1 General Jacob Smart, 'Strategic implications of space activities', *Strategic Review*, Autumn 1974, p. 20.
2 *Military Review*, Oct. 1978, p. 50.
3 *Colorado Springs Sun*, 10 Oct. 1977.
4 Quoted by John Markoff in 'Outer space — the military's new high ground', *Baltimore Sun*, 6 July 1980.
5 Clarence A. Robinson, 'Space-based systems stressed', *Aviation Week and Space Technology*, 3 Mar. 1980.
6 Martin Ince, *Space* (Sphere Books, London, 1981), p. 139.
7 Forooq Hussain and Curtis Peebles, 'Military space systems', in *The Illustrated Encyclopedia of Space Technology* (Salamander, London, 1981), p. 76.
8 R. W. Bruce, 'Satellite orbit sustaining techniques', *American*

Rocket Society Journal, Vol. 31 (Sept. 1961), p. 1237, cited in SIPRI, *Outer Space — Battlefield of the Future?* (Taylor and Francis, London, 1978), p. 20.

9   M. Ince, *op. cit.*, p. 140.

10 Anti-satellite warfare techniques are discussed later, but it is worth noting that as early as 1975 a US satellite was blinded while passing over Siberia. At first the Pentagon feared the satellite had been attacked by a Soviet laser weapon, though subsequently a gas-pipeline was blamed. See *Business Week*, 4 June 1979.

11 SIPRI, *op. cit.*, pp. 14–16.

12 Ted Greenwood, 'Reconnaissance and arms control', *Scientific American*, Feb. 1973, in B. Russett and B. Blair (eds), *Progress in Arms Control?* (W. H. Freeman & Co., San Francisco, 1979), p. 97.

13 *Ibid.*

14 Christopher Lee, *The Final Decade* (Hamish Hamilton, London, 1981), p. 101.

15 See articles by Barry Miller in *Electronic Warfare/Defense Electronics*, Sept.–Oct., and Nov.–Dec. 1977.

16 This description of satellite orbital characteristics follows those presented in 'Military applications of space', *RAF Quarterly*, Vol. 13 (1973), pp. 273–5 and SIPRI, *op. cit.*, pp. 98–102.

17 SIPRI, *op. cit.*, p. 101.

18 *Ibid.*

19 *Illustrated Encyclopedia of Space Technology, op. cit.*, pp. 81–2.

20 SIPRI, *op. cit.*, p. 106.

21 The USA is clearly ahead in at least one aspect of the arms race. It has succeeded in opening up a significant 'acronym gap' over the Soviet Union.

22 *International Encyclopedia of Space Technology, op. cit.*, p. 82.

23 *Ibid.*

24 SIPRI, *op. cit.*, p. 109.

25 Nicolae Ecobescu, 'The need to halt the arms race in outer space', *Revue Roumaine D'Etudes Internationales*, Vol. 13, No. 4 (Bucharest, 1979), p. 542; *Aviation Week, op. cit.*, p. 25.

26 *Illustrated Encyclopedia of Space Technology, op. cit.*, p. 82.

27 Alfredo Civetta, 'Un Sistema di navigazione per il futuro', *Rivista Marittima*, nr. 1, 1978, pp. 51–8. Quoted in Ecobescu, *op. cit.*, p. 543.

28 SIPRI, *op. cit.*, p. 137.

29 Ecobescu, *op. cit.*, p. 544.

30 SIPRI, *op. cit.*, p. 149.

31 *Illustrated Encyclopedia of Space Technology, op. cit.*, p. 72.

32 Clarence A. Robinson, 'Space-based systems stressed', *Aviation*

Week and Space Technology, 3 Mar. 1980.

33 Foreign and Commonwealth Office, *Foreign Policy Document No. 44* (London, 1979), p. 2.

34 Geoffrey E. Perry, 'Russian hunter-killer satellite experiments', *Military Review*, Oct. 1978, p. 51.

35 *Ibid.*, p. 55.

36 SIPRI, 'Outer space — battlefield of the future?', *passim*. Only two of the 73 electronic reconnaissance satellites and two of the 30 navigation satellites launched by the USA between 1959 and 1976 had a 62° orbital inclination.

37 Representative Robert Carr, quoted in *Aerospace Daily*, 25 Nov. 1977.

38 *Business Week, op. cit.*, p. 145.

39 *Business Week, op. cit.*, p. 145.

40 *Ibid.*, p. 142.

41 *Financial Times*, 18 Oct. 1980.

42 *Business Week, op. cit.*, p. 142.

43 *Illustrated Encyclopedia of Space Technology, op. cit.*, p. 84.

44 *Flight International*, 2 Feb. 1980, p. 297.

45 Foreign and Commonwealth Office, *Foreign Policy Document No. 44* (1979), p. 3. $80 million went for ASAT.

46 *Flight International*, 7 Apr. 1979, p. 1046.

47 *Detroit News*, 5 Oct. 1977.

48 *RAF Quarterly, op. cit.*, p. 280.

49 J. Markoff, *op. cit.*

50 R. Hansen, 'Freedom of passage on the high seas of space', *Strategic Review*, (Fall, 1977), p. 85.

51 Frank Asbeck, 'The militarisation of space', *Armament and Disarmament Information Unit Report*, Vol. 2, No. 2 (University of Sussex, 1980), p. 2.

52 *Business Week, op. cit.*, p. 138.

53 Asbeck, *op. cit.*, p. 2.

54 *Financial Times*, 18 Oct. 1980.

55 *Wall Street Journal*, 22 Dec. 1980.

56 *Ibid.*

57 *New Scientist*, 1 Jan. 1981, p. 3.

58 *Flight International*, 16 Aug. 1980, p. 577.

59 Asbeck, *op. cit.*, p. 2.

60 *Aviation Week and Space Technology*, 2 May 1977. p. 16.

61 Useful articles on this subject are Richard Garwin, 'Charged particle beam weapons?', *Bulletin of the Atomic Scientists*, Oct. 1978; Clarence A. Robinson, 'Soviets test beam technologies in space', *Aviation Week and Space Technology*, 13 Nov. 1978; Donald M.

Snow, 'Lasers, charged-particle beams and the strategic future', *Political Science Quarterly*, Vol. 95, No. 2, Summer 1980; and Barry L. Thompson, 'Directed energy weapons and the strategic balance', *Orbis*, Fall, 1979.

62 James W. Canan, *The Superwarriors* (Weybright & Talley, New York), pp. 253-4.

63 *International Defence Review*, No. 4, 1979.

64 *Business Week*, *op. cit.*, p. 138.

65 *Aviation Week and Space Technology*, 28 July 1980, p. 57.

66 *Aviation Week and Space Technology*, 8 Dec. 1980, p. 36.

67 *Ibid.*

68 *The Daily Telegraph*, 20 Dec. 1980.

69 *The Times*, 25 Mar. 1983.

70 *Aviation Week and Space Technology*, 28 July 1980.

71 *St Louis Post-Despatch*, 11 Jan. 1980.

72 *Aviation Week and Space Technology*, 28 July 1980.

73 Donald M. Snow, *op. cit.*, p. 288.

74 K. Gatland, M. Hewish & P. Wright, *The Space Shuttle Handbook* (London, 1979), p. 77.

75 *Philadelphia Inquirer*, 8 Feb. 1980.

76 *The Times*, 7 Jan. 1981.

77 *Ibid.*

78 *Baltimore Sun*, 6 July 1980.

79 Lt Col C. A. Forbrich, 'The Soviet space shuttle program', *Air University Review* (May–June 1980), p. 56.

80 *Ibid.*, p. 60.

81 Forbrich, *op. cit.*, pp. 57-8.

82 Walter C. Clemens, 'Strategy and arms control', *Bulletin of the Atomic Scientists*, Nov. 1967, p. 28.

5
NUCLEAR WEAPONS IN EUROPE

1 For example, E. P. Thompson quoted in *The Daily Telegraph*, 2 Sept. 1981. Non-governmental fears of a European arms race have also surfaced in East Germany. See Ronald D. Asmus, 'New peace initiative in the GDR', *Radio Free Europe Background Report No. 39*, 15 Feb. 1982.

2 SIPRI, *World Armaments and Disarmament 1980*, p. 185.

3 *The Guardian*, 5 Sept. 1981.

4 Michael Mandelbaum, *The Nuclear Revolution* (Cambridge, 1981), Ch. 6, *passim*.

5 P. Williams, 'Deterrence', in J. Baylis, *et al.*, *Contemporary Strategy* (London, 1975), pp. 80–1.
6 Freedman, 'NATO myths', *Foreign Policy No. 45* (Winter 1981–2), p. 50.
7 L. Freedman, *op. cit.*, p. 51.
8 L. Freedman, *op. cit.*, p. 55.
9 G. Treverton, *RUSI Journal*, Sept. 1980, pp. 3–4.
10 J. Jordan, *et al.*, *The Balance of Military Power* (London, 1981), p. 175.
11 B. Gunston, *Rockets and Missiles* (London, 1979), p. 34.
12 Gunston, *op. cit.*, p. 40.
13 Two-thirds of NATO's members have nuclear-capable 155 mm self-propelled howitzers. Almost as many have the 203 mm self-propelled howitzer.
14 Source: R. Kennedy, 'Soviet theatre-nuclear forces: implications for NATO Defense', in *Orbis*, Vol. 25 (Summer 1981), pp. 333; 335.
15 Source: IISS, *The Military Balance 1981–82*.
16 Lynn E. Davis, 'A proposal for TNF arms control', *Survival*, Vol. XXIII, No. 6, Nov.–Dec. 1981, p. 245.
17 Paul Buteux, 'Theatre nuclear forces – modernisation plan and arms control initiative', *NATO Review*, Vol. 28, No. 6 (Dec. 1980).
18 P. Corterier, 'Modernization of TNF and arms control', *NATO Review*, Vol. 29, No. 4 (Aug. 1981), p. 6.
19 See ch. 4, pp. 93–4.
20 Thomas W. Wolfe, *Soviet Power and Europe 1945–1970* (Baltimore and London, 1970), p. 173.
21 Wolfe, *op. cit.*, p. 198.
22 *Ibid.*
23 This problem has grown even more difficult for the USSR in the 1970s with the advent of a significant Chinese IRBM capability also targeted on the Soviet Union.
24 Richard Burt, 'The SS-20 and the Eurostrategic balance', *World Today* (Feb. 1977), p. 47.
25 R. Kennedy, *op. cit.*, p. 332.
26 Gunston, *op. cit.*, p. 26.
27 L. Freedman, 'The dilemma of theatre nuclear arms control', *Survival*, Vol. XXIII, No. 1 (1981), p. 5. (Hereafter cited as Freedman, 'TNF dilemma'.)
28 *Ibid.*
29 Freedman, 'TNF dilemma', p. 10.
30 SIPRI, *World Armaments and Disarmament 1980*, p. 177.
31 *Ibid.*, p. 177.
32 The SS-20 is based on the two upper stages of the 3-stage SS-16.

33 *Soviet News* (London), 3 Nov. 1981, p. 358.
34 *The Sunday Times*, 2 Aug. 1981.
35 Sources: R. Kennedy, *op. cit.*, pp. 333–5; SIPRI, *The Arms Race and Arms Control* (Taylor and Francis, London, 1981), p. 144.
36 Sources: R. Kennedy, *ibid.*; SIPRI, *ibid.*; IISS, *The Military Balance 1982–83*, pp. 136–7.
37 Source: IISS, *The Military Balance 1981–82*.
38 *The Times*, 19 Nov. 1981.
39 *Soviet News*, 1 Dec. 1981.
40 P. Corterier, *op. cit.*, p. 6.
41 P. Corterier, *op. cit.*, p. 7.
42 *The Times*, 24 July 1981.
43 *The Times*, 23 Oct. 1981.
44 *The Times*, 20 Nov. 1981.
45 R. Ranger, 'NATO's new great debate, theatre nuclear force modernisation and arms control', *Orbis*, Vol. 36, No. 3 (1981), p. 562.
46 President Leonid Brezhnev, *Soviet News* (London), 3 Nov. 1981, p. 358.
47 *Ibid.*
48 *Ibid.*
49 *Soviet News*, 3 Nov. 1981, p. 358.
50 Lev Semeiko, 'Strategy of parity and "Eurostrategy" of superiority', *Co-existence*, Vol. 17, No. 1 (1980), p. 159.

6

THE EUROPEAN CENTRAL BALANCE

1 *The Military Balance 1981–82* (IISS, London, 1981), p. 123.
2 Harold Brown, 'A review of US defense posture', quoted in Frank Blackaby, 'The unequal contest'; *ADIU Report*, Vol. 1, No. 2 (Aug. 1979), p. 1.
3 Statement on the Defence Estimates (HMSO, 1977).
4 General Alexander Haig, 13 Oct. 1976, cited in Henry Stanhope, 'New threat — or old fears', in Derek Leebaert (ed.) *European Security: Prospects for the 1980s* (Lexington Books, Lexington, 1979), p. 42.
5 S. Nunn and D. Bartlett to Senate Armed Services Committee, 24 Jan. 1977.
6 Senators Nunn and Bartlett, *loc. cit.*
7 J. Record, *Force Reductions in Europe: Starting Over* (Cambridge, Massachusetts, Institute for Foreign Policy Analysis, 1980), p. 27.

8 Source: *The Military Balance 1981–82, op. cit.*, pp. 124–5.
9 Excluding units in USSR, which appear as mobilizable reserves.
10 *In extremis*, NATO could press a further 1,104 armed helicopters into service.
11 Source: Stanhope, *op. cit.*, p. 46.
12 Stamhope, *op. cit.*, p. 47.
13 *Ibid.*, p. 48.
14 *Ibid.*, p. 47.
15 Barry M. Blechman *et al.*, *The Soviet Military Build-up and US Defence Spending* (Washington, 1977), p. 30.
16 Blechman, *op. cit.*, p. 10.
17 Blechman, p. 9.
18 D. Miller, W. Kennedy, J. Jordan and D. Richardson, *The Balance of Military Power* (London, 1981), p. 53.
19 J. Record, *op. cit.*, p. 27.
20 Philip A. Karber, 'The Soviet anti-tank debate', *Survival*, Vol. XVIII, No. 3 (May–June 1976), p. 108.
21 Miller *et al.*, p. 62.
22 *Ibid.*, p. 149.
23 John Erikson, 'The Warsaw Pact — the shape of things to come?' in K. Dawisha and P. Hanson (eds), *Soviet East European Dilemmas* (Heinemann, London, 1981), p. 163.
24 *Ibid.*, p. 149.
25 Blechman, *op. cit.*, p. 13.
26 Miller, *op. cit.*
27 *NATO and the New Soviet Threat*, Report of Senator Sam Nunn Senator Dewey F. Bartlett to the Committee on Armed Services, United States Senate (83-803-0), (Washington, United States, GPO, 1977), p. 5.
28 D. Miller, *op. cit.*, p. 105.
29 Stanhope, p. 40.
30 W. J. Koenig, *Weapons of World War Three* (Hamlyn, London, 1981), p. 124.
31 Blechman, p. 27.
32 Marshall A. A. Grechko, *The Armed Forces of the Soviet State* (2nd edn, Moscow, 1975), p. 198, quoted in Philip A. Karber, 'The Soviet anti-tank debate', *Survival*, Vol. 18, No. 3 (May–June 1976), p. 106.
33 Blechman, p. 27.
34 Miller, p. 81.
35 Miller, p. 72.
36 David Greenwood, 'Paying for defence: will NATO's strength decline?', *NATO Review*, Vol. 30, No. 2 (Brussels, 1982), p. 32.

37   North Atlantic Council, Final Communiqué, 31 May 1978; *NATO Review*, Vol. 26, No. 4 (Brussels, 1978), p. 29.

38   David Greenwood, 'NATO's three per cent solution', *Survival*, Vol. 23, No. 6 (Nov.–Dec. 1981).

39   Bill Mumford, 'NATO defence at the summit', *NATO Review*, Vol. 26, No. 3 (June 1978), p. 4.

40   Robert Komer, 'The origins and objectives' [of LTDP], *NATO Review*, Vol. 26, No. 3 (June 1978), p. 9.

41   Quoted in *The Times*, 13 May 1982.

42   Robin Ranger, *Arms and Politics 1958–1978* (Gage, Toronto, 1979), p. 190.

43   Linda P. Brady, 'Negotiating European security: mutual and balanced force reductions', *International Security Review*, Vol. 6, No. 2 (Summer 1981), p. 193.

44   Speech by Leonid Brezhnev, 23 Oct. 1973, quoted in John G. Keliher, *The Negotiations on Mutual and Balanced Force Reductions* (Pergamon Press, New York, 1980), p. 50.

45   US Ambassador Stanley R. Resor to MBFR Conference, 31 Oct. 1973, in Keliher, *ibid.*, p. 51.

46   Lothar Ruehl, '"MBFR": lessons and problems', *Adelphi Paper 176* (IISS, London, 1982), p. 9.

47   *Ibid.*, p. 13.

48   Ruehl, *op. cit.*, p.28.

49   Keliher, *op. cit.*, p. 123.

50   Ruehl, p. 24.

51   Quoted in Keliher, *op. cit.*, p. 142.

52   Hans Gunther Brauch, 'CBMs and the CSE', *Arms Control Today*, Vol. 10, No. 10 (Nov. 1980), p. 1.

53   SIPRI, *Armaments and Disarmament in the Nuclear Age* (Almqvist and Wiksell, Stockholm, 1976), pp. 261–2.

54   *Ibid.*, p. 263.

55   Les Aspin, 'Surprise attack', *NATO Review*, Vol. 25, No. 4 (Aug. 1977), p. 12.

56   Alton Frye, 'A defense outline for Carter', *International Herald Tribune*, 16 May 1978.

57   Jonathan Alford, in Alford (ed.), 'The future of arms control, Part III — Confidence building measures', *Adelphi Paper No. 149* (IISS, London), p. 1.

7

THE CHEMICAL ARMS RACE

1   Lt Gen P. Krasota, 'Who is against a ban on chemical weapons?' *Soviet News*, 26 Jan. 1982, p. 27.

2 Christy Campbell, *War Facts Now* (London, Fontana, 1982),
   p. 100.
3 The Convention on the Prohibition of the Development, Production and Stockpiling of Bacteriological (Biological) and Toxin
   Weapons and Their Destruction, signed 10 Apr. 1972.
4 Quoted in *Daily Bulletin*, US Mission, Geneva, 20 Oct. 1977, p. 4,
   and cited in Charles H. Bay, 'The other gas crisis — chemical
   weapons', Part I, *Parameters*, Vol. 9, No. 3 (1979), p. 72.
5 J. Goldblat, 'Status of US–Soviet negotiations for a chemical
   weapons convention', in *Chemical Weapons: Destruction and
   Conversion* (Taylor and Francis, London, 1980), pp. 157–64.
6 Quoted in Charles H. Bay, *op. cit.*, p. 72.
7 Austin Bay, 'Chemical warfare: perspectives and potentials',
   Strategy and Tactics (No. 62, May–June 1977), p. 31.
8 Austin Bay, *loc. cit.*
9 *Ibid.*
10 Letter to the US Delegates to the Hague Conference, 18 Apr. 1899.
   In T. N. Dupuy and Gay M. Hammerman (eds), *A Documentary
   History of Arms Control and Disarmament* (Bowker, New York,
   1973), p. 53.
11 Calvin D. Davis, *The United States and the First Hague Peace Conference* (New York, 1962), p. 119.
12 Austin Bay, *op. cit.*, p. 25.
13 G. Winthrop Young, *The Grace of Forgetting* (no date), p. 233.
   Quoted in Philip Noel-Baker, *The Arms Race* (John Calder, London,
   1958), p. 320.
14 Austin Bay, *op. cit.*, p. 25.
15 J. P. Perry-Robinson, 'Chemical weapons for NATO?' in M. Meselson (ed.), *Chemical Weapons and Chemical Arms Control*, (Carnegie, New York, 1978), p. 22.
16 R. Harris and J. Paxman, 'How close is chemical warfare?' *Sunday
   Telegraph Magazine*, No. 286, 21 Mar. 1982, p. 23.
17 *Protocol Prohibiting the Use in War of Asphyxiating, Poisonous or
   Other Gases and of Bacteriological Methods of Warfare*, Geneva,
   17 June 1925.
18 John H. Barton and Lawrence D. Weiler (eds), *International Arms
   Control* (Stanford UP, 1976), p. 117.
19 M. Mandelbaum, *The Nuclear Revolution* (Cambridge, UP, 1981),
   p. 38.
20 *Ibid.*, pp. 3–4.
21 Quoted in Harris and Paxman, *op. cit.*, p. 23.
22 Gwynne Roberts, 'Hitler's deadly secrets', *The Sunday Times*,
   22 Feb. 1981.

23 *Ibid.*

24 *The Guardian*, 2 May 1981.

25 E. C. Mayer, L. B. Lennon and J. E. Leonard, 'Defence planning for chemical warfare', in M. Meselson, *op. cit.*, p. 1.

26 Blood agents enter through the throat and lungs. They kill by interfering with the body's oxygen supply to the tissues.

27 Harris and Paxman, *op. cit.*, p. 25.

28 Austin Bay, *op. cit.*, p. 28.

29 This list is taken from SIPRI, *Armaments and Disarmaments in the Nculear Age* (Almqvist and Wiksell, Stockholm, 1976), p. 117.

30 Meselson, *op. cit.*, p. 9.

31 *Ibid.*, p. 11.

32 SIPRI, *CB Weapons Today* (Almqvist and Wiksell, Stockholm, 1973), p. 150.

33 A. M. Hoeber and J. D. Douglass Jr, 'The neglected threat of chemical warfare', *International Security*, 3 (Summer 1978), p. 59.

34 James F. Dunnigan, *How To Make War* (Arms and Armour Press, London, 1982), p. 271.

35 SIPRI, 1976, *op. cit.*, p. 118.

36 J. Erikson, 'The Soviet Union's growing arsenal of chemical warfare', *Strategic Review*, Vol. 7, No. 4 (1979), p. 66.

37 J. P. Perry-Robinson, 'Chemical warfare capabilities of the Warsaw and North Atlantic Treaty Organisations', in SIPRI, *Chemical Weapons, Destruction and Conversion, op. cit.*, p. 17.

38 *Ibid.*, p. 20.

39 Austin Bay, *op. cit.*, p. 30.

40 Erikson, *op. cit.*, p. 70.

41 Austin Bay, *op. cit.*, pp. 29–30.

42 Erikson, p. 65.

43 *Ibid.*

44 From Austin Bay, p. 29.

45 J. P. Perry-Robinson, 'CW capabilities of WTO and NATO', *op. cit.*, p. 28.

46 D. M. Kyle, 'NATO's chemical warfare defense: improving but inadequate', *Armed Forces Journal International*, Nov. 1980, p. 33.

47 A. Hay, *et al.*, 'The poison cloud hanging over Europe', *New Scientist* (11 Mar. 1982), p. 630.

48 Kyle, *op. cit.*, p. 33.

49 D. M. O. Miller, *et al.*, *The Balance of Military Power* (Salamander, London, 1981), p. 111.

50 J. P. Perry-Robinson, 'CW capabilities of WTO and NATO', p. 20.

51 J. P. Perry-Robinson, 'CW capabilities of WTO and NATO', p. 21.

52 *The Times*, 18 Sept. 1981.

53 *The Guardian*, 5 Jan. 1981.
54 *The Observer*, 19 July 1981.
55 J. Taylor, 'US chemical warfare ability lagging Russians', *Sunday Oklahoman* (26 Oct. 1980), p. A18.
56 Taken from D. M. O. Miller, *op. cit.*, p. 111.
57 J. P. Perry-Robinson, 'CW capabilities of WTO and NATO', p. 37.
58 *Ibid.*
59 Harris and Paxman, *op. cit.*, p. 25.
60 *Ibid.*
61 J. P. Perry-Robinson, 'CW capabilities of WTO and NATO', p. 39.
62 *Ibid.*, p. 39; SIPRI, *The Arms Race and Arms Control* (Taylor and Francis, London, 1982), p. 12.
63 *The Times*, 18 Sept. 1981.
64 *The Times*, 5 Feb. 1982.
65 Johan Lundin, 'The scope and control of chemical disarmament treaties particularly with regard to binary chemical weapons', *Cooperation and Conflict*, 3 Apr. 1973, p. 148.
66 J. P. Perry-Robinson, 'Binary nerve-gas weapons', in SIPRI, *Chemical Disarmament: New Weapons for Old* (Almqvist and Wiksell, Stockholm, 1975), pp. 53-5.
67 Hearings before Senate Armed Services Committee Part 5 (Washington, 1974) in J. P. Perry-Robinson, SIPRI, 1975, p. 33.
68 A. Hal, *et al.*, *op. cit.*, p. 631.
69 J. P. Perry-Robinson, 'Chemical and biological warfare: analysis of recent reports concerning the Soviet Union and Vietnam', *ADIU Occasional Paper No. 1* (Brighton, University of Sussex, 1980), p. 42.
70 See above, ref. 45.

8

ARMS CONTROL AND DISARMAMENT

1 'Disarmament conference in ancient China', in T. N. Dupuy and G. M. Hammerman (eds), *A Documentary History of Arms Control and Disarmament* (Bowker, New York, 1973), pp. 3-4.
2 H. Bull, *The Control of the Arms Race* (Weidenfeld & Nicolson, London, 1961), p. ix.
3 Ken Booth, 'Disarmament and arms control', in J. Baylis, K. Booth, J. Garnett and P. Williams, *Contemporary Strategy* (Croom Helm, London, 1975), p. 89.
4 Lord Grey of Falloden, *Twenty Five Years*, Vol. I (Hodder & Stoughton, London, 1925), pp. 91-2.

5 The Bible, Isaiah, 2.4.

6 Quoted in Booth, *op. cit.*, p. 109.

7 J. Bentham, 'A plan for universal and perpetual peace' (1789), in Dupuy and Hammerman, *op. cit.*, p. 28.

8 See chapter 7.

9 On the use of disarmament proposals as Cold War propaganda see J. W. Spanier and J. L. Nogee, *The Politics of Disarmament: A Study in Soviet American Gamesmanship* (Praeger, New York, 1962).

10 *Proposals for Fixing Numerical Limitations of All Armed Forces,* 28 May 1952, UN Document DC/10, 1952.

11 Philip Noel-Baker, *The Arms Race* (Calder, London, 1958), p.23, on whose description of the 1952–55 negotiations this section is based.

12 A phrase used to describe the fear of nuclear weapons by Charles Hansen, *New York Times*, 18 Sept. 1979.

13 T. C. Schelling and M. H. Halperin, *Strategy and Arms Control* (Twentieth Century Fund, New York, 1961), p. 2.

14 K. Booth, *op. cit.*, p. 89.

15 Francois de Rose, 'European concerns and Salt II', *Survival*, Vol. XXI, No. 5 (Sept.–Oct. 1979), p. 206.

16 *Treaty between Great Britain, Denmark, France, Italy, Japan, the Netherlands, Norway, Sweden and the United States of America, relative to the Archipelago of Spitzbergen*, 9 Feb. 1920. Norway gained full sovereignty over Spitzbergen but Article IX stated that the islands 'may never be used for warlike purposes'.

17 James E. Dougherty, *How To Think About Arms Control and Disarmament* (New York, 1973), p. 131.

18 *Treaty on Principles Governing the Activities of States in the Exploration and Use of Outer Space, Including the Moon and Other Celestial Bodies*, 27 Jan. 1967.

19 *Convention of the Prohibition of the Development, Production and Stockpiling of Bacteriological (Biological) and Toxin Weapons and on their Destruction*, signed 10 Apr. 1972.

20 *Convention on the Prohibitions of Military or Any Other Hostile Use of Environmental Modification Techniques*, signed 18 May 1977.

21 *Convention on Prohibitions or Restrictions on the Use of Certain Conventional Weapons which May be Deemed to be Excessively Injurious or to Have Indiscriminate Effects* (UN Document A/Conf/95/15), 1981.

22 Quoted in UN press release DC/1025, 14 Oct. 1981, p. 1.

23 P. Towle, 'Disarmament and arms control agreements in wartime',

Bulletin of Peace Proposals, Vol. II, No. 2 (1980).

24 A. Brayton Abbott, 'Confidence building measures in European security', *The World Today* (Oct. 1980), p. 382.

25 *Ibid.*, pp. 388–9.

26 *Ibid.*, p. 384.

27 Leslie H. Gelb, 'The future of arms control: a glass half full', *Foreign Policy*, No. 36 (Fall 1979), p. 21.

28 For example, Colin S. Gray, 'Nuclear strategy: the case for a theory of victory', *International Security* (Summer 1979), pp. 54–87, and Carl H. Builder, 'Why not first-strike counterforce capabilities?', RAND Paper P-6312 (Rand Corporation, Santa Monica, California, 1979).

Bibliography

GENERAL

Alford, J. 'The East–West Balance: A Position of Unstable Equilibrium' *Round Table* (January 1980), pp. 18–27.

Blackaby, F. 'World Arsenals 1982' *Bulletin of the Atomic Scientists* Vol. 38 (June 1982), pp. 21–6.

Blainey, Geoffrey, *The Causes of War* Sun Books, Melbourne, 1977.

Blechman, Barry M. *et al.*, *The Soviet Military Build up and U.S. Defense Spending* Brookings Institution, Washington, 1977.

Cockle, Paul, 'Analysing Soviet Defense Spending: The Debate in Perspective' *Survival*, Vol. XX No. 5 (September–October 1978), pp. 209–19.

Cox, John, *Overkill* Penguin, Harmondsworth, 1977.

Cusack, Thomas R. and Ward, Michael D. 'Military Spending in the U.S., USSR and China' *Journal of Conflict Resolution* (September 1981), pp. 429–69.

Einhorn, Robert J. 'Treaty Compliance' *Foreign Policy* (Winter 1981–82), pp. 29–47.

Garnett, John (Ed), *Theories of Peace and Security* Macmillan, London, 1970.

Hagan, Lawrence S. (ed.), *The Crisis of Western Security* Croom Helm, London, 1982.

Holzman, Franklyn D. 'Soviet Military Spending: Assessing the Numbers Game' *International Security* (Spring, 1982), pp. 78–101.

International Institute for Strategic Studies, *Strategic Survey 1981–82* IISS, London, 1982.

International Institute for Strategic Studies, *The Military Balance 1982–83* IISS, London, 1982.

Kohler, G. 'The Soviet/Russian Defense Burden 1862–1965' *Bulletin of Peace Proposals*, Vol. 11 No. 2 (1980), pp. 131–8.

Leebaert, Derek (ed.), *Soviet Military Theory* Allen and Unwin, London, 1981.

Mandelbaum, Michael, *The Nuclear Revolution* Cambridge University Press, Cambridge, 1981.
Millar, T. B. *The East–West Strategic Balance* Allen and Unwin, London, 1981.
Miller, D. M. O., Kennedy, William, Jordan, John and Richardson, Douglas, *The Balance of Military Power* Salamander, London, 1981.
Noel-Baker, Philip, *The Arms Race* John Calder, London 1958.
Palme Commission, *Common Security* Pan Books, London, 1982.
Wright, Quincy, *A study of War* University of Chicago Press, Chicago, 1942.
Zuckerman, S. *Science Advisers, Scientific Advisers and Nuclear Weapons* Menard Press, London, 1980.

1
ARMS RACES AND MILITARY POWER

Art, Robert J. 'To What Ends Military Power?' *International Security* (Spring 1980), pp. 3–35.
Baylis, John, Booth, Ken, Garnett, John, Williams, Phil, *Contemporary Strategy* Croom Helm, London, 1975.
Bird, L. A. *Costa Rica: A Country Without an Army* Northern Friends Peace Board, York, 1979.
Blechman, Barry M. and Kaplan, Stephen, *Force Without War: U.S. Armed Forces as a Political Instrument* Brookings Institution, Washington, 1978.
Brooks, Harvey, 'The Military Innovation System and the Qualitative Arms Race' in Long, Franklin & Rathjens, George (eds) *Arms, Defense Policy & Arms Control*, Norton, New York, 1976, pp. 99–129.
Erikson, J. *Soviet Military Power* Royal United Services Institute, London, 1971.
Gray, Colin S. 'Action and Reaction in the Nuclear Arms Race' *Military Review* Vol. 51 No. 8 (August 1971), pp. 16–26.
Gray, Colin S. 'The Arms Race Phenomenon' *World Politics* Vol. 24 (1972) pp. 39–79.
Gray, Colin S. *The Soviet American Arms Race* Saxon House, Farnborough, 1976.
Handel, Michael, 'Numbers Do Count: The Question of Quality versus Quantity' *Journal of Strategic Studies* (September 1981) pp. 225–60.
Kaplan, Stephen S. *Diplomacy of Power: Soviet Armed Forces as a*

Political Instrument Brookings Institution, Washington 1981.

Kissinger, H. *Nuclear Weapons and Foreign Policy* Harper and Row, New York, 1957.

Lambelet, John C. 'Do Arms Races Lead to War?' *Journal of Peace Research* Vol. 12 No. 2 (1975), pp. 123–8.

Millis, Walter, 'The Uselessness of Military Power' in Goldin, Robert A. (ed.), *America Armed* Rand McNally, Chicago, 1961.

Morganthau, Hans J. *Politics Among Nations* (5th edn) Knopf, New York, 1973.

Posen, Barry R. and Van Evera, Stephen W. 'Overarming and Underwhelming' *Foreign Policy* No. 40 (Fall 1980), pp. 99–118.

Quester, George H. *Offense and Defense in the International System* Wiley & Sons, New York, 1977.

Schelling, Thomas C. *Arms and Influence* Yale University Press, New Haven, 1966.

Singer, J. David, 'Threat Perception and the Armament-Tension Dilemma', *Jounral of Conflict Resolution* Vol. 2, No. 1 (1958), pp. 90–105.

Tammen, Ronald L. 'The Reagan Strategic Programme', *Arms Control Today* Vol. 11 No. 11 (December 1981), pp. 1–3, 5–6.

Warnke, Paul C. 'Apes on a Treadmill' *Foreign Policy* No. 18 (Spring 1975), pp. 12–29.

Wohlstetter, Albert, 'Rivals, But No Race' *Foreign Policy* No. 16 (Fall 1974), pp. 48–81.

2

THE STRATEGIC NUCLEAR BALANCE

Alford, J. and Nailor, P. 'The Future of Britain's Deterrent Force' *Adelphi Paper 156* International Institute for Strategic Studies, London, 1980.

Arnett, Robert L. 'Soviet Attitudes Towards Nuclear War: Do they really think they can win?' *Journal of Strategic Studies* Vol. 2, No. 2 (September 1979), pp. 172–91.

Ball, Desmond, 'The MX Basing Decision' *Survival* (March–April 1980), pp. 58–63.

Ball, Desmond, 'Can Nuclear War be Controlled?' *Adelphi Paper 169* International Institute for Strategic Studies, London, 1981.

Bertram, Christoph (ed.), *Strategic Deterrence in a Changing Environment* International Institute for Strategic Studies, London, 1981.

Beukel, E., 'Analysing the Views of Soviet Leaders on Nuclear Weapons' *Co-operation and Conflict* Vol. 15 No. 2 (1980), pp. 71–84.

Builder, Carl H. 'Why Not First-Strike Counterforce Capabilities?' *RAND Paper P-6312* (Rand Corporation, Santa Monica, California, 1979.

Carnesdale, Albert, 'Reviving the ABM Debate' *Arms Control Today* Vol. 11 No. 4

Carnesdale, Albert and Glazer, Charles, 'I.C.B.M. Vulnerability: The Cures are Worse than the Disease' *International Security* (Summer 1982), pp. 70-85.

Erikson, John, 'The Soviet View of Deterrence: A General Survey' *Survival* Vol. XXIV No. 6 (Nov-Dec 1982), pp. 242-9.

Feld, Bernard T. and Tsipis, Kosta, 'Land-based Intercontinental Ballistic Missiles' *Scientific American* Vol. 241 No. 5 (November 1979), pp. 51-62.

Freedman, Lawrence, *U.S. Intelligence and the Soviet Strategic Threat* Macmillan, London, 1977.

Goure, Leon and Deans, Michael J. 'The Soviet Strategic View' *Strategic Survey* (Fall 1981), pp. 90-109.

Gray, Colin S. 'Nuclear Strategy: The Case for a Theory of Victory' *International Security* (Summer 1979), pp. 54-87.

Gray, Colin S. 'A New Debate on Ballistic Missile Defence' *Survival* Vol. XXIII No. 2 (March-April 1981), pp. 60-71.

Jervis, Robert, 'Why Nuclear Superiority Doesn't Matter', *Political Science Quarterly* Vol. 94 No. 4 (Winter 1979-80), pp. 617-33.

Kaplan, Fred. M. *Dubious Specter: A Skeptical look at the Soviet Nuclear Threat* Institute for Policy Studies, Washington, 1980.

Labrie, Roger P. *SALT Handbook: Key Documents and Issues 1972-79* American Enterprise Institute, Washington, 1979.

Mandelbaum, Michael, *The Nuclear Revolution: International Politics Before And After Hiroshima* Cambridge University Press, Cambridge, 1981.

Martin, Laurence, *Strategic Thought in the Nuclear Age* Heinemann, London, 1979.

Zuckerman, Solly, *Nuclear Illusion and Reality* Collins, London, 1982.

3
THE SPREAD OF NUCLEAR WEAPONS

Adelman, K. L. and Knight, A. W. 'Can South Africa Go Nuclear?' *Orbis* Vol. 23 (Fall 1979), pp. 633-47.

Baker, Stephen J. 'The International Political Economy of Proliferation' in Carlton, D. and Schaerf, C. (eds) *Arms Control and Technological Innovation* Croom Helm, London, 1977, pp. 70-101.

Barnaby, F., Goldblat, J. and Levinson, M. (eds), *The NPT: The Main Political Barrier to Nuclear Weapon Proliferation* SIPRI, Taylor and Francis, London, 1980.

Betts, Richard, 'A Diplomatic Bomb for South Africa?' *International Security* (Fall, 1979), pp. 99–115.

Camiller, J. A. 'The Myth of the Peaceful Atom' *Millenium* Vol. 6 No. 2 (1977), pp. 111–27.

Harkavy, R. E. 'Pariah States and Nuclear Proliferation' *International Organisation* Vol. 35 (Winter 1981), pp. 135–63.

Kapur, Ashok, *International Nuclear Proliferation: Multinational Diplomacy & Regional Aspects* Praeger, New York, 1979.

Kapur, Ashok, 'The Nuclear Spread: A Third World View' *Third World Quarterly* Vol. 2 No. 1 (January 1980), pp. 59–75.

Kapur, Ashok, 'Nuclear Proliferation in the 1980s *International Journal* (Summer 1981), pp. 535–55.

Kincade, William H. 'Missile Vulnerability Reconsidered' *Arms Control Today* Vol. 11 No. 5 (May 1981), pp. 1–2, 5–8.

Lewis, Kevin N. 'The U.S.–Soviet Strategic Balance in the 1980s — Missing the Trees for the Leaves' *Survival* Vol. XXIV No. 3 (May–June 1982), pp. 108–16.

Lodgaard, S. 'Nuclear Proliferation: Critical Issues' *Bulletin of Peace Proposals* Vol. 12, No. 1 (March 1981), pp. 11–20.

Lovins, Amory B., Lovins, L. Hunter and Ross, Leonard, 'Nuclear Power and Nuclear Bombs' *Foreign Affairs* (Summer 1980), pp. 1137–77.

Millett, Stephen M. 'Soviet Perceptions of Nuclear Strategy and Implications for U.S. Deterrence' *Economics and Policy Analysis Occasional Paper No. 18* Columbus, Ohio, 1981.

Payne, Keith B. 'Deterrence, Arms Control and U.S. Strategic Doctrine' *Orbis* (Fall 1981), pp. 747–70.

Quester, George H. 'Reducing the Incentives to Proliferation' *Annals of the American Academy of Political and Social Science* 430 (March 1977), pp. 70–81.

Robinson Jnr, Clarence A. 'Administration Pushes I.C.B.M. Defence' *Aviation Week and Space Technology* 11 October 1982, pp. 113–118.

Saleff, Stephen, 'The Plutonium Connection: Energy and Arms' *Bulletin of the Atomic Scientists* (September 1980), pp. 18–23.

Schilling, Warner R. 'U.S. Strategic Nuclear Concepts in the 1970s: The Search for Sufficiently Equivalent Countervailing Parity' *International Security* (Fall 1981), pp. 49–79.

Snow, Donald M. 'Current Nuclear Deterrence Thinking' *International Studies Quarterly*, Vol. 23 No. 3 (September 1979), pp. 445–86.

Waltz, Kenneth N. 'The Spread of Nuclear Weapons: More may be better' *Adelphi Paper No. 171* International Institute for Strategic Studies, London, 1981.

Yost, David S. 'Ballistic Missile Defense and the Atlantic Alliance' *International Security* (Fall 1982), pp. 143-74.

4

THE ARMS RACE IN SPACE

Asbeck, Frank, 'The Militarisation of Space' *ADIU Report* Vol. 2 No. 2 (April–May 1980), pp. 1-3.

Baker, David, *The Shape of Wars to Come* Patrick Stevens, Cambridge, 1981.

Ebobescu, N. 'The Need to Halt the Arms Race in Outer Space' *Revue Roumaine d'Etudes Internationales* Vol.13 No. 4 (1979) pp. 535-49.

Forbich, Carl A. 'The Soviet Space Shuttle Programme' *Air University Review* Vol. 31 (May–June 1980), pp. 55-62.

Garwin, Richard L. 'Charged-particle beam weapons' *Bulletin of the Atomic Scientists* (October 1978), pp. 24-7.

Garwin, Richard L. 'Are we on the Verge of a New Arms Race in Space?' *Bulletin of the Atomic Scientists* (May 1981), pp. 48-55.

Gatland, Kenneth *et al.*, *Illustrated Encyclopaedia of Space Technology* Salamander, London, 1981.

Hafner, D. L. 'Arms Control Measures for Anti-Satellite Weapons' *International Security* Vol. 5 No. 3 (Winter 1980-81), pp. 41-60.

Jasani, Bhupendra M. *Outer Space — Battlefield of the Future?* SIPRI, Taylor and Francis, London, 1978.

Jasani, Bhupendra M. *Outer Space: A New Dimension of the Arms Race* SIPRI, Taylor and Francis, London, 1982.

Jasani, Bhupendra M. and Lunderius, Maria A. 'Peaceful Uses of Outer Space — Legal Fiction and Military Reality' *Bulletin of Peace Proposals* (1980 No. 1), pp. 57-70.

Kane, F. X. 'Anti-Satellite Systems and U.S. Options' *Strategic Review* Vol. 10 (Winter 1982), pp. 56-64.

Oberg, James, *Red Star in Orbit* Random House, New York, 1981.

Robinson Jnr, Clarence A. 'Defense Department Backs Space-Based Missile Defense' *Aviation Week and Space Technology* 17 September 1982, pp. 14-16.

Smernoff, Barry J. 'The Strategic Value of Space-Based Laser Weapons' *Air University Review* (March–April 1982), pp. 2-17.

Snow, Donald M. 'Lasers, Charged-particle beams and the Strategic

Future' *Political Science Quarterly* Vol. 95 No. 2 (Summer 1980), pp. 277–94.

Stares, Paul, 'The Military Uses of Outer Space: Does Britain Have Any Choice?' *RUSI Journal* Vol. 127 No. 4 (December 1982), pp. 47–52.

Tsipis, Kosta, 'Laser Weapons' *Scientific American* (December 1981), pp. 51–7.

5
NUCLEAR WEAPONS IN EUROPE

Bertram, Christoph, 'The Implications of Theatre Nuclear Weapons in Europe' *Foreign Affairs* (Winter 1981–82), pp. 305–26.

Betts, Richard K. *Cruise Missiles: Technology, Strategy, Politics* Brookings Institution, Washington, 1981.

Corterier, Peter, 'Modernisation of Theatre Nuclear Forces and Arms Control' *NATO Review* Vol. 29 No. 4 (August 1981), pp. 4–9.

Freedman, Lawrence, *Britain and Nuclear Weapons* Macmillan, London, 1980.

Freedman, Lawrence, 'The Dilemma of Theatre Nuclear Arms Control' *Survival* Vol. XXIII No. 1 (January–February 1981), pp. 2–10.

Freedman, Lawrence, 'NATO Myths' *Foreign Policy* (Winter 1981–82), pp. 48–68.

Frye, Alton, 'Nuclear Weapons in Europe: No Exit from Ambivalence' *Survival* (May–June 1980), pp. 98–106.

Hanmer, Stephen, 'NATO's Long-Range Nuclear Forces: Modernisation in Parallel with Arms Control' *NATO Review* Vol. 28 No. 1 (February 1980), pp. 1–6.

Hyland, William G. 'Soviet Theatre Forces and Arms Control Policy' *Survival* (September–October 1981), pp. 194–9.

Jones, Christopher, 'The Soviet View of I.N.F.' *Arms Control Today* Vol. 12 No. 3 (March 1982), pp. 4–5, 10.

Lunn, Simon, 'Cruise Missiles and the Prospects for Arms Control' *ADIU Report* University of Sussex (October 1981), pp. 1–5.

Ranger, Robin, 'NATO's New Great Debate: Theatre Nuclear Force Modernisation and Arms Control' *International Journal* (Summer 1981), pp. 556–74.

Semeiko, Lev, 'Strategy of parity and "Eurostrategy" of superiority' *Co-Existence* Vol. 17 No. 2 (1980), pp. 156–63.

Stockholm International Peace Research Institute *Tactical Nuclear Weapons: European Perspectives* SIPRI, Taylor and Francis, London, 1978.

Treverton, Gregory F. 'Nuclear Weapons and the "Gray Area"' *Foreign Affairs* Vol. 57 No. 5 (Summer 1979), pp. 1075–89.

Treverton, Gregory F. 'Nuclear Weapons in Europe' *Adelphi Paper 168* International Institute for Strategic Studies, London, 1981.

Vayrynen, Raimo, 'Eurostrategic Arms Race: Doctrine and Their Implications' *Current Research on Peace and Violence* No. 1 (1981), pp. 1–32.

Warnke, Paul C. 'Theater-Nuclear Forces and NATO Security' *Orbis* (Fall 1981), pp. 501–4.

6

THE EUROPEAN CENTRAL BALANCE

Alford, Jonathan, 'NATO's Conventional Forces and the Soviet Mobilisation Potential *NATO Review* (June 1980), pp. 18–22.

Borawski, J. 'Mutual Force Reductions in Europe from a Soviet Perspective' *Orbis* Vol. XXII No. 4 (Winter 1979), pp. 845–73.

Brady, Linda P. 'Negotiating European Security: Mutual and Balanced Force Reductions' *International Security Review* Vol. 6 No. 2 (Summer 1981), pp. 189–208.

Brayton, Abbott A. 'Confidence Building Measures in European Security' *The World Today* (October 1980), pp. 381–91.

Dean, Jonathan, 'MBFR: Ten Years of Negotiating Security in Europe' *Arms Control Today* Vol. 12 No. 8 (September 1982), pp. 1–3, 8.

Greenwood, David, 'NATO's Three per cent solution' *Survival* (Nov.–Dec. 1981), pp. 252–60.

Hanning, Norbert, 'The Defence of Western Europe with Conventional Weapons' *International Defence Review* No. 11 (1981), pp. 1439–43.

Herspring, Dale R. and Volgyes, Ivan, 'How Reliable are Eastern European Armies?' *Survival* (September–October 1980), pp. 208–18.

Holst, Johan Jurgen, 'Arms Control in Europe: Towards a New Political Order?' *The Bulletin of Peace Proposals* Vol. 13 No. 2 (1982), pp. 81–90.

Holst, Johan Jurgen and Melander, Karen Alette, 'European Security and Confidence Building Measures' *Survival* Vol. XIX No. 4 (July–August 1977), pp. 146–54.

Jung, Ernst, 'The Vienna MBFR Negotiations after Seven Years' *NATO Review* (July–August 1977), pp. 146–54.

Karber, Philip A. 'The Soviet Anti-Tank Debate *Survival* Vol. XVIII No. 3 (May–June 1976), pp. 105–11.

Keliher, John G. *The Negotiations on Mutual and Balanced Force*

Reductions: The Search for Arms Control in Central Europe Pergamon, Oxford, 1981.

Macdonald, H. 'Conventional Arms Control in Europe' *Arms Control* Vol. 2 (December 1981), pp. 284–312.

Mearsheimer, John M. 'Why the Soviet Can't Win Quickly in Central Europe?' *International Security* (Summer 1982), pp. 3–39.

Record, Jeffrey, *Force Reductions in Europe: Starting Over* Institute for Foreign Policy Analysis Inc., Cambridge, Massachusetts, 1981.

Walker, Paul F. 'Precision Guided Weapons' *Scientific American* (August 1981), pp. 36–45.

Wolfe, Thomas W. *Soviet Power and Europe 1945–1970* Johns Hopkins Press, Baltimore, 1970.

7

THE CHEMICAL ARMS RACE

Bay, Austin, 'Chemical Warfare: Perspectives and Potentials' *Strategy and Tactics* No. 62 (1977), pp. 23–33.

Bray, Charles H. 'The Other Gas Crisis — Chemical Weapons' Part I, *Parameters* Vol. 9 No. 3 (September 1979), pp. 70–8. Part II, *Parameters* Vol. 9 No. 4 (December 1979), pp. 65–74.

Dick, Charles, 'The Soviet Chemical and Biological Warfare Threat' *RUSI Journal* Vol. 126 No. 1 (March 1981), pp. 45–51.

Erickson, John, 'The Soviet Unions Growing Arsenal of Chemical War' *Strategic Review* Vol. 7 No. 4 (1979), pp. 63–71.

Graveley, A.F. 'Defence or Deterrence? The Case for Chemical Weapons' *RUSI Journal* Vol. 126 No. 4 (December 1981), pp. 13–20.

Hoeber, Amoretta M. *The Chemistry of Defeat: Asymmetries in the U.S. and Soviet Chemical Warfare Postures* Institute for Foreign Policy Analysis Incorporated, Cambridge, Massachusetts, 1981.

Krasota, P. 'Who is Against a Ban on Chemical Weapons?' *Soviet News* (26 January 1982), pp. 27–8.

Lundin, S. J. 'Chemical Weapons: Too Late for Disarmament?' *Bulletin of the Atomic Scientists* (December 1979), pp. 33–7.

Meselson, Matthew (ed.) *Chemical Weapons and Chemical Arms Control* Carnegie Endowment for International Peace, Washington, 1978.

Meselson, M. and Perry-Robinson, J.P. 'Chemical Warfare and Chemical Disarmament' *Scientific American* Vol. 242 No. 4 (April 1980), pp. 34–43.

Miettinen, Jorma K. 'Chemical Weapons and Chemical Disarmament Negotiations' *Bulletin of Peace Proposals* Vol. 13 No. 2 (1982), pp. 119–26.

Perry-Robinson, J. P. 'Chemical and Biological Warfare: Analysis of Recent Reports Concerning the Soviet Union and Vietnam' *ADIU Occasional Paper No. 1* University of Sussex, Brighton, 1980.

Perry-Robinson, J.P. 'Chemical Weapons and Europe' *Survival* (January–February 1982), pp. 9–18.

Stockholm International Peace Research Institute (SIPRI) *The Problem of Chemical and Biological Warfare* Vol. IV CB Disarmament Negotiations 1920–1970 Almqvist and Wiksell, Stockholm, 1971.

SIPRI *Chemical Disarmament: New Weapons for Old* Almqvist and Wiksell, Stockholm, 1975.

SIPRI *Chemical Weapons: Destruction and Conversation* Taylor and Francis, London, 1980.

United Nations, 'Chemical and Bacteriological (Biological) Weapons. Report of the Secretary-General' *United Nations General Assembly Document A/37/259* (1 December 1982), UN, New York.

8
ARMS CONTROL AND DISARMAMENT

Allison, Graham T. and Morris, Frederick A. 'Armaments and Armaments: Exploring the Determinants of Military Weapons' in Long, Franklin A. and Rathiens, George (eds) *Arms Defense Policy and Arms Control*, Norton, New York, 1976, pp. 99–129.

Barton, John H. and Weiler, Lawrence D. *International Arms Control* Stanford University Press, Stanford, California, 1976.

Barton, John H. *The Politics of Peace: An Evaluation of Arms Control* Stanford University Press, Stanford, California, 1981.

Bertram, Christoph, 'Rethinking Arms Control' *Foreign Affairs* Vol. 59 No. 2 (Winter 1980–81), pp. 352–65.

Bowie, Robert R. 'The Bargaining Aspects of Arms Control: The SALT Experience' in Kintner, W. R. and Pfaltzgraff, R. L. (Eds) *SALT – Implications for Arms Control in the 1970s* Pittsburg, 1975, pp. 127–39.

Brauch, H.G. 'Confidence Building Measures and Disarmament Strategy' *Current Research on Peace and Violence* Vol. 2 No. 3–4 (1979), pp. 114–45.

Caldwell, D. 'CTB (Comprehensive Test Ban Treaty): An Effective SALT Substitute' *Bulletin of the Atomic Scientists* Vol. 36 No. 10 December 1980), pp. 30–3.

Carlton, David and Schaerf, Carlo (eds) *Arms Control and Technological Innovation* Croom Helm, London, 1975.

Carlton, David and Schaerf, Carlo (eds) *The Dynamics of the Arms Race* Croom Helm, London, 1977.

Clarke, Duncan L. *Politics of Arms Control: The Role and Effectiveness of the U.S. Arms Control and Disarmament Agency* Free Press, New York, 1979.

Clarke, Duncan L. 'Arms Control and Foreign Policy Under Reagan' *Bulletin of the Atomic Scientists* (November 1981), pp. 12–19.

Draper, G.I.I.A. 'The New Law of Armed Conflict' *RUSI Journal* Vol. 124 No. 3 (September 1979), pp. 3–11.

Dumas, L. J. 'The Impact of the Military Budget on the Domestic Economy' *Current Research on Peace and Violence* Vol. 3 No. 2 (1980), pp. 73–84.

Dumas, L. J. 'Disarmament and Economy in Advanced Industrialized Countries: The U.S. and the USSR' *Bulletin of Peace Proposals* Vol. 12 No. 1 (1981), pp. 1–10.

Dupuy, Trevor N. and Hammerman, Gay M. (eds) *A Documentary History of Arms Control and Disarmament* Bowker, New York, 1973.

Finan, J. S. 'Arms Control and the Central Strategic Balance: Some Technological Issues' *International Journal* (Summer 1981), pp. 430–59.

Freedman, Lawrence, 'SALT II and the Strategic Balance' *The World Today* (August 1979), pp. 315–23.

Garthoff, Douglas F. 'The Soviet Military and Arms Control' *Survival* Vol. 19 (1979), pp. 242–50.

Garthoff, Raymond L. 'Negotiating with the Russians: Some Lessons from SALT *International Security* Vol. 1 No. 4 (1977), pp. 3–24.

George, R. 'The Economics of Arms Control' *International Security* Vol. 3 (Winter 1978–79), pp. 94–125.

Goldblat, Josef, 'The Laws of Armed Conflict: Restrictions and Limitations on the Methods and Means of Warfare' *Bulletin of Peace Proposals* Vol. 13 No. 2 (1982), pp. 127–34.

Goldblat, Josef, *Agreements for Arms Control: A Critical Survey* Taylor and Francis, London, 1982.

Howard, Michael (ed.) *Restraints on War: Studies in the Limitation of Armed Conflict* Oxford University Press, Oxford, 1979.

Hussain, Farooq, 'The Impact of Weapons Test Restrictions' *Adelphi Paper 165* IISS, London, 1981.

Ikle, F. C. *How Nations Negotiate* Harper, London, 1964.

Lellouche, Pierre, 'Science and Disarmament' *NATO Review* (February 1982), pp. 12–17.

Lodal, Jan M. 'Verifying SALT' *Foreign Policy* No. 24 (1976), pp. 40–64.

Lodgaard, Sverre, 'The Functions of SALT' *Journal of Peace Research* Vol. XIV No. 1 (1977), pp. 1-21.

Myrdal, Alva, *The Game of Disarmament: How the United States and Russia run the Arms Race* Manchester University Press, Manchester, 1977.

Perry, Robert, 'The Faces of Verification: Strategic Arms Control for the 1980s' *RAND p-5986* Rand Corporation, Santa Monica, California, 1977.

Russell, Bruce M. and Blair, Bruce G. *Progress in Arms Control?* W.H. Freeman, San Francisco, 1979.

Singer, J. David, 'Slowing and Reversing the Strategic Arms Race: Some Possible Alternatives' *Bulletin of Peace Proposals* Vol. 13 No. 2 (1982), pp. 69-72.

Spanier, J. and Nogee J. L. *The Politics of Disarmament: A Study in Soviet American Gamesmanship* Praeger, New York, 1962.

Steinberg, Gerald M. 'Informal Arms Control: Restraint Without Ceremony' *Arms Control Today* Vol. 12 No. 6 (June 1982), pp. 4-5.

Sykes, Lynn R. and Evernden, Jack F. 'The Verification of a Comprehensive Test Ban' *Scientific American* (October 1982), pp. 47-55.

Talbott, Strobe, 'Scrambling and Spying in SALT II' *International Security* (Fall 1979), pp. 3-21.

Tampere Peace Research Institute, *International Detente and Disarmament: Contributions by Finnish and Soviet Scholars* Tampere PRI, Helsinki, 1977.

Towle, P. 'Disarmament and Arms Control Agreements in Wartime' *Bulletin of Peace Proposals* Vol. 11 No. 2 (1980), pp. 111-17.

Tsipis, K. 'Scientists and Weapons Procurement' *Bulletin of the Atomic Scientists* Vol. 36 (June 1980), pp. 41-3.

Vernon, Graham D. 'Controlled Conflict: Soviet Perceptions of Peaceful Co-existence' *Orbis* Vol. 23 No. 9 (Summer 1979), pp. 271-97.

Warnke, Paul C. 'Dare We End the Arms Race?' *Arms Control Today* Vol. 12 No. 5 (May 1982), pp. 4-5, 8-9.

Weiler, Lawrence D. 'The Arms Race, Secret Negotiations and the Congress' *Occasional Paper No. 12* The Stanley Foundation, Muscatine, Iowa, 1976.

Wrenn, Harry L. 'The Benefits and Risks of a Comprehensive Nuclear Explosions Test Ban' *CRS Report No. 79-260F* Congressional Research Service, Washington, 1979.

Young, Elizabeth and Wayland, 'Marxism–Leninism and Arms Control' *Arms Control* Vol. 1 No. 1 (May 1980), pp. 3-39.

Index